Women in Polish Cinema

Women in Polish Cinema

Ewa Mazierska and Elżbieta Ostrowska
With a supplementary chapter by Joanna Szwajcowska

Berghahn Books
NEW YORK · OXFORD

First published in 2006 by

Berghahn Books
www.berghahnbooks.com

Library of Congress Cataloging-in-Publication Data

Mazierska, Ewa.
    Women in Polish cinema / Ewa Mazierska and Elżbieta Ostrowska;
with a supplementary chapter by Joanna Szwajcowska.
        p. cm.
    Filmography: p.
    Includes bibliographical references and index.
    ISBN 1-57181-947-9 (alk. paper) ISBN 1-57181-948-7 (pbk.)
        1. Women in the motion picture industry—Poland. 2. Women in
motion pictures. 3. Motion pictures—Poland. I. Ostrowska, Elżbieta,
1967. II. Title.
PN1995.9.W6M368 2006
791.43'65209438—dc22   2005057004

British Library Cataloguing in Publication Data

A catalogue record for this book is available
from the British Library.

Printed in the United States on acid-free paper.

ISBN 1-57181-947-9 hardback
ISBN 1-57181-948-7 paperback

The well-known difference of opinions in Poland concerns what is 'serious' and what is 'unserious'. The dominating way of thinking of the opposition in the 1970s and 1980s was that the struggle for independence was serious, the struggle for women's rights was not. ... This kind of unifying reasoning was, at that time, in a way, close to mine. I remember when, during a feminist discussion in an international gathering in West Berlin at the end of the 1980s, I maintained that Solidarity, first, had to win independence and democracy for all of society and only then would it be able to deal with women's questions and improvement of women's situation.

Maria Janion, *Kobiety i duch inności*

Contents

List of Illustrations

Acknowledgements

We wish to express our gratitude to Adam Wyżyński and Grzegorz Balski from the National Film Archive, Poland, who assisted us with finding the films, journals and stills used in the book; to Janina Falkowska for her warm support and help with the preparation of the final version of the manuscript; to Helena Goscilo and Dorota Ostrowska for reading parts of the text and for their insightful comments; and to Peter Stevenson, Elizabeth Nazarian and Oscar Swan for helping us with the editing of the text. Our special thanks go to Gifford Kerr and Michael Stevenson who have encouraged the project at every stage of its development and offered us perceptive comments, as well as helping us with its editing.

The authors and publishers wish to thank the following institutions and individuals: SF 'Oko', SF 'Kadr', SF 'Perspektywa', SF im. Karola Irzykowskiego, SF 'Indeks', SF 'Tor', Wytwórnia Filmów Oświatowych w Łodzi, Andrzej Stempowski, Arthur Reinhart for their permission to reproduce illustrative material, and Wiesław Zdort, Henryk Czepek, Zbigniew Stanek and Dorota Kędzierzawska for helping us to obtain them. All stills were provided by the National Film Archive.

The research for the section written by Ewa Mazierska was funded by the Leverhulme Trust.

A preliminary version of Chapter 5 was published with the title, 'Agnieszka and Other Solidarity Heroines of Polish Cinema', in *Kinema*, No. 17, Spring 2002; Chapter 8 with the title, 'Wanda Jakubowska's Cinema of Commitment', in *European Journal of Women Studies*, No. 2, May 2001, published by Sage Publications Ltd (website address www.sagepub.co.uk); Chapter 9 with the title, 'Ambitions, Temptations and Disappointments: The Cinema of Barbara Sass', in *Feminist Media Studies*, No. 3, November 2003; and Chapter 11 with the title 'Devils, Crows, Women: the Cinema of Dorota Kędzierzawska', in *Canadian Slavonic Papers*, No. 4, December 2001. Reprinted with permission of the publishers.

All translations from English are by us, unless indicated otherwise.

Introduction

EWA MAZIERSKA AND ELŻBIETA OSTROWSKA

In the several books about Polish cinema that have been published in the last twenty or so years, both in Poland and abroad, women's contribution to cinema and women's issues as represented on screen are either omitted from the authors' discussion or have only a token presence. This treatment of women is by no means unique to scholars and critics dealing with Polish cinema. Many authors examining women in cinemas of other nations, such as Julia Knight in her book, *Women and the New German Cinema* (1992) and Susan Martin-Márquez in *Feminist Discourse and Spanish Cinema* (1999), draw attention to similar absences or inadequate treatment. While there are some common reasons why women are underrepresented or dismissed in the specific publications concerning national cinemas – the main one being the simple fact that female filmmakers represent a minority in the community of filmmakers – virtually in all countries in the world, there are also some reasons that are country specific. In Poland the main cause seems to be regarding women's issues, which, as Maria Janion, whose words we use as an epigraph to our book, puts it, are regarded as 'unserious', as opposed to issues concerning nation, state and religion, which were treated as 'serious'. The consequences of this approach are manifold. One of the most important is the unwillingness of Polish filmmakers of both sexes to give prominence to gender issues because of their fear of entering the domain of an unserious art. Another consequence found in the critical examinations is the repression or at least neglect of the gender dimension of those Polish films that foreground women and their concerns. It appears that this oversight and denigration of women in Polish films on both sides of the camera is unjustifiable, both as an artistic strategy and a critical approach. The aim of this book is to help to rectify it.

The collapse of communism brought hope that other discourses, including those concerned with gender and sexual differences, would replace what

Janion labelled as the domain of 'serious' discussion. So far this hope has been only partially realised. In particular, 'the struggle for independence' still occupies a central position in Polish culture, although it is typically understood in a new way: not as a fight against communism, but against a corrupting Western influence which threatens Polish identity (see Jackowski 1993), pushing to the margins other problems including the question of position of women in Poland, which is central to this book. Accordingly, it is as important now as it was before 1989, if not more so, to reveal and assess the ideologies which determine how women in Poland live, are perceived and represented.

In postcommunist Poland, feminism has been often perceived as one of the most serious threats to the traditional notion of Polish femininity, which was developed during the period of Romanticism and then 'saved' for the welfare of the whole country despite communist attempts to undermine it. In Polish academic circles this populist and nationalistic critique of feminism is avoided; there is, however, a conspicuous distrust of feminism, inasmuch as it is seen as a product of an 'aberrant Western mindset'. This is evident in an editorial of a special issue, devoted to film and feminism, of the journal *Film na świecie* (*Film in the World*) published in 1991:

> We bring this volume of *Film na świecie* to our female and male readers not without a certain anxiety. We devote it, almost wholly, to women's cinema, i.e. to films about Women, made by Women, watched by Women and analised by Women. Our scepticism over the subject of feminism in cinema does not stem from intellectual or cultural conservatism. We simply think that people cannot be divided into women and men, but, rather, into the wise and stupid, the poor and rich, the good and bad, etc. (*Film na świecie* 1991: 13)

This statement is symptomatic of the 'exorcisms' that are performed on feminism in Polish film studies. Authors writing about women in cinema demonstrate, more or less vehemently, their distance from feminist approaches to film. In an anthology, edited by Grażyna Stachówna, *Kobieta z kamerą* (*Woman with the Camera*, 1998a), which includes a number of essays devoted to female directors, this distance or even opposition to feminism emerges at many points. Although it is clear that the very concept of the volume stems from a supposed feminist approach, the editor does not even once use the word 'feminism' in her preface and some of the chapters' authors warn the reader not to locate their essays and the films they discuss in relation to feminism. Tadeusz Lubelski, for example, in his essay on Agnès Varda, claims that her films cannot be properly understood in relation to feminist film studies (Lubelski 1998: 21); Tadeusz Miczka informs us that Lina Wertmüller 'did not identify herself with the feminist movement' (Miczka 1998: 35); and Joanna Korska says, 'I do not want to prove that Barbara Sass is a feminist and I do not think this issue matters for an understanding of her films' (Korska 1998: 84). In order to support their scepticism towards feminism, almost all of these authors quote female directors' interviews in which they oppose labelling their films as 'feminist' or 'women's cinema'.

Distrust of feminism has been openly expressed by Alicja Helman in her introduction to a collection of essays devoted to the representation of women in cinema, *I film stworzył kobietę... (And Film Created Woman...*, Stachówna 1999). In her general characterisation of the essays in the volume she concludes: 'These essays reveal problems specific to women with a greater complexity and subtlety than when they are approached in a way typical to feminism' (Helman 1999: 15). Given the diversity of approaches within feminist analysis, it is not clear which of its strands Helman regards as unsatisfactory. But this can probably be discerned through considering two main ways in which feminism has been employed in Polish film studies. The first attempted to familiarise the Polish reader with translations of seminal feminist texts on film, such as Laura Mulvey's 'Visual Pleasure and Narrative Cinema' (Mulvey 1992), as well as with more general surveys of its basic notions or assumptions. The second way consisted of applying feminism to specific films. In general, the feminist approach in Polish film studies emerged through its poststructuralist variant founded on psychoanalysis and semiotics.

Surprisingly, those who have employed a feminist approach in Polish film studies have rarely, until very recently, undertaken analyses of Polish cinema. A pioneering attempt to look at indigenous films from a feminist perspective has been made by Wiesław Godzic in his book *Film i psychoanaliza (Film and Psychoanalysis*, 1991). He applied the methods of feminist-oriented psychoanalysis to *Przygoda na Mariensztacie (An Adventure at Marienstadt*, Leonard Buczkowski, 1954). Undoubtedly, his interpretation shed a new light on this canonical example of socialist realism in Polish cinema. However, Polish film scholars have commonly regarded his discussion, divorced from a historical and ideological context, as a significant drawback. After Godzic Polish film scholars have applied a feminist approach almost exclusively to Western cinema, as if convinced that it can only be useful in relation to texts that originate from the same cultural tradition as the method used. Hence, the majority of their potential readers diagnosed a feminist approach towards Polish cinema as inappropriate. Simultaneously, the modifications and changes in feminist discourse itself have not been generally acknowledged. Polish film scholars only familiarised themselves with and tried to use feminist concepts and ideas that were developed up to the first half of the 1980s. Later stages in the development of feminist film theory, beginning in the second half of the 1980s, have been overlooked in film studies in Poland. This is particularly unfortunate in light of the fact that the second half of the 1980s brought a significant change in feminist film theory. As Susan Hayward observes,

By then feminists felt that the focus on the textual operations of films was too narrow and that a film needed to be examined within its various contexts –

that is, the historical and social contexts of its production and reception
...There was a need to move on from questions of gender and broaden the
debate to include questions of class and power relations between women, of
differences among the spectating female subjects, of the film industry as more
than just an ideological institution or apparatus of patriarchy that renders
women invisible and constructs Woman – and also to see these questions in
relations to history. Only after this broadening of the debate could gender be
reintroduced. (Hayward 2000: 120–23)

This criticism led to three new strands in feminist film theory. The first was
developed in the United Kingdom, inspired by British cultural studies and
its historical-materialist approach. The new analysis of popular culture
linked the issues of gender with those of class and race in their relation to
power.

The problem of power and possible resistance to it was also a merit of
analyses undertaken by American feminists who, in turn, based their theories on Michel Foucault's work. They offered a new understanding of film
spectatorship that replaced the earlier binary opposition of the
masculine/feminine spectator, arguing that an individual can be positioned
within a cultural discourse in many different ways. In this new approach to
the problem of spectatorship the factors of age, gender, race, class and sexual orientation were regarded as significant modifiers of the process of
reading and interpreting texts.

The third new strand in feminist film theory can be seen as the most radical polemic with the earlier feminism. It was initiated by black feminists,
who argued that so far feminism had been developed as a discourse of
white, middle-class woman which did not contain the experience of women
of colour. As bell hooks claims:

Feminist analyses of woman's lot tend to focus exclusively on gender and do
not provide a solid foundation on which to construct feminist theory. They
reflect the dominant tendency in Western patriarchal minds to mystify
women's reality by insisting that gender is the sole determinant of woman's
fate. (hooks 1984: 12)

It ought to be emphasised here that psychoanalytically oriented feminist
theory offered an essentialist notion of female identity characteristic of
modernism. Contrary to modernist psychology and philosophy, 'recent
approaches to the problem of identity', as Craig Calhoun claims, 'have
stressed the incompleteness, fragmentation and contradictions of both collective and personal existence' (Calhoun 1994: 14). Consequently, the
notion of singular female identity defined through sexual difference has
been gradually replaced by feminism with the category of gender discourse,
which develops within a particular culture and under specific historical,
political and social conditions. This transition that has occurred within
feminism has barely been recognised in Polish film studies. As a consequence, the pragmatic trend that emerged in feminist film criticism in the

last twenty or so years has not been applied as an analytical strategy to examine Polish cinema.

Our book is an attempt to fill this gap. We argue that to examine women's issues in Polish cinema in a comprehensive way it is necessary to go beyond the level of textual analysis and situate the films within a broader system of representation in Polish culture. The latter has been influenced to a significant extent by the national discourse and as such we will pay special attention to it.

Women in Polish Cinema has two principal objectives. Firstly, to examine the main types of female characters in Polish feature cinema, from its beginnings after the First World War to contemporary times. Secondly, to analyse the work of the most prominent Polish women film directors against the background of the roles played by women in Polish history, and their positions within society. For this reason, we begin by considering the most important and enduring female figure in Polish culture: the Polish Mother. We look at the historical origin of this paradigm of femininity and various factors that shaped it, albeit in different ways, such as the Catholic Church, the socialist state and the anti-totalitarian opposition.

The second part of the book, 'Women According to Men' examines the main types of women represented in Polish films. Chapter 2 considers the presence of the myth of the Polish Mother in Polish cinema from its beginning until recent years. In order to demonstrate the stability of this myth we concentrate on two films with distinctive images of the Polish Mother. The first, *Huragan* (*Hurricane*, 1928), directed by Józef Lejtes, is a model of the cinematic representations of the myth in pre-Second World War cinema. The second, *Skarga* (*The Complaint*, 1991), directed by Jerzy Wójcik, is examined as a testimony to the persistence of the myth in postwar culture, including the period after the collapse of communism in 1989.

Chapter 3 analyses a number of Polish cinematic heroines of the early 1950s in order to deconstruct the propagandistic message they were meant to convey. The main issue addressed in this part is whether the idea of a 'New Woman' as presented in such films as, for example, Jan Zelnik's documentary, *Kobiety naszych dni* (*Women of Our Days*, 1951), Maria Kaniewska's *Niedaleko Warszawy* (*Not Far from Warsaw*, 1954), Jan Rybkowski's *Autobus odjeżdża 6.20* (*The Bus Leaves at 6.20*, 1954), and Leonard Buczkowski's *An Adventure at Marienstadt*, successfully challenged the feminine roles prescribed by a supposedly defunct patriarchal hegemony. The chapter concludes with an examination of the figure of the 'Superwoman', which recurred in films made during the 1980s, offering a revisionist perspective on the Stalinist period in both Polish history and cinema.

Chapter 4 focuses on the representations of women in films belonging to the Polish School of the late 1950s, when the rigorous schemata of socialist realism were replaced by films of directors such as Andrzej Wajda,

Andrzej Munk and Kazimierz Kutz, who offered more individualised vision of reality. All of their films dealt with the same theme: a certain type of experience of the Second World War that had been either suppressed or distorted in socialist realist work. This chapter reassesses the portrayals of women in these films, like, for example, Andrzej Wajda's *Pokolenie* (*A Generation*, 1955) and *Lotna* (1959), Andrzej Munk's *Eroica* (1957) and *Pasażerka* (*The Passenger*, 1962), and Wojciech Jerzy Has's *Jak być kochaną?* (*How to be Loved?*, 1963) in order to see whether they reflect with some equality the war experience of both genders.

Chapter 5, devoted to Solidarity heroines, focuses on Agnieszka, the main female character in Andrzej Wajda's *Człowiek z marmuru* (*Man of Marble*, 1976) and *Człowiek z żelaza* (*Man of Iron*, 1981), as a paradigm of Polish woman fighting against communist oppression. Special attention is given to the political background of Agnieszka's 'birth' and her transformation from an independent and strong-headed woman in *Man of Marble* to the thwarted and submissive Polish Mother in *Man of Iron*. This chapter also examines later portrayals of a Solidarity heroine, comparing them to Agnieszka, and reflects on the phenomenon of the actress who played her part, Krystyna Janda, the greatest star of Polish postwar cinema.

In Chapter 6 we discuss the representation of women in Polish postcommunist cinema, arguing that in the 1990s and in the first decade of the new century they are as marginalised in Polish cinema as ever before. More importantly, patriarchal and sexist attitudes, which in earlier periods of Polish cinema were typically masked as the consequence of appropriating a nationalistic and patriotic stance, have been expressed openly since 1989. Moreover, the conflict between the two sexes, which before was hardly articulated in Polish films, now erupted with a vengeance. This led to the proliferation of some female stereotypes such as the witch and the bitch to which the audiences of Polish films had rarely been exposed before. We suggest that this portrayal of women is particularly influenced by the rise of masculinism and the crisis of masculinity which affected Polish society after the collapse of communism.

The last chapter in the second part of the book is devoted to the portrayal of Jewish women, who serve as an archetypal figure of 'the Other woman' in Polish culture, in order to analyse the intersection of the issue of gender and nationality. As analysis of Andrzej Wajda's films *Ziemia obiecana* (*The Promised Land*, 1974) and *Wielki Tydzień* (*Holy Week*, 1995) demonstrates, Jewish women are often constructed in film as an opposition to the femininity created and developed in the Polish national discourse that has its perfect embodiment in the myth of the Polish Mother. The chapter concludes with an analysis of Jan Jakub Kolski's film, *Daleko od okna* (*Far From the Window*, 2000), which offers a revisionist reading of the relationship between Polish and Jewish femininity dominant in Polish cinema.

   To sum up, in the second part of the book we examine how films belonging to the main schools and paradigms of Polish cinema reflected the situation of women in Poland, to what extent their portrayals were stereotyped, how they deviated from other cultural representations of Polish women and what ideological purposes women in Polish films served. Our principal argument, based on the assumption that cinematic representations (as with all other cultural representations) are not neutral but fulfil various ideological functions, is that the main types of female heroines were introduced and developed to support the dominant ideology of the day. These ideologies changed in step with the political and social changes in Poland and abroad, but they also contained some constant elements. In our opinion, Polish women were defined in relation to the state or nation, and to their families, and morally judged according to their success or failure as citizens, fighters for their homeland's independence and welfare, as well as wives and mothers. The burden of responsibility placed on the shoulders of the average Polish woman was very heavy. She was expected to make sacrifices which in many other societies were attributed only to men, including fighting against the nation's enemies, contributing to material production by working in the factories and on the land, as well as fulfilling the traditional female obligations, such as childbearing and homemaking. This position of Polish women had both advantages and drawbacks. The main advantage was the relatively high status of (at least some) women in Poland. They were figures of authority, widely admired – even revered – in art and literature, as well as respected in the domestic setting. The crucial disadvantage of this specific situation was their constrained subjectivity, combined with widespread disregard by state institutions of their individual, private needs. On the whole, patriarchy to a large extent shaped and policed the lives of Polish women. Similarly, representations of women in the majority of Polish films were firmly rooted in patriarchal discourse. It is worth emphasising that the collapse of communism in 1989 did not fundamentally change either the position of women in society or the way they are depicted in films. Paradoxically, the introduction of democracy not only failed to set women free, but undermined the special position Polish women had enjoyed in sociocultural life for several centuries.

   Although the representation of women is the focus of our discussion in this part, we also tackle the way men are portrayed in Polish films. Men cannot be ignored in this context because gender operates dialectically: the position of women must be measured in relation to the situation of men. It must be added that the second part of the book focuses on films directed by men. To paraphrase Lucy Fischer, who once wrote that 'women have no monopoly on feminist art' (Fischer 1989: 18), male directors do not have a monopoly on cinema, advocating patriarchy or misogyny. However, it must equally be stressed that male directors played a dominant role in promoting and elaborating numerous stereotypes of both women and men that conveyed patriarchal ideology. For example, they created various types of noble, patriotic Polish men: sons, husbands and fiancés, for whom Polish Mothers wanted to sacrifice their personal happiness and even life. Similarly, in the period of socialist realism they 'gave birth' to high-minded and generous male Party secretaries who helped young women to reach higher positions on the professional ladder (but never as high as that which they occupied themselves). Furthermore, after the collapse of communism male cinema made the audience believe that Polish males suffered multiple crises because of women's selfishness and greed. Hence, cinema (more than any other area of national art) expects women to pay for the various disappointments which the political, social and economic transformation brought to Polish men. The structure of the second part of *Women in Polish Cinema* reflects how in different periods of Polish cinema male directors used and transformed ideas and images of both sexes in a way that was beneficial to male causes.

In the third part of the book, 'Women behind the Camera', we examine whether patriarchy was also conveyed in the films directed by female filmmakers, as well as discuss other topics and motives of their films relevant to the problem of representing women. This part is devoted to the work of four female directors: Wanda Jakubowska, Barbara Sass, Agnieszka Holland and Dorota Kędzierzawska. They were chosen primarily because of their important place in Polish cinema. Jakubowska and Holland also gained some recognition abroad, the former mainly thanks to the topical subjects of her films, made soon after the Second World War, the latter as a result of making some of her best films abroad.

Chapter 8, devoted to Wanda Jakubowska, explores two main topics of her films: life in the concentration camps during the Second World War and changes in Polish society and culture after the introduction of communism. It pays particular attention to Jakubowska's advocacy of the communist cause, reflecting her personal beliefs and her professional standing as one of the highest-profile filmmakers to join the Polish Communist Party after the Second World War. We also attempt to establish whether and how her films reflected problems specific to women, such as motherhood.

Discussion of films directed by Barbara Sass in Chapter 9 considers her as an author of women's films, namely films about and for women – the only Polish director who was ever regarded this way. We discern in Sass's work two distinctive strands. In one, which coincides with the early part of her career, she is concerned with the position of women in contemporary Polish society. In the second strand she chooses women from earlier epochs as the main characters, and represents them as melodrama heroines. By looking at the various aspects of Sass's films belonging to these strands, such as the construction of the heroines, *mise-en-scène*, and the mode of addressing the spectator, we attempt to establish whether and to what extent the label 'an author of women's films' is justified in regard to this director.

Chapter 10 examines the Polish films by Agnieszka Holland, who is undoubtedly the most renowned Polish female director. Although she does not perceive herself as a representative of 'women's cinema', thanks to the diversity of themes, styles and ideological positions she achieves an effect of remarkable heterogeneity which may well be considered symptomatic of cinema made by women. Moreover, the chapter shows that in her Polish films Holland deals with the subject matter and motives that pertain to the dilemmas experienced by contemporary women. The persistence of these themes allows her to be located in the context of 'women's cinema' understood in the broadest way.

The final chapter is devoted to the cinema of Dorota Kędzierzawska. Due to her interest in those who live at the margins of society – ethnic minorities, children and single mothers – and her use of formal rupture and visual stylisation, we regard her work as closest to a paradigm of feminist cinema, identified with the critical work of Laura Mulvey and Claire Johnston, often described as 'feminist counter-cinema'. The second main frame of reference applied in this chapter is a radical version of postmodernism, associated with the work of Jean-Luc Godard. We suggest that these two approaches are in an important sense similar, as both encourage deconstruction and decentring as a means to interrogate reality and cinema. Our list of female directors is short, reflecting our decision to concentrate only on the most distinctive examples of Polish women's cinema, but also the fact that only a handful of women succeeded in making films in Poland and even fewer achieved national recognition. It must also be added that female directors in Poland were often confined – by informal means or simply by tradition – to making low-budget films, addressed to an audience of children, or dealing with problems affecting children. Three of the directors discussed in this book, Wanda Jakubowska, Agnieszka Holland and Dorota Kędzierzawska, also made films for or about children. We mention this fact not to undermine their overall achievements or to suggest that children's films deserve less attention than adult films, but to emphasise a specific ghettoisation that Polish women risked when embarking on a career in filmmaking. This was the fate of, amongst others, Maria Kaniewska and Anna Sokołowska, two accomplished female directors, who barely entered the 'male' territory of making films about adults and continued to be treated as second-class citizens in the community of Polish filmmakers. Similarly, if it was not for her third film, *Nic* (*Nothing*, 1998), which was the first in Kędzierzawska's career to depict mainly adult characters, this highly original director would probably have remained regarded simply as a director of 'small, obscure films' which do not deserve wider distribution, let alone publicity. The fear of being marginalised in the Polish cinematic world was a crucial factor in why Polish women filmmakers rarely produced films directed specifically at women, such as films about adolescence, childbearing or avant-garde films addressing women's sensibilities, and instead concentrated on general social issues. The desire to be part of a wider artistic or political movement within Polish cinema and to be treated as a serious filmmaker also explains to a large extent why female directors avoided certain genres such as criminal film and comedy. Until the collapse of communism generic cinema in general, and these genres in particular, were treated with contempt by film critics – as pure entertainment. Hence, if women embarked on making comedies and thrillers, they would risk double marginalisation: as female filmmakers and as producers of low art.

The directors whose work we choose to analyse represent different generations. The first to be discussed, Wanda Jakubowska, was born in 1907 and started her cinematic career in the 1930s; the last one, Dorota Kędzierzawska, was born in 1957 and made her début in the 1990s. On the one hand, this suggests that female directors, however rare, were somehow present in all periods of the cinematic history of Poland; on the other, that there was never a 'women's movement' in Polish cinema. Polish female filmmakers, not unlike women playing prominent roles in other spheres of culture, played down gender divisions. This view also applies to post-communist times, when there are more female directors in Poland, both in absolute terms and as a proportion of all directors (which is, however, still low in comparison with other European countries, such as Germany). At the same time, the chosen directors played a significant role in Polish cinema. Jakubowska, Holland and Sass participated in the important movements in Polish national cinema: Jakubowska in START and socialist realism, Sass and Holland in the Cinema of Moral Concern. The youngest director discussed here, Dorota Kędzierzawska, who began her career after the collapse of communism, is also, in many senses, the most marginal. One of our objectives in the third part of the book is to analyse what subjects interested these four directors and how they tackled them. Consequently, we would like to explore their attitude to national and international history, politics and culture, including the previously mentioned myth of the Polish Mother. By doing this we also wish to establish whether belonging to some particular movement in Polish cinema, or, conversely, placing oneself in opposition to them, and favouring certain genres and styles, was compatible with, or perhaps even conducive to advancing the female cause and using specifically feminist aesthetics. In other words, we wish to examine whether Jakubowska, Holland, Sass and Kędzierzawska can be regarded as creators of 'women's cinema'. Yet, this is not a straightforward task, as the concept of women's cinema is notoriously difficult to define. It suggests, as Alison Butler observes in her study of this phenomenon, films made by, addressed to, or concerned with women, or all three. Moreover, various authors emphasise different and sometimes even contradictory features as essential qualities of women's films. However, for the purpose of our research into the work of Polish directors, we will refer to Butler's definition of women's cinema as minor cinema: cinema that uses the same language as mainstream cinema, but with different concerns. Butler argues for considering women's cinema as minor cinema, as opposed to 'counter-cinema' (which was favoured by earlier authors, especially Laura Mulvey), because 'the plurality of forms, concerns and constituencies in contemporary women's cinema now exceeds even the most flexible definition of "counter-cinema"' (Butler 2002: 19).

While we accept Butler's arguments for using this term, we will also point to another reason, which is specific to the situation of Polish female directors (with the possible exception of Dorota Kędzierzawska) – namely, their previously mentioned desire to play a pivotal role in the main paradigms and debates in the national cinema, while simultaneously creating films conveying interests rarely expressed in male films. Consequently, this book will concentrate not on a comparison of the work of Jakubowska, Holland, Sass and Kędzierzawska with some abstract 'women's cinema', but rather will attempt to establish whether and in what sense their work can be treated as an alternative discourse to the male one. As a result, the reader of our book can treat the second and third parts as complementary.

Our book utilises a variety of approaches and methods. It looks both at text and context, at the director's work and her biography, at the film itself and its importance for different generations of viewers. There were several reasons for producing such a heterogeneous work rather than using a uniform method of research. Firstly, we felt that each phenomenon, be it a type of representation or a body of work of a particular director, deserves a specific approach because of its particularities in terms of subject, style and ideology, as well as the unique set of circumstances in which it was born. We share Bakhtin's belief that 'just as lava differs from the rock it will become, so the two states of lived experience, on the one hand, and systems of registering such experience on the other, are fundamentally different from each other' (Holquist 1999: x). In other words, disunity and heterogeneity is built into the nature of things and any form of depiction should account for what is particular and situational in the world, the 'once occurent event of Being' (Bakhtin, quoted in Farmer 1999: 381). In our analyses we try to employ Bakhtin's notion of 'architectonics' which is 'a way to generalise the particular without compromising its very particularity, its concretness' (Farmer 1999: 381).

Secondly, research on women's issues in general and women's cinema in particular is in a state of flux, and as we have already suggested, few assumptions and theses go uncontested. Moreover, a substantial number of feminist film critics suggest that rather than employ a rigid theory or methodology, those interested in feminist art should embrace a multitude of approaches and perspectives or even reject theory (see Wallace 1994: 5). Nevertheless, we feel that we owe the reader an explanation of how we use the biographies of female filmmakers – especially which aspects and moments of the women filmmakers' lives we regard as constitutive to their development as filmmakers. Our conviction, which arises from the contemporary concept of identity as fluid and shaped by a multitude of factors, is that for each director these aspects and moments were different, as each biography was a result of different set of circumstances. For example, in the case of Wanda Jakubowska's becoming a film director, a particular role was played by her involvement in the communist movement and incarceration in a concentration camp; for Holland it was having a Jewish father who opposed the communist regime. In addition, we refer to the directors' biographies to emphasise the obstacles Polish women (not unlike their Western 'sisters') have to overcome to enter the mainly masculine world of filmmaking. On the whole, by considering biography we embrace the feminist conviction that every piece of knowledge and every opinion is a 'located knowledge' and a 'located opinion', formed and developed in a particular set of historical circumstances.

Theoretical debate concerning 'women's cinema' is usually conducive to creating such a cinema as a distinctive phenomenon. In countries in which such a debate has been widespread, particularly Britain in the 1970s, the ideas discussed were put into practice by a stream of female directors, including Sally Potter and Laura Mulvey. In contrast, until recently Poland has had no significant feminist theory or critique – not one that would inspire female directors to make films deliberately different from their male colleagues. We hope that our discussion, albeit in a minor way, will play a positive role in encouraging other Polish scholars and perhaps female filmmakers to take part in a debate concerning the existence, character and status of women's cinema in Poland.

The Polish Mother

CHAPTER 1

The Myth of the Polish Mother

JOANNA SZWAJCOWSKA

Let the Mother, the Queen, the Handmaid make every Polish woman live like a Mother, be adored like a Queen, sacrifice for the Nation like a Handmaid.
Stefan Cardinal Wyszyński (1978: 190)

The Historical Sources of the Myth

The myth of the Polish Mother, like many other Polish national myths, emerged in the nineteenth century in partitioned Poland. In its original version it referred to the position and role that Polish women allegedly played in that period. While general statements about the Polish Mother have usually been qualified as reconstructions of a model, the model itself seems to have delineated areas on which more meticulous research focused. As Grażyna Borkowska points out, most of the research has been geared towards uncovering the patriotic-martyrological aspect of women's lives to the neglect of other areas of their activity. This is expressed, on the one hand, in the frequency with which descriptions of women's suffering and sacrifice appear in historical writing and, on the other, in the ease with which all kinds of public activity are subsumed under the label of political-patriotic (Borkowska 1996: 33–38).

Bearing this in mind, I shall try to account for the historical circumstances which allowed the myth to arise. First of all, we must remember that in its nineteenth-century version the myth pertained to women of the gentry (*szlachta*) to include, by the end of the century, the newly formed stratum of intelligentsia. It is interesting, therefore, to refer briefly to the earlier gentry tradition and the implications its form might have had for women. According to Nora Koestler, the specific position that the gentry occupied in the 'republic of nobles' had a positive influence on the self-awareness of the female part of this stratum. The author argues that the privileges and freedoms that the gentry enjoyed, although in a strictly political sense concerning only men, awakened women's emancipatory needs (Koestler 1992: 31–42; Kuchowicz 1990: 7–50). One should not overrate the progressiveness of the 'gentry democracy', which was limited to one closed, social group and had little to do with modern ideas of individual freedom;[1] however, it remains true that the privileged status, at least in part, extended also to women.

Discussing the position of Polish women in the nineteenth century, particularly in the context of the mythical figure of the Polish Mother, one has to take into account the role which in the occupied country was ascribed to the home, the family – in other words, to the private sphere. With some differences between the three partitioned areas, Poland remained a predominantly agricultural country, which contributed to maintaining a traditional family model.[2] Within this model, the family in the time of partitions was assigned specific tasks. This pertains particularly to the territories controlled by the Russians and Prussians, where the policy of the occupiers was most repressive, although the intensity of political repression and extent of denationalising practices fluctuated over time. In the Russian part the anti-Polish policy tightened as a consequence of the insurrections. The efforts at russification included severe censorship on the works of Polish history and literature and restrictions on school curricula concerning the teaching of the Polish language, history, geography and literature. After 1864, teachers were forced to teach Polish in Russian to Polish children. The situation in the Prussian part deteriorated after 1872, when germanisation acquired a more systematic character. Where formerly Polish would be used in teaching German, in 1872 German was made compulsory in all state-run schools and Polish was forbidden except for religious instruction. In such a situation home became the main refuge of 'Polishness' and women began to play an important role in the transmission of national traditions and culture. The education of children gained the status of a patriotic task. Autobiographies and memories often refer to the role that the home played in the patriotic education of their authors:

> Mother, a stubborn patriot, didn't even try to conceal her pain and disappointment caused by the failure of the insurrection. She was educating us placing a stress on the necessity of a further struggle with the enemy of the Patriae. From earliest childhood we were made familiar with the poetry of our 'bards', with particular attention to the forbidden works. We were taught Polish history, only Polish books were bought. (Piłsudski, quoted in Zygmuntowicz 1989: 5)

Jan Prokop draws attention to a number of possible consequences of the annexation of the public sphere by the occupiers and the transfer of some of its functions to the private sphere of the home and family. First, the fact that national identity was shaped at home, in the circle of the family, rendered to it a particularly intimate dimension. Instilled in childhood, it referred to the roots of the identity of an individual and thanks to it gained strong emotional underpinnings. In 'normal' circumstances the awareness of belonging to a nation, of being a citizen of a state, is somehow more external as it is taught as a part of school education, or through entering into other state structures. Therefore, it refers more to the sense of the common interests of the community rather than being a personal issue. Prokop argues that this way of perceiving national identity endowed Polish patriotism with specifically intimate tones which allowed people to think of Poland in very personal, family terms (Prokop 1993: 22–23). This phenomenon is certainly not unique to Polish culture; it is probably common to all nationalities whose identity is threatened by external factors.

The shift between public and private, according to Prokop, also had consequences for the balance of gender relations. Not only did women preside in homes, which became so important to the national survival, but as a consequence of restrictions on recruiting Polish men to higher administrative offices, the men – if they did not become insurgents or conspirators – lost some of the social prestige normally associated with their public activity. Moreover, no matter how limited the public involvement of men might be, it still often required some compromise with the foreign authorities. Women, who did not have to face officialdom, could afford a more steadfast attitude (Prokop 1991: 414–17). Some authors observe that a similar phenomenon took place later in socialist Poland, where the distortion of the channels of professional promotion and mechanisms of social recognition had a frustrating effect on men, leading sometimes to a sense of emasculation (Watson 1993: 471–87). At the same time political and economic circumstances led to the increase of the role of the family and therefore also women.

Let us return to the question of women's roles in partitioned Poland. The realisation of the role of an educator in the patriotic tradition was but one of the fields of women's activity which contributed to the construction of the myth. Equally important was the heroic aspect referring to women's participation in the insurrections, in which they mainly shouldered such tasks as caring for the wounded, or giving shelter and helping the insurgents. The examples of women who, after the collapse of successive insurrections, followed their husbands or sons in exile to Siberia fostered the martyrological aspect of the myth, which stresses the selflessness and capacity to sacrifice. Others, who remained at home, faced the hardships and responsibilities of maintaining the household on their own (see Śliwowska 1990: 207–26; Caban 1994).

The patriotic consciousness of women found expression also on a more symbolic level. Jewellery, often donated for the needs of the insurrections, was substituted by rings coined from handcuffs or other pieces decorated with national symbols. The black clothes that women wore after the defeats of insurrections denoted not only mourning for the deaths of relatives, but the symbolic death of the motherland.

The autobiographical material of Eliza Orzeszkowa (a famous writer of the period of positivism) provides an exemplary portrait of a Polish female patriot, and although biographers claim that Orzeszkowa often idealised the motivations underlying her decisions, or made declarations which were not confirmed by facts, she did so to comply with the standing norms of patriotic behaviour. Let us look at a few examples in which she presents the autobiographical facts to convey an image of a model patriot. Orzeszkowa's activity during the January insurrection of 1863 is beyond doubt: she transported food, bandages and mail, she gave shelter to Romuald Traugutt, one of the leaders of the insurrection and then helped him to escape (Żmigrodzka 1965: 55). As a consequence, her husband, who was much less involved than her, was sentenced to exile. Orzeszkowa didn't follow him and a few years later wrote in a letter:

> No matter what, I didn't go with my husband to Siberia, and it was because I didn't love him. At that time I didn't understand well what I was doing; then it became for me a pang of conscience which lasts until today. I consider this lack of generosity for a man who suffered for the dearest cause as one of the most important ethical errors I have ever made. (Orzeszkowa, quoted in Jankowski 1980: 11–12)

Orzeszkowa clearly subscribes to the view that personal reasons should not prevail over the requirements of 'the Cause', and if personal happiness interferes with the patriotic duties, the first has to be sacrificed. It is exactly in such terms that she presents her failure to remarry: 'It may well be that I will be forced to choose between the duty to remain in the country, which I consider an enormous one in the present circumstances, and my heart's desires, as well as prospects of family happiness. Needless to say, I will choose the first' (Orzeszkowa, quoted in Żmigrodzka 1965: 72). How sincere Orzeszkowa was in such declarations (see Żmigrodzka 1965: 65; Jankowski 1980: 11) is of less importance in this case; what matters is that they point to the fact that choices could be considered in this light. In other words, there existed a defined model to which a woman should aspire. This model required sacrifice of personal life for the good of the nation.

The conflict between the 'heart's desires' and the demands of the patriotic code, which Orzeszkowa alludes to in her testimony, is incorporated into the myth of the Polish Mother. Within the nationalist discourse women-mothers face an irresolvable dilemma between motherly love and the need to protect a child, on the one hand, and the duty of a patriot, on the other. The latter calls for them not only to produce as many children as possible, but then to send their sons to war for the Patriae. Therefore, the concept of the Polish Mother refers also to the sacrifice that women had to make of their children and the suffering connected to that.

These remarks concerning the historical background against which the myth arose allow us to define the main aspects or themes to which it pertains. First, it concerns the role of women in the transmission of culture and language in the conditions of repressive policy of foreign occupiers. Second, it incorporates the heroic aspect connected to women's participation in the direct struggle with the oppressors. The final theme relates to the suffering women experience as mothers, wives and sisters losing their relatives in the insurrections, and as patriots mourning the misfortunes of their country.

The Romantic Roots and Civil Religion

The period of Romanticism, during which artistic production multiplied the mythical figures and realities, contributed largely to establishing conceptions of Polish nationalistic discourse. Before focusing on the artistic representations of the myth of the Polish Mother it is worthwhile, therefore, to examine the role that Romanticism has played in Polish cultural and national life. Maria Janion refers to Romanticism as the 'basic and almost obligatory system of dialogue in Polish literature'. Its role has gone beyond the sphere of artistic influence to become a shared code of the nation enabling an expression of symbolic values. Moreover, Janion argues, the period of Romanticism marks the beginning of the modern era in Poland, shaping the Polish mentality much more effectively than the ideas of the Enlightenment (Janion 1975: 23). Marta Piwińska, the author of an interesting analysis of the reception of Romanticism in Poland, claims that the Romantics' language has become a 'metalanguage, by means of which every Pole can enter a field of community and communicate with another' (Piwińska 1973: 37).

The common language created by Romantic literature concerned, first of all, patriotic values. In the face of the loss of statehood, the Romantic poets took upon themselves the task of maintaining and developing the national identity. This led to a production of grand theories of the destiny of nations and the role of the individual, as well as to a rich literary output which translated the ideas into a poetic language. In the context of Polish Romanticism particular attention has to be drawn to the development of messianism. Not only were the ideas of messianism dominant in the Romantic interpretation of the role of Poland in the world's history, but they seem to have provided a basis for the development of the Polish civil religion.

The messianic ideas of Polish Romanticism can be summarised, in a crude outline, as follows. God reveals himself in the universal history of humanity through the repetition of the sacred story of sacrifice and redemption. The history of Poland, persecuted by tyrants, is a replication of Christ's martyrdom and, therefore, Poland becomes identified with the figure of Christ. The role that she is to play in the history of the world is analogous: her 'crucifixion' and sacrifice will end in the defeat of her oppressors and her resurrection will give a beginning to a new era of freedom and justice on earth (Piwińska 1973: 30; see also Janion 1975: 81). The role of an individual, or rather his destiny, is closely connected to the destiny of the nation – Adam Mickiewicz said: 'to be Polish is not a nationality, it is a destiny' – and requires sacrifice and the abandoning of private life and individual pursuits. These two themes: messianic/sacrificial and heroic/ insurrectionist provided a literary base for the formulation of 'Polish patriotic style' (Janion 1979: 78).

The religious underpinnings were well assimilated by society and reinforced by the particular situation of religion in the occupied country. For us the most interesting aspect of the development of civil religion (see Morawska 1984: 29) is the one that relates to the Marian cult: a particularly strong trend in the Polish Catholicism. There seem to be two overlapping factors that have strengthened and granted a particular status to the worship of the Virgin Mary in Poland. On the one hand, the cult of Mary is a stable and prominent element of popular religion, which undeniably has been an important part of religiosity in Poland (Hamington 1995: 11–29). On the other, and what is perhaps more interesting in our case, is the national dimension of worship which made the Virgin Mary a part of Polish history. In fact, it is the figure of the Virgin Mary which has most persistently functioned in the double role of a religious and a national symbol. Numerous chapels and shrines all over Poland may be an expression of the popular cult of Our Lady; however, the chapels erected in the courtyards of Warsaw houses during the insurrection of 1944 appealed to the collective image of Mary as a patroness of Polish combat against invaders. The Black Madonna of Jasna Góra is an addressee of thousands of individual prayers and a performer of miraculous recoveries, but at the same time she is believed to have lent her support at crucial moments in Polish history, such as the defence of the Monastery against Swedish troops in 1655, or the battle with the Soviet army in 1920, known as the 'miracle over the Vistula river'. The best known piece of Polish poetry, which every child learns at school by heart, is the Invocation in *Pan Tadeusz*, which reads:

Panno Święta, co Jasnej bronisz Częstochowy
I w Ostrej świecisz Bramie! Ty! Co lud zamkowy
Nowogródzki ochraniasz z jego wiernym ludem!
Jak mnie dziecko do zdrowia powróciłaś cudem ...
Tak nas powrócisz cudem na Ojczyzny łono ...

O Holy Virgin, who dost oversee
Bright Częstochowa and in Wilno shinest
Above the Ostra Gate! Thou who inclinest
To shelter Nowogródek with its folk
In faithfulness. When I, in youth, bespoke
Thy help, by miracle thou didst restore

My failing health
So by miracle thou wilt decree
That we regain our country. (Mickiewicz 1981: 9)

The power of the symbol in its extrareligious dimension was confirmed in the postwar period. Perhaps the most spectacular example of this was the 'arrest' of the icon by the regime authorities during its peregrination through Poland, organised in connection with the celebrations of the *Millennium* (the tenth centenary of Poland's conversion to Christianity) in 1966. The massive gatherings of people on the arrival of the painting clearly indicated a failure of the secularising policy of the state and as such became a political act. The personal devotion to the Virgin Mary of the Primate Wyszyński, as well as of the former Archbishop of Cracow, Pope John Paul II – both perceived as important figures on the political scene – certainly contributed to the strengthening of the cult and further appropriation of the symbol into the political realm, as did the badge of the Black Madonna in Lech Wałęsa's lapel, or the icons hung on the shipyard's gates during the workers' strikes in Gdańsk in the 1980s.

How does it relate to the development of the myth of the Polish Mother? The Romantic poetry, permeated with religious imagery, initiated the formulation of the myth on the level of artistic expression. One of the recurring aspects of the representations of the female figure is associated with suffering and sacrifice, and more or less explicitly refers to the symbolism of the Dolorosa, the Mother of Sorrows. It is interesting to relate the metaphorical pronouncements to Adam Mickiewicz's assertions concerning women's emancipation:

> Such is the inevitable way of humanity: first, one has to make a sacrifice to gain a right. It is in this way that the woman liberates herself in Poland; she has here a greater liberty than anywhere else, she is more respected, she feels she is the man's companion. It is not through arguing about women's rights, not through announcing of invented theories that women will acquire value in society, but through sacrifice. (Mickiewicz, quoted in Janion 1996b: 96–97)

Although Mickiewicz's poetic output often transgressed the boundaries of Catholic dogma, it would be hard to deny in this case a clear endorsement of the idea of salvation through suffering and sacrifice. Perpetuated in poetry, the model of a sacrificing, suffering woman constitutes one of the layers of the myth of the Polish Mother.

On the other hand, the most popular Polish icon, the Black Madonna, is associated with a different symbolic area: as the Queen of Poland and her patroness,[3] she is not only a comforter of the 'crucified' nation, but a figure representing power, authority and heroism. It is difficult to establish a direct link between the literary images of Polish heroines and this interpretation of the religious symbol; however, strong, heroic and unwavering female figures appear in abundance in Polish cultural texts, building another layer of the myth.

Why is the religious imagery so important for the analysis of the myth of the Polish Mother? It is clear that associations of the myth with the figure of the Virgin Mary can be established. On the one hand, it takes us to the debate over the role of the single most significant female religious symbol in Western civilisation. On the other, it allows some insights into the ways in which the universal meanings of the symbol have been adapted in Poland, and into the implications that the insistence on the particular meanings and interpretations has had for Polish culture. Before we focus on the interpretations of the universal meanings of the figure of the Virgin Mary, let us refer briefly to the position of sociologists of religion.

The question concerning the religious dimension of the myth can be placed in a broader framework of sociological studies of religion. In traditional approaches, one way of defining the main aspects of religiosity were survey techniques that closed religious phenomena in a number of indices or parameters (see Piwowarski 1975). This method, however, was criticised for its inadequacy in accounting for the religious aspects of modern life. As Wade Clark Roof argues, in the modern world, religion, whose functions have been changing in the process of secularisation, is more than ever diffused throughout the culture and no longer contained by formal institutions (Roof 1985: 76). It may be claimed that in case of Polish religiosity, in which the institutionalised forms are relatively well preserved, the traditional methods are not entirely anachronistic. At the same time, however, it is obvious that religion, like anywhere else and, in fact, at any historical time, has permeated to other areas of culture. The religious connotations contained in the myth of the Polish Mother, which by now functions well in secular contexts, may be an example of this process.

The overall meaning of the myth goes far beyond a particular representation of the figure of the Virgin Mary; however, as I have indicated, the presence of religious content is detectable. While the general, many-layered construction of the myth is of most interest to us, it seems useful to place its religious undertones in the context of a broader debate concerning the role that the symbol of the Virgin Mary has had in shaping the gender order. Let me begin, however, with drawing attention to the aspect of feminist criticism that highlights the process of a 'social construction' of Mary (see Daly 1973; Warner 1976; Kristeva 1986; Hamington 1995), which provides an interesting commentary to our hypothesis about possible adaptations or interpretations of the symbol in particular cultural environments. In its universal articulations, the symbol, in the form in which it is present in contemporary discourse, is, in fact, a compound of different meanings built over the course of centuries. Maurice Hamington, offering a step-by-step reconstruction of the growth of the Marian cult and of the pluralistic nature of dogmatic development, concludes:

Mary became an objectified reality of mythic proportions in the early Church. She was subsequently reified on an unofficial level by the faithful who adored her, and was later reified on a dogmatic level through the infallible papal pronouncements. Mary's constructed reality was perpetuated by the internalisation of Catholics in their faith education and the abundance of stories that circulated about her. Through Marian apologetics, she has been legitimised in each age by various dogmas and pronouncements. The continuing phenomenon of apparitions serves to further legitimise Mary as an ongoing powerful religious force. (Hamington 1995: 25)

Developing over time, Mary has been a part of religion which in Clifford Geertz's words is 'a system of symbols which acts to establish powerful, pervasive, and long-lasting moods and motivations ... which cast a derivative, lunar light over the solid features of a people's secular life' (Geertz 1973: 90). Moreover, the resplendent growth of the Marian cult, whose extent, at some point, began to alarm the Church hierarchy (see Hamington 1995: 22), testifies to a particular popularity and appeal of the figure of Our Lady.

What is, therefore, the message that the symbol conveys? The feminist criticism directed against the figure of the Virgin Mary pertains to many aspects which in their comprehensive meaning constitute a very limiting and frustrating model of femininity and women's roles. Firstly, the figure of Mary fixes the essence of being a woman on motherhood, which reduces the field of women's self-fulfilment to the realisation of a biological function. The association of femininity with motherhood has been strongly pronounced in the discourse of the Church (see Camp 1990; Caldwell 1991: 19–27; Hamington 1995) and on a symbolic level has led to a situation where 'the *consecrated* (religious or secular) representation of femininity is absorbed by motherhood' (Kristeva 1986: 163). Secondly, through a simultaneous valorisation of virginity, the symbol sets up constraints on female sexuality, as well as embodying an impossible ideal – motherhood and virginity being mutually exclusive, thus condemning real women to a position of imperfection (Caldwell 1991: 19). Thirdly, it reserves for a woman, at best, the place of a mediatrix with the divine (male) power. In fact, it situates her in an inferior position even in relation to her son, which hierarchical model, among others, feeds into the concept of asymmetrical parenting (Hamington 1995: 120–22). Additionally, the alternative model of femininity present in Western culture, expressed in the myth of Eve, ensnares women in a model of moral dichotomy, which relegates sexual desires into the realm of the evil and sin, thus reinforcing Mary's asexuality as an ideal.

This admittedly most cursory punctuation of the main tenets of feminist criticism concerning the figure of the Virgin Mary aims at drawing attention to the universal implications ascribed to the symbol, which will enable us to refer to some of these meanings in the analysis of the myth of the Polish Mother.

Representations of the Polish Mother in Cultural Texts

In so far as historical discourse or religious symbols (to which I have referred in the two previous sections) can be treated as cultural texts, here I refer specifically to works of art. What I seek to present are the main recurring themes, the imagery which refers us to the myth of the Polish Mother and the scenes which in a changed form reappear in successive representations in films, iconography and literature.

Ever since the Romantic literature and fine arts introduced the image of the Polish Mother it has been exploited in Polish art, whether with due respect to the values it represented, or with the sneering irony of critics of the Romantic 'national religion'. This has been the lot, too, of male Romantic heroes, with the difference, perhaps, that the Kordians, Wallenrods, Gustaw-Konrads[4] have met with a parallel interest of literary criticism. The fact that the figure of the Polish Mother has not merited enough attention to meet with a comprehensive analysis seemingly does not prevent a common understanding of allusions to it in academic literature, art, as well as in everyday life. Jan Prokop, writing about the tradition of the Polish home, which for generations has been a school for future soldiers of freedom, comments upon the tasks of the parents: 'It is to such risky enough career, how different from the success in trade of the Buddenbrocks, that many of the Polish fathers and mothers wanted to prepare their children. And the Polish Mother in particular!' (Prokop 1993: 28). Renata Siemieńska, referring to the female partisans, insurgents and members of resistance movements of the Second World War writes: 'The memory of women's participation in the struggle against the Nazis lingers on as memory of the Polish Mother who struggled and sacrificed her life during the war, side by side with men' (Siemieńska 1986: 16). Bogdan Cywiński, drawing a literary portrait of the Polish Catholic suggests that the Polish Mother may be his female counterpart: 'This figure, usually equipped with Slavic comeliness, combines familiarity of a girl not fearing even the most prosaic tasks with the pride of the future Polish Mother, stability of feelings with capacity to sacrifice them for the good of the motherland' (Cywiński 1971: 213). Kazimierz Kutz, in his film *Perła w koronie* (*A Pearl in the Crown*, 1972), presents a scene in which a representative of striking miners who goes to negotiate with the management says, 'Give me a woman with some medals: a Polish Mother type.'

One of the ways in which the myth is kept alive is through artistic representations. Let us look at some of the literary, film and iconographic works to see how the myth has been reproduced over the time. In his poem written after the fall of the November insurrection of 1830, 'Do Matki Polki' ('To a Polish Mother') Mickiewicz draws a poignant picture of the destiny of a Polish mother, whose son is doomed to defeat and death in the unfair struggle with the invader. In the face of his future fate, the mother has to prepare herself, as well as her son, for the awaiting martyrdom. Her own suffering becomes associated with the suffering of the Virgin Mother, and the Mother Dolorosa comes to symbolise the fate of Polish women:

O matko Polko! źle się twój syn bawi!
Klęknij przed Matki Boleśnej obrazem
I na miecz patrzaj, co jej serce krwawi:
Takim wróg piersi twe przeszyje razem!

O Polish Mother, here great griefs are stored.
Before the Mother of Our Sorrows kneel;
look on her heart with its tranfixing sword
and read the blows your bosom must feel. (Mickiewicz 1957: 28–30)

A concrete personification of the poetic image of the suffering mother, embedded in a narrative structure of a drama, is found in Mickiewicz's *Dziady* (*The Forefathers' Eve*, 1832) in the figure of Mrs Rollison. Here, an old, blind woman, a widow, comes to a representative of the tsarist authorities to beg for mercy for her imprisoned and tortured son. On her second visit, when she thinks her son has been killed, she seems to find supernatural powers to force the entrance to the senator's room in a desperate attempt at a revenge for her son's death. Although the figure of Mrs Rollison appears in two brief episodes, it has grown into a powerful symbol of a mother's pain, suffering and courage, which is reflected in the permanent presence of references to these scenes in contemporary representations of mothers.

The figure has a nearly literal replica in the character of Mrs Soerensen, from a drama by Leon Kruczkowski, *Niemcy* (*The Germans*), written in 1949. This time, the woman comes to negotiate her son's lot with a Nazi officer, hoping that a precious golden necklace may aid her in winning his help. In Agnieszka Holland's film of 1981, *Kobieta samotna* (*A Woman Alone*), a desperate mother, who lives with her son in terrible material conditions, tries to get access to the offices of the Party authorities to seek help. The scene takes place in a completely different context; however, her fight with a guard on the steps inevitably brings to mind Mrs Rollison's entrance to the Russian senator's room. *Matka Królów* (*Mother of the Kings* 1982; *król* in Polish means *king*), from Janusz Zaorski's film, probably the most famous mother of the postwar cinema, in a scene with a cynical lawyer defending her rebellious son, tries to bribe him with jewellery. In another scene we see her waiting patiently at the foot of a staircase for an 'audience' with a representative of the authorities. Maria Nurowska, a popular writer whose novels are a mine of Romantic clichés, draws a couple of portraits of Mrs Rollison, whether of the epoch in characteristically entitled *Panny i wdowy* (*Maidens and Widows*), or in the context of Stalinist Poland in *Innego życia nie będzie* (*There Will Be No Other Life*).

A mother defending, protecting or taking up the role of intermediary for her children is not in any way specific to Polish culture. What, however, allows us to identify her as the Polish Mother is the repetitive political context in which her interventions take place. Her children are victims of repressive systems and the constant actualisation of the setting in the Polish history stimulates the recurrence of the image.

The episodic role of Mrs Rollison takes us to further representations of the female world in the patriotic canon of Polish art. Apart from a couple of exceptions, the Romantic main protagonist is male and women usually appear in the same limited way: as mothers, wives, sisters who share the patriotic ideas of their men and are ready to accept the consequences of their involvement.

In the artistic representations of the Polish Mother to which I have referred, there is another common element, which one cannot but notice. The female protagonists are all lonely figures – apart from the character from Holland's film, which in fact is a critical deconstruction of the myth – and they are all widows. This not only brings an immediate association with 'mourning widows' (a phrase from a poem by Cyprian K. Norwid) from the time of the partitions but replicates the image of a strong, resisting woman, coping on her own.

Mourning attire, a symbol of loss and suffering, is a stable attribute of the Polish Mothers in nineteenth-century representations. The women in black appear in poems by Juliusz Słowacki, Cyprian K. Norwid, Maria Konopnicka, in novels by Eliza Orzeszkowa, in paintings and drawings by Artur Grottger. Grottger devoted a number of works to the theme of the insurrection of 1863, which make up a series entitled *Polonia*. They present scenes from various moments of the insurrection; we may find a scene of a farewell between a woman and an armed insurgent leaving on a horse, scenes of battles, a scene of a house search by Russian soldiers, scenes of mourning and images of defeat. Women are often the subject of his pictures and their representations inevitably refer to various elements of the myth of the Polish Mother. Figure 1.1 (*The Mourning*) presents a group of women who, in the presence of a messenger from a battlefield, cry over the death of a relative. The central figures in Figure 1.2 (*On the Battlefield*) are two women who come to take care of the dead and the wounded after a battle (note the black mourning clothes and crosses as a substitute for jewellery).

The imagery of the myth of the Polish Mother may overlap with representations of the nation. Poland is often seen as a woman, but unlike numerous representations in other cultures where the female figure is victorious or rebellious (see Janion 1996b: 5–49), Mother Poland is a suffering, enslaved woman (see Figure 1.3, Artur Grottger, *Polonia*; similar allegories of Poland were painted by Jan Matejko and Stanisław Wyspiański). Dorota Siwicka, who points also to other ways of 'intimate representations of the Patriae', defines this personification of a country in

Figure 1.1 Artur Grottger, *Żałoba* (*The Mourning*), 1863, from *Polonia* cycle

Figure 1.2 Artur Grottger, *Na pobojowisku* (*On the battlefield*), 1863, from *Polonia* cycle

Figure 1.3 Artur Grottger, *Polonia*, 1863, title page of the *Polonia* cycle

family figures as characteristic of Polish Romanticism and, as suggested also by Jan Prokop, crucial to the formation of identity (Siwicka 1993: 70–72). Moreover, it is possible to find links between this type of representations and religious imagery of the Virgin Mary (Einhorn 1993: 221), the prototype of a mother's suffering and sacrifice.

At the same time, Polish art does not renounce the representation of women in a knightly, heroic tradition. The myth of the Polish Mother is often referred to in the context of women fighting and sacrificing lives for the motherland on an equal footing with men. In literature portraits of female knights became fashionable at the turn of the eighteenth century (for an analysis of female representations in the knightly tradition, see Janion 1996b: 78–102). However, it was the Romantic poets who introduced a number of heroines into the patriotic literary canon. Two of the best-known examples of poetic representations of women knights are Mickiewicz's *Śmierć pułkownika* (*The Death of a Colonel*, 1832), a poem to the memory of a legendary female insurgent, Emilia Plater, and *Grażyna* (c. 1825). The latter is the story of a Lithuanian princess who challenges her husband's compromising decision and herself goes on a mortal fight with the enemy.

Both Emilia Plater and Grażyna fit into the convention of deploying the female figure as an allegory of revolutionary struggle, an image so much more powerful for contrasting the weakness and vulnerability of the good, personified by the woman, with the strength and cruelty of the evil, the enemy. Maria Janion points to the fact that this kind of symbolism, although not as popular as that of the French Revolution, has been present in the representations of Polish rebellions. To prove that point she quotes a few examples of witnesses' descriptions of revolutionary episodes. The first one concerns events from Lviv, 1848: 'The people ... didn't want to leave the barricades and the defenceless began to be murdered in the streets. My sister Julia was standing on one of the barricades; holding a red banner she encouraged the people to defend; several shots were fired and the virgin-martyr fell shattered by the bullets' (Łusakowski, quoted in Janion 1996b: 45). The second, a recollection presented in a film documentary, refers to the workers' demonstrations in Poznań, 1956: 'At the head of the marching people there was a woman ... maybe a tram driver as she was wearing a uniform ... She was carrying a white and red flag ... She seemed to be wounded' (A voice-off commentary to a documentary film of 1981, *Niepokonani* [*Unbeatable*] by Andrzej Marek Drążewski, quoted in Janion 1996b: 44). According to some testimonies, in Gdańsk in 1970, a group of workers who were carrying the body of a boy killed by the militia, was led by a young woman holding a Polish flag.[5]

Grażyna, Mickiewicz's Romantic heroine, who leads the troops against the Teutonic Knights, is interesting for yet another reason. She not only transgresses the boundary of her female role by dressing up and fighting as a man, but she does it doubly, transgressing also the role of a wife who owes obedience to her husband. In that, she is one of the female characters of the Romantic period who, like their male counterparts, make decisions of their own. These decisions involve renunciation of their personal life in the name of the good of the country. Another example is Queen Wanda, whose legend was revived by the Romantics and survives today in stories for children known under the title *The Legend of Wanda Who Didn't Want a German*. There exist many different versions of the story;[6] in one of them, which provided a source for many of the later artistic elaborations, Wanda refuses to marry a German prince and to avoid his courting drowns herself in the Vistula river.[7] Another Polish queen around whom a similar patriotic legend was constructed, was Queen Jadwiga (*c.* 1374–99), who in turn loved a German but for the good of Poland married a Lithuanian.

This model of female patriotic behaviour (men usually do not seem to fall into the trap of falling in love with someone of the wrong nationality; if they do, however, they are still invaders and thus the problem does not have to be considered in terms of national betrayal) was updated in the time of the partitions, when women could be divided into those who remained faithful to their patriotic mission and those who by having affairs with the Russian occupiers contributed to the fall of Poland. During the Second World War those who 'sexually collaborated' with the Germans had their hair shaved off by the members of the resistance.

Let us return to the representations of Polish Mothers in the socialist period to try to answer what happened to the myth at that time. With its roots reaching back to the tradition of the gentry and by the end of the nine-teenth century inherited to a large extent by the intelligentsia, in socialist Poland the myth began to hold cross-class significance, undergoing a process that could be called 'democratisation' and like many other national myths, was used both by the regime authorities and by the opposition.

Its revival within the opposition was part of a more general phenomenon which consisted in alluding, by the civil society movement, to the national legacy and to the continuity of the tradition of liberationist struggles. It coincided with the political involvement of the Church and with the increasing significance of civil religion. On the one hand, within the civil movement, women's roles extended and their participation in political activity could be referred to the traditions of the Polish Mother. On the other, in the democratic version of the myth the heroic aspect began to cover a broader area than a direct involvement in the struggle, and began to refer to much more prosaic tasks, which, in fact, required no little forti-tude. Like the persecutions by the occupiers, the hardships of everyday life in the socialist country might have been perceived as the common lot of both men and women. It is worth quoting at length a recollection of one of the Solidarity activists, which not only illustrates how this transfer of mean-ings worked, but raises the problem, to which I shall return below, of how feminism could be viewed in the given political context:

> If we lead miserable lives in this country, it's because we live under a terrible system, the regime is to blame; it's not the law that's wrong, because we have equal rights with men. But life in Poland is not only hard for women. It is just as hard for the men. This is not my imagination. I am a mother of three. Both my husband and I were teachers, with the lowest income in the lowest income bracket in the country. With three children to take care of and with standing in queues for hours on end, the battle of sexes didn't come into it. We didn't argue over who should wash the dishes and who should stand in the queue. It was simply a choice: whoever was nearer, say, the kindergarten, went and collected the children and stood in the queue, and the first person home peeled the potatoes and cooked the dinner. We had to complement each other. So do most Polish couples, except that it may be that our history has given Polish women a sense of mission. Our situation doesn't date back to just the postwar period, but to the time of the insurrections, when Poland was not free and when women played an important and major role in this country. (Nowakowska 1988: 51–52)

This heroisation of everyday survival seems to have had an ambiguous effect on the myth. The above statement idealises gender relations but, in fact, in most representations the Polish Mother, rather than being a partner in a harmonious relationship, remains a lonely figure. As such, she deserves respect and admiration, but at the same time she meets with pity. Thus, the image of the Polish Mother of the socialist period is often connected with the doubly burdened woman, who tries to reconcile her job with the demands of the family.

Anna Reading, in her book *Polish Women: Solidarity and Feminism* (1992: 18–22), discusses 'the Polish Mother role', referring to a fragment of Aleksandra Piłsudska's memories of her grandmother:

> My grandmother was a woman of great intelligence and strength of character, and in the breadth of her mind and reading undoubtedly excelled the majority of her contemporaries. After her husband's death she ran the estate herself, controlling the servants and the workmen with an iron hand ... Patriotism was the main motor of her life. The entire passion in her intense powerful nature was devoted to the cause of her country's freedom ... and in her conspirational work of the January rising she played a prominent part in the neighbourhood, chairing secret meetings in the house and carrying guns. She took danger with utter contempt. The failure of the rising provoked the greatest trauma of her whole life. Hence forward, she always wore the same black dress with its white lace at the neck and cuffs, and on her finger a ring, decorated with a white cross in pearls on black enamel. (Piłsudska, quoted in Reading 1992: 20)

Through an analysis of this model description of the Polish Mother, Reading questions whether the partitioning of Poland really made women central to Polish society in terms of the material work they did and in terms of historical/textual representations. She observes that the symbolism of the ring denotes patriotism, Catholicism and marriage, and therefore the woman's being married to the nation, the Church, and to her husband. It can be worn only by a true patriot, which is defined by Piłsudska's grandmother as 'someone who loves Poland above everything else in the world ... and who will abandon everything, even life itself for freedom' (Piłsudska, quoted in Reading 1992: 21). Referring to the mourning attire of Polish Mothers, Reading passes on to the analysis of the symbolism of widowship ('widow' in Sanskrit meaning 'empty'), to conclude: 'The Matka-Polka places woman on a pedestal whilst simultaneously chaining her to the family and the hearth. The Polish Mother is a figure of courage and great strength and at the same time an ideal of woman in which she is empty, with no meaning of her own' (Reading 1992: 21). The chapter in which the author draws parallels between the fate of Poland and the fate of women ends with a conclusion: 'Subject nation/Subject woman.'

It is true, as Reading says, that women remained primarily responsible for family life, but it seems to me that the position which the myth of the Polish Mother has offered to women should be interpreted in a broader perspective. On the one hand, one may ask how it compares to the roles contained in the Cult of True Womanhood (Welter 1978), created more or less at the same time, or to the later 'feminine mystique' (Friedan 1963). On the other, it should be considered in the context of the areas of freedom that a defined social and political system offers to an individual in general. It may be argued, as in the case, for example, of racial minorities, that generally oppressive conditions result in a double discrimination against women: in this example racial and sexual. This may also be the case, as Reading suggests, of a subject nation, or of any society in which individual freedom is subject to obvious limitations. However, a general pattern of power relations in society undoubtedly has an impact on the self-perceptions of women and may weaken awareness of sexual discrimination or establish a different hierarchy of desired 'freedoms'.

The question pertaining to Polish women concerns the conditions in which their cultural identity has been shaped in a historical process. First, we must take into consideration the persistence of nationalism, which Peter A. Heltai and Zbigniew Rau argue 'should be understood as a rational preference of societies which in the last two centuries faced, first, the loss of independence and, second, the imposition of the Soviet type system. ... nationalism, unlike social democracy or liberalism, was the political current which posed the most powerful long-term challenge to both these calamities and which eventually would manage to overcome them' (Heltai and Rau: 1991: 133). As has been argued, throughout that period – that is, in the time of the partitions and in the postwar near-totalitarian system – the public sphere in which civil society could develop was suppressed. Following Rau's definition of civil society as providing: 'a space in which individuals and their associations compete with each other in the pursuit of their values' (Rau 1991: 4), we may conclude that the absence of this historically evolved form of society constrained the possibility not only of articulation, but also of full development of individual interests. The mobilisation of society could take place under a unifying banner of patriotism/ nationalism, or, often understood in similar terms, 'anti-communism'.

Many researchers point to the fact that the feminist movement that developed in Poland at the end of the nineteenth century had to deal with the problem of precedence of national cause over women's struggles for their rights (Siemieńska 1986: 13). Similar attitudes prevailed in the circles of the anti-regime opposition. Maria Janion, in a book published in 1996, writes:

> The well-known difference of opinions in Poland concerns what is 'serious' and what is 'unserious'. The dominating way of thinking of the opposition in the 1970s and 1980s was that the struggle for independence was serious, the struggle for women's rights was not. ... This kind of unifying reasoning was, at that time, in a way, close to mine. I remember, when during a feminist discussion in an international gathering in West Berlin at the end of the 1980s, I maintained that Solidarność, first, had to win independence and democracy for all of society and only then it would be able to deal with women's question and improvement of women's situation. (Janion 1996b: 326)

From the present perspective, Janion admits, this way of thinking did not take women far, and as we have seen, the companions from Solidarity have shown little solidarity with women.

All this, however, cannot deny the fact that women felt involved in the 'most important issue' and while it impeded the development of Western feminist consciousness, it did so, at least partly, because the women's experience of exclusion from the public sphere was of different nature and so was their view on power relations.

Notes

1. A decidedly critical view on the progressiveness of the era of 'golden freedom' of Polish nobility is presented by Jerzy Szacki in *Liberalizm po komunizmie* (1994: 54–60).
2. 'Traditional' has here the sense of 'preindustrial' that is, without the sharp division between the public and the private sphere which at that period began to characterise Western societies.
3. Mary was assigned the title of the Queen of the Polish Kingdom in 1656. After the coronation of the icon of the Black Madonna of Częstochowa in 1717, the queenly patronage over Poland became more and more associated with this particular representation of Our Lady. It is worth mentioning that analogous ceremonies of Mary's coronation took place also in other countries at around the same period, e.g. in France, in 1683; in Austria, 1674; in Portugal, in 1648 (see Kopeć 1983).
4. The male figures mentioned here are all protagonists of Romantic poetic works, which constitute the basis of Polish literary canon: Adam Mickiewicz, *Dziady* (1823–32); *Konrad Wallendrod* (1828); Juliusz Słowacki, *Kordian* (1833).
5. This scene is described by Bronisław Baczko (1984: 185–92).
6. According to some calculations there exist 165 dramas, ballads and articles, as well as numerous paintings and drawings (see Kopaliński 1985: 351).
7. This is a version by Jan Długosz (1415–80) (Kopaliński 1985: 351).

PART II

Women According to Men

CHAPTER 2

Filmic Representations of the Myth of the Polish Mother

ELŻBIETA OSTROWSKA

Cultural representations of the Mother are of central importance to the life of all historical societies. These representations range from degraded and entrapped images to the most sublime and exalted. These contradictory possibilities may, at times, even be interwoven. The discourse of the 'maternal' is therefore a site of contestation, ready to be filled with those meanings which a society needs to ascribe to both the social role and subjectivity of real mothers and their representations. It is my task here to locate the meanings of a particular Polish sub-structure within these more general debates about the representation of women as mothers. I will argue that the Polish discourse on maternity is not completely dissimilar to its Western equivalents, but we should locate Polish connotations of this term on the margin of what is commonly understood in the West as 'motherhood'.

However, what should be stressed here is that this chapter does not analyse the generality of representations of motherhood in Polish cinema, but focuses on a specific cultural icon of the Polish Mother. As discussed in the previous chapter, the figure of the Polish Mother is not necessarily a real mother making a personal choice and going through the biological and psychological experience of motherhood, but, rather, a woman whose maternal tasks, whether they are presently fulfilled by her or expected from her in the future, are directly related to the demands of the national ideology. Therefore, the prolific critical literature in the West on the issue of the representation of motherhood in cinema, concentrating, as it does, mainly on the personal, cannot be directly applied to the Polish myth of the Mother. Moreover, its focus on the representations of motherhood in genre cinema and popular culture (see Kaplan 1992 and Fischer 1996) also limits its applicability to the Polish context, because in communist Poland generic cinema existed only in a residual form. The inappropriateness of applying the analytical tools employed in examining images of mothers in Western systems of representation when discussing this issue in relation to other cultures is noted by, among others, Lucy Fischer, who writes in her book *Cinematernity*: 'the conclusions I reach are applicable only to the Western tradition, and additional work must be done to explore their relevance to other cultures' (Fischer 1996: 29). Thus, this chapter is an effort to rework these analytical strategies in an examination of the dominant discourse of motherhood as epitomised in the figure of the Polish Mother.

In Polish cinema, as in the West, the presence of the mother can be discerned, as E. Ann Kaplan puts it: 'as a prevailing cultural discourse ... of the Ideal "angel" Mother pitted against her evil "witch" opposite ...' (Kaplan 1992: 9). Yet, within Polish culture there has been a specific set of requirements imposed on maternity stemming from national ideology that masked their patriarchal origin. The difference might be explained through, for example, the theme of maternal sacrifice discussed by Molly Haskell and which she regards as the most prevalent motif in relation to Motherhood to be found in Hollywood films: 'Children are an obsession in American movies – sacrifice of and for children, the use of children as justification for all manner of sacrifice ...' (Haskell, quoted in Fischer 1996: 11). Sacrifice is also the most stable aspect of the figure of the Polish Mother, yet it exceeds the demand to sacrifice 'of and for children'. The Polish Mother not only has to sacrifice her life for her children, but she also has to sacrifice her children for the freedom of the Motherland. In other words, she has to instil in her offspring, regardless of gender, this readiness for sacrifice. This ideological requirement is relevant to sons in particular, as mothers bring up their sons knowing from the very beginning that they will perish in the fight for liberation of their country. If she refuses to accept this task of inculcation, she will be labelled 'a bad, selfish mother'. This punishing but gladly accepted contradiction is engrained in the figure of the Polish Mother, who is obliged to take care of her children but at the same time to accept the potential and likely loss of them in the name of the national cause. If maternity is always a social necessity, its related cultural requirements in the Polish case, as with many others, demonstrate that these are modified by various factors, among which nationality plays the most important role. Therefore my examination of the myth of the Polish Mother in Polish cinema does not focus on general issues in the representation of motherhood, but rather aims at describing its Polish specificity, demonstrating how 'ideologies of gender are imbricated with those of nation' (Butler 2002: 92).

As demonstrated in the previous chapter, representations of the Polish Mother have been remarkably stable since their initial formulation as an element in the response to the various occupations of Poland during the last two hundred years. No doubt, each period during that time used images of the Polish Mother in quite specific ways, but all depended on a central and unchanging principle of resistance to the oppressors of the Polish nation. Because of their ideological power, these representations became central to the popular culture available to Polish audiences. In Polish cinema, in contrast to other representations of Polish women that only appeared at particular moments in Polish history, the Polish Mother is enduring. She was introduced at the beginning of Polish cinema, and since then, can be traced in films in every decade up to the present. Of course, because of its oppressive power, there are examples of the films that attempt to deconstruct this national icon of femininity, most powerfully in the third part of Kazimierz Kutz's *Krzyż Walecznych* (*Cross of Valour*, 1958) and in *Kobieta samotna* (*A Woman Alone*, 1981) by Agnieszka Holland, analysed elsewhere in this book (Chapter 10). Here, however, the main goal is to demonstrate the stability of the icon across time as evidenced in two films widely separated in the history of Polish cinema. The first, *Huragan* (*Hurricane*, 1928), directed by Józef Lejtes, is a model of the cinematic representations of the myth in pre-Second World War cinema. The second, *Skarga* (*The Complaint*, 1991), directed by Jerzy Wójcik, will be examined as a confirmation of the persistence of the myth in postwar culture, including the period after the collapse of communism in 1989. Examples from other films will be used to reconstruct the filmic representation of the myth as fully as possible. As a strategy to enable an understanding of the complexity of its formal and thematic specificity I made close textual readings of the two films, rather than giving a general survey of filmic images of the Polish Mother.

Józef Lejtes's films are an important part of the historical and patriotic strand of Polish prewar cinema that employs familiar melodramatic structures, adapting them to the national tradition (see Madej 1994: 137–57). These films reflect on both the narrative and visual level the national mythology, in which the ideal image of Polish Woman, the Polish Mother, plays a particularly important role. What distinguishes films by Lejtes from others belonging to this strand is his mastery in using the classical modes of melodramatic narrative, as codified by David W. Griffith, as well as his efficient way of employing stylistic devices common in world cinema at that time. His début, the silent film *Hurricane*, is particularly interesting in regard to the mythologisation of women's figures in Polish prewar cinema, as it presents the whole range of iconic images of femininity, all of them derived from the Romantic 'master' figuration of the Polish Mother. The context of the Romantic tradition is introduced at the very beginning of the film, in the initial credit: 'Year 1863. Mickiewicz's songs have been silenced, but have rendered a flame of self-sacrifice in all hearts. Everywhere the nation finds an eagerness to find unity and independence.'

The action of *Hurricane* (Figure 2.1) takes place during the January Uprising of 1863. The Polish characters are divided into two groups.

Figure 2.1 Zbigniew Sawan as Tadeusz Orsza and Renata Renée as Helena Zawisza (in the middle) in *Huragan* (*Hurricane*), 1928, dir. Józef Lejtes © Filmoteka Narodowa w Warszawie

Margrave Wielopolski (Aleksander Zelwerowicz) leads the first group, which promotes a policy of conciliation and cooperation with the Russians. He also advises the Moscow government on the conscription of young Polish males into the tsarist army. The second group includes conspirators who plan to organise an uprising. Their leader is Tadeusz Orsza (Zbigniew Sawan). After escaping impressment, he finds himself by accident in the palace of a Russian nobleman, Gortschakov, whilst a ball is taking place, to which young Polish women have been forcibly invited. Amongst them is Helena Zawisza (Renata Renée), a proud noblewoman, who is being pestered by a Russian officer, Count Ignatov. In this dramatic situation the first meeting of the two main characters occurs, and the beginning of their irresistibly romantic love, marked with tragedy from the first encounter. Soon the uprising erupts, with Tadeusz participating. When his squad, exhausted by battle, gets near to the Zawisza's family manor house, he is sent there to get some food for his starving comrades. At the same time Ignatov has followed Helena and decides to invade the house, where he unexpectedly finds the group of emaciated insurgents. A battle arises, in the course of which the injured Tadeusz loses consciousness. When he comes round, he finds Helena dead. His initial despair is transformed into a rebellious fury that takes him to barricades to fight not only for the freedom of the Motherland, but also to take revenge for his lover's death (see Madej 1994: 145).

Helena Zawisza is not the only female character in the film. Before she appears a number of women play episodic, yet important, roles in terms of the cinematic representation of the collective notion of Polish femininity. The very first appears in the opening scene of the film. She takes part in the political demonstration that takes place near to Wielopolski's abode, organised by Poles to manifest their disagreement with his policy of appeasement. An initial long shot is of the demonstrating crowd, in which there are several women. In the next medium shot, two figures, male and female, are distinguished. This image visualises the information contained in the first credit, that the 'whole nation' comes together to seek independence. It is worth noting here that the frame composition in this static shot is entirely neutral; neither the male nor the female figure is privileged, as both of them occupy the same amount of space in the frame. Woman is therefore presented from the very beginning as having an equal occupancy of public space and, in addition, plays an active role in it. In short she is in distinct opposition to the image of a 'domesticated woman', only to be found in private space.

This initial image proposes a pattern for all the female characters that may be presented later. The context, in which a woman appears on the screen for the first time, along with the kinds of activities she undertakes, define the social roles that the viewer might expect. If a female character is at home at the commencement of the narrative, it is more than likely that the audience will perceive her as a 'domesticated' woman who can at most violate a certain canon of behaviour. This schematisation is an important factor of film reception, an indispensable element in the constant process of constructing and verifying expectations in the fictional world. The image of a woman demanding freedom with men is an important semantic clue that will influence a viewer's potential point of view on subsequent female characters.

The first feature of the Polish woman, represented in Lejtes's film, is therefore her political activity, equal to that of the man. Soon, however, another woman is presented as a victim of the oppressor. Violence against her is explicit: the title reads 'Women are raped.' The following scene shows a woman and a man walking on a dark street, observed by Russian soldiers, who suddenly approach the couple and pull the woman away. The man's protest is merely an empty gesture of disagreement. In this situation he is as helpless as his partner. Humiliated by the oppressors, he also becomes a victim. This scene, which has no connection with the main plot, serves as a symbolic brief image of brutal violence inflicted on the Polish nation. Lejtes's decision to represent it by a scene of the sexual oppression of woman makes reference to the most pertinent metaphoric image of Poland as a woman, violated by invaders (see Madej 1994: 144). Clearly, this episode is a reference to the feminised image of Poland popular in nineteenth-century Polish paintings, the most popular of which are by Jan Matejko and Artur Grottger (see Chapter 1).

This motif of visually juxtaposing an image of martyred Poland with the tragic experience of a woman is developed in the next scene, which takes place after the demonstration is brutally crushed by tsarist soldiers. The first shot presents the suddenly emptied square. The only trace of the hundreds protesting a moment before is four dead bodies. A black-clothed woman is leaning over one of them. Her costume symbolically identifies her as a Polish Mother despairing after her son has died for the Motherland. Her pose and magnified gesture of lament create a Polish *pieta*, invoking the religious content of the myth associated with the cult of the Virgin Mary, typical of Polish Catholicism. An intertwining of religious and patriotic elements is essential in the image structure. The Polish specificity of the suffering experienced by this mother places her squarely with the allegorical image of the suffering Motherland, which will lose her sons in subsequent uprisings. Permeated by the feminine, the Motherland becomes the object of intimate experience. As Jan Prokop writes, 'it is a mother calling for help, not a structure of power ordering collective life' (Prokop 1991: 415).

The symbolic image of the mother in Lejtes's film cannot be simply identified with the icon of the Mater Dolorosa. The mother's initial despair and pain are transformed immediately into a gesture of anger and rebellion. She majestically rises from her knees and raises her fist as if she were shaking it at her son's killer. The shots showing the mother are connected through parallel editing with images of Wielopolski, who observes all the events from his balcony. Initially his face seems to express fear or at least astonishment with everything that has happened. After a while, however, it freezes in a gesture of obstinacy and cruel indifference. This device results in an impression that it is he who is an object of the mother's anger. Soon a Russian soldier on a horse approaches the woman and shoots her; she falls next to her son. What is worth noting here is that in this scene a woman is presented not only as a victim of the oppressor, but conversely she dies because she has actively expressed her anger.

All the female characters that appear on the screen before Helena create a significant context for her. She is not dancing when we see her for the first time at the ball. Her face expresses her aversion to this obligatory 'entertainment'. Noticing Ignatov's eyes staring at her, she proudly turns her back to him. When Ignatov asks one of his comrades to introduce him to the beautiful Polish woman, he receives the answer, 'It is useless to try, sir. She is a Polish woman faithful to her ideals'. This opinion, expressed by a Russian soldier, indicates that Polish Woman gets respect from everybody, even from the invaders. Helena is faithful to her ideals until the very end, that is until her death. She refuses Ignatov's courtship with contempt suitable for a brutal and ruthless oppressor, even if she has to pay for it with her own life. Because of her pride and intransigence, she is similar to the legendary Wanda, who preferred to die rather than to marry a German, the 'eternal enemy of Poles' (see Chapter 1).

Legendary Wanda is not the only icon of femininity present in Polish culture that should be mentioned while analysing the character of Helena. Proud and contemptuous of Ignatov, she is caring and tender towards Tadeusz; it could be even said that she looks after him like a mother. This is particularly striking in the scene when, emaciated, he arrives at her home. They behave as lovers for only a short time and after a while she begins to act as a mother and thus changes him from a heroic insurgent into a helpless boy. His helplessness is confirmed later on when he loses his consciousness and because of this is unable to protect Helena from the Russian officer's violence. This narrative resolution echoes the scene in which the man was unable to protect his female partner from rape.

Woman's maternal attitude towards man is certainly not exclusive to Polish nineteenth-century society and culture. This representation of feminine behaviour was also relatively common in Western Europe in the period, in which the most perfect realisation of femininity – the cult of motherhood – was developed and refined. What should be stressed here is that the maternal role was not limited to looking after children, but was complemented by a broadly understood duty of care of men (see Badinter 1981). In the context of Polish culture and history, feminine protective behaviour acquires the value of a patriotic deed. This is at the very core of the myth of the Polish Mother.

As the religious factor is also a key aspect of the myth of the Polish Mother, a scene confirming the strong attachment of the main heroine to the Catholic religion had to be included in the film. This is to be found in a scene in which Helena and Tadeusz ardently pray in the local church and then sing one of the best-known religious-patriotic hymns, 'Boże coś Polskę' ('God, you protected Poland for Centuries'), along with the congregation. This situation serves also as a legitimisation of the relationship between the couple. The rhetorical message is to build up a contrast between the pure love of Helena and Tadeusz, expressed under the gaze of the Church, and Ignatov's oppressive violence. A later title confirms that Helena is closely connected to the national mythology. '[Tadeusz] swears revenge. He goes not only to fight for the freedom of the Motherland but also to take revenge for the desecrated honour of his beloved.' This juxtaposition of Helena with the idea of the motherland clearly insists on an allegorical interpretation by the audience.

Other women in the film complement this mythologised image of Polish femininity. The first is Helena's younger sister, Janka, who incarnates the icon of a woman-knight in both her outlook and behaviour. She has short hair, dresses herself in a masculine way and neglects all the norms of a 'proper' femininity. Her favourite activity is cleaning her rifle. When Tadeusz is about to leave for the uprising, she asks him to take her with him. She serves as another example of women's involvement in the national cause, but is overshadowed by the figure of her suffering elder sister. This engagement with the national cause also characterises a peasant woman, whom we first see watching her child in a cradle. When she sees a proclamation of the uprising through the window, she wakes her husband and sends him to the battle with the words, 'It is time. Go! Our brothers are waiting for you.' Finally, a woman-conspirator takes part in a secret meeting at an inn. Three people, one of them the woman, are bending over the table in a pose typical of male conspirators. Not only is the woman inscribed into this masculine iconography, but also she is again presented in a public space traditionally reserved for men.

The plot does not motivate the presence of these women. They complement the catalogue of features of the main character's idealised femininity. Thus each appears on the screen only once to signify virtues to be shared by women in the collective myth of the Polish feminine. This is then further built into a wider ideological construction: the national-patriotic myth of Polishness, supportive of the nationalistic policy of the Polish interwar government. This pattern is very typical of the historic-patriotic genre in Polish prewar cinema. Similar heroines can be found in *Rok 1863* (*Year 1863*, 1922) by Edward Puchalski, *Na Sybir* (*To Siberia*, 1930) by Henryk Szaro and in *Florian* (1938) by Leonard Buczkowski. In other genres before the Second World War, such as melodrama and comedy, female characters were deprived of individual features; instead they incarnated the idea of 'eternal femininity'. Therefore, it can be said that the representations of women in Polish prewar cinema articulate a strictly specified pattern, whether it is a universal myth of femininity, or the national-patriotic myth. This specificity, or a limitation, of Polish cinema of that time becomes striking when it is compared with the Polish literature of the period in which the 'women's cause' was a matter of relatively great significance, and in the work of female writers in particular, such as Narcyza Żmichowska and Eliza Orzeszkowa (see Borkowska 1996).

The relative fixity of Polish cinema in comparison with the achievements of world cinema at that time, seen for example in its female characters, is explained by the ideological discourses of the period. On the one hand, the origins of the new Polish state were connected with nineteenth-century uprisings, rather than global changes taking place in twentieth-century Europe. On the other hand, the independence regained after 123 years of partitions was endangered once again, this time by the Bolsheviks. As is often the case, external danger usually results in an intensification of nationalistic attitudes and behaviour, which can be easily legitimised through references to the national mythology. Originating in the national

Romantic ideology, the myth of the Polish Mother once again turned out to be an important factor in the process of strengthening the notion of national identity and thus continued as a desirable model for contemporary women. Prewar Polish cinema, in which traditional narrative and icono-graphical patterns were widely used, could fulfil the role of preserving and reproducing the national mythology more efficiently than Polish literature, which was strongly influenced by the ideas and concepts of European modernism.

During the Second World War, and the decades of Soviet oppression that followed, this national Romantic myth again affected Polish women through its representations. During this period there occurred a clear reworking of the main lineaments of the structures of meaning relating to the Polish Mother. This involved a further movement away from the dom-inant notions of the mother familiar in Western representations of mother-hood. A main determinant of this restructuring was firstly the drastic separation of Poland from the West, and secondly, the need for the image of the Mother to be part of the defence against yet another 'occupation', that of the Soviet Union, even if this came in the guise of International Brotherhood and Communism. Even though much was still shared, in terms of meaning, with the Western maternal discourse, the carapace of extra, protective meanings, specifically needed in Poland at that time, hard-ened. This process, resulting finally in a kind of ossification, was eventually to place actual Polish mothers at some considerable risk from the extraor-dinary constraints that it required. At the same time this image-system was adapted to the demands of the new communist ideology. This appropriation of elements derived from the national patriotic tradition into the discourse of communist ideology was a very efficient strategy to establish the illusion of continuity in national life, an attempt to convince society of the correct-ness of the new political situation. Indeed, there is a strange compatibility, probably rooted in a shared patriarchal nexus, between the older Polish national discourse and that of the communists in relation to female sexual-ity. Though for different reasons, both deprived women of their sexuality or rather subsumed it into different, 'higher' values, patriotic and proletarian aims respectively. This process of the sublimation of sexuality resulted in a virtual absence of its representation in Polish cinema.

The figure of the Polish Mother barely appears in the first postwar films and never occupies a central position within their narratives. This is evident very early in *Ostatni etap* (*The Last Stage*), made by Wanda Jakubowska in 1947 (see Chapter 8). In the socialist realist films of the 1950s the Polish Mother is also virtually absent and is replaced by her emancipated 'daugh-ter', a Superwoman (see Chapter 3). This absence, however, did not last long as the character of the suffering mother returned to the Polish screen after 1956, for example in *Zagubione uczucia* (*Lost Feelings*, 1957) (see Chapter 3). The national icon of femininity also appeared in Tadeusz

Makarczyński's short film Noc (Night, 1961). The leitmotif of this poetic impression is a repeated image of an old woman in black mourning clothes awaiting the return of her children, lost during the war. The ideological meanings are achieved in an Eisensteinian 'intellectual montage' that allows a contrast between images of fireworks in the sky, triumphantly announcing the end of the war, and portrayals of mothers, whose facial expressions convey an eternal tragedy. The images are juxtaposed with a multilingual commentary (in Polish, Russian, German, French, English) of announcements of mothers searching for their children lost during the war. The combination of the soundtrack with the repeated image of suffering mothers explicitly produces a propagandistic pacifist message. The figure of a suffering mother, rather than referring to an individual, subjectively experienced loss of a child, seems to represent the 'objective', historical collective experience (see Iskierko 1980: 232). Makarczyński's film clearly reveals the image of the Polish Mother as a still stable signifier, whereas the signified depends on the specific historical discourse in which it is placed.

The films of the 1960s, in the period of the so-called 'small stabilisation', presented a somewhat 'degraded' image of the national myth of femininity, in which she is reduced to being a hardworking mother patiently wearing her 'double burden'. Later films, made in the 1970s and 1980s, by directors connected with the political opposition, relate to the traditional image of the Polish Mother much more directly. It is apparent that the figure again became a symbol of struggle against political oppression, this time against the communist system that was seen as a continuation of the partitions of the nineteenth century.

Particularly interesting evidence of the stability and persistence of the myth can be found in two films by Andrzej Wajda: Człowiek z marmuru (Man of Marble, 1976) and its sequel, Człowiek z żelaza (Man of Iron, 1981). The main female character, Agnieszka (Krystyna Janda), undergoes a very symptomatic metamorphosis between the first and the second film. If in Man of Marble she appears as an independent, rebellious and emancipated woman, in Man of Iron she 'matures' into a wife and a mother, who passively accepts suffering and puts the national issue above her individual needs and desires (see Chapter 5).

However, the most famous filmic version of the myth of the Polish Mother is in the film Matka Królów (Mother of the Kings) (Figures 2.2 and 2.3), made by Janusz Zaorski in 1982. The director tells us the tragic and shocking saga of the Król (King) family, during the paradoxes and absurdity of the war and the Stalinist period. The main character, Łucja Król (Magda Teresa Wójcik), is in an extremely difficult situation. Her husband, the only breadwinner, is killed in a car accident, leaving her with three sons and with a fourth baby on the way. With no professional training, she is forced to become the provider for her family. A job as a cleaning lady, childbirth, the difficulties of wartime and grinding poverty, are all faced with a

Figure 2.2 Magda Teresa Wójcik as Łucja Król and Franciszek Pieczka as Cyga in *Matka Królów* (*Mother of the Kings*), 1982, dir. Janusz Zaorski © Filmoteka Narodowa w Warszawie

familiar patience and 'inborn' dignity. She does not think about herself; her only concern is her family. As in Mickiewicz's play *Forefathers' Eve* we are given, once again, a familiar scene: Łucja goes to the Communist Party[1] headquarters to plead for the freedom of her son, imprisoned for his political activity on behalf of the nation (see Chapter 1).

For all her life this woman has performed only one role: that of a Polish Mother, although in its proletarian variant, ready for sacrifice, full of love and internal purity. She safeguards what is most important for the survival of the national identity: her family. In times of ideological confusion, she seems to be the only one who is able to live according to elementary moral rules. Her sons' involvement in political activity leads them to violate the moral code. Once more men make mistakes and a woman is pure and innocent. Her moral superiority is shown to be a result of her acceptance of suffering. The last line spoken by Łucja Król is especially symptomatic of her attitude. When a friend says, 'You have had a really hard life', she answers 'Others have had harder'. This sentence fits perfectly that common understanding of 'maturity', which is supposed to mean an ability to go beyond one's own misery and tragedies and see them as a realisation of 'the collective lot of Polish women'. The acceptance of this perspective inevitably

Figure 2.3 Łucja Król (Magda Teresa Wójcik) and her children in *Matka Królów* (*Mother of the Kings*), 1982, dir. Janusz Zaorski © Filmoteka Narodowa w Warszawie

excludes an individual from full participation in history and renders her as a sublime yet entrapped myth (see Umińska 1992: 9).

If the figure of the Polish Mother can be regarded as the icon of idealised Polish femininity, Magda Teresa Wójcik became an icon of the Polish Mother figure in Polish cinema due to her role in *Mother of the Kings*. This phenomenon is evident in Jerzy Wójcik's film, *The Complaint*, made in 1991, which embodies a revival of the myth of the Polish Mother in Polish cinema after 1989. In contrast to the Polish economy as a whole, which, after the collapse of communism, quickly adopted the 'free market' model, significant strands of cinema still remain linked to the previous mode of production and its traditional role in national culture. After 1989, 'liberated' Polish film directors could have enthusiastically used the opportunity to enter the realm of 'pure' and simple entertainment, or 'art for art's sake'. This only partly came true as a significant number of movies made at that time were still dominated by 'national matters'. These films were made mostly, but not only, by the older generation of directors and concerned historical issues which, for obvious reasons, had been almost entirely absent in cinema of the previous period, or had to be misrepresented according to the demands of communist propaganda. Needless to say, both the narratives and style of these films were shaped by the national patriotic mythology. For example, the myth of the Polish Mother is central to the narrative in Janusz Zaorski's *Panny i wdowy* (*Maidens and Widows*, 1991), Robert Gliński's *Wszystko, co najważniejsze* (*Everything, That Really Matters*, 1992), Jerzy Kawalerowicz's *Za co?* (*For What?* 1995). In many others this mythological figure appears as a marginal character in the main narrative, still, however, retaining its great significance in terms of the overall meanings produced within the text.

It can be said that these films exemplify a very important process in the liberation, recovery and reuse of a collective memory. It would be too naïve, of course, to think that the process of liberating this collective mythos was not underpinned by pragmatic reasons, related to the political struggles of their contexts. As Bronisław Baczko says:

> Each authority attempts to monopolise certain emblems and control, or even govern others. Therefore, processes of authority, the political in particular, are also performed through the collective imagination. Holding symbolical power does not mean adding an element of illusion to the 'real' power, but duplicates it, reinforcing actual domination as a result of this appropriation of symbols. (Baczko 1994: 23)

The process of once again 'awakening' the collective memory and other national myths after 1989 might also have been aimed at recovering the national collective identity. This, in turn, would consequently have helped to propose at an ideological level regressive political and social options for Poland. The myth of the Polish Mother became a very important element in this process, contributing significantly to the revival, yet again, of a Polish idealisation of the feminine.

The Complaint (Figure 2.4) is one of the most interesting examples of this trend in post-1989 Polish cinema, for again its heroine is presented as an almost pure embodiment of the myth of the Polish Mother. Maria Teresa Wójcik appears on the screen as a dramatis persona taken from ancient tragedy rather than a film character in a realistic movie, as was the case of Łucja Król from *Mother of the Kings*. The strongly expressed iconic aspect of the character is a result of the mode of narration and the stylistic devices employed by the director. The plot, based on a true story, is presented in a flow of loosely connected episodes, some semi-documentary and some highly visionary, almost oneiric. Historical accuracy, in terms of representing the tragic events in Szczecin in 1970, when the shipyard strike was brutally put down by the communist government and many people were killed, works together with metaphorical images, to bring about, once again, the transformation of history into History as myth.

Figure 2.4 Magda Teresa Wójcik as Stefa Sawicka and Henryk Boukołowski as Stanisław Sawicki in *Skarga* (*The Complaint*), dir. Jerzy Wójcik © Studio Filmowe 'Indeks', photo: Witold Sobociński

The film opens with images of the shipyard at dusk, followed by a flow of short close-ups of small objects, vases, flowers, a small model airplane and photographs. All of them are shaking. In medium close-up a frightened woman runs through a flat. Suddenly we hear a shot and the glass in the windows breaks. An older woman runs in with a pillow and says that this has to be placed in the window. She seems to be well accustomed to this kind of situation. Then, a young girl runs into the flat and nervously says, 'I've been looking for him everywhere'. The woman tries to calm herself by saying that this does not mean that something has happened to him, to her teenage son Stefan. Eventually, the three women start tidying up the broken glass from the floor. This scene easily lends itself to an allegorical reading as it again stands for the endangered Polish home. Of course, the women, who represent three generations, are witnessing this and trying to prevent it. The 'absent man', for whom all they are waiting and whom they are worried about, is to be an indispensable element of this iconic situation. Fortunately, this time they do not have to wait for him too long as he returns shortly. His mother (Maria Teresa Wójcik), grandmother (Danuta Szaflarska), and his girlfriend, Anka (Karolina Lutczyn), are visibly relieved. Not entirely though, as the next morning when Stefan (Rafał Zwierz) leaves for school, his mother asks him not to take the path close to the shipyard. He calmly replies that he is no longer a child.

The realistic code used in this scene is continued in the next, in which the father (Henryk Boukołowski) comes back from the night shift, only to be distressingly disturbed by visionary images of Stefan. First we see the father with his colleagues on a barge, on which he recognises his son. Initially his son seems to be a part of this highly realistic situation, however, soon he starts to move from place to place in a supernatural way. Finally he transcends the limits of physical time and space. This is shown in a visionary image of him shown in close-up against bright, blue sky, as if he managed to escape the reality of gloomy and dark Szczecin and to enter a different world. This unrealistic image of Stefan will be a recurrent motif in the film and it is worth noting that it does not function as a subjective vision of any of the characters, but appears entirely independently as if belonging to another ontological order. The scene with the father can be read as presaging something that will happen to him in the near future. The mother has a vision of her son as well, when, on her way back home from work, she goes to his school. She stands behind the fence and observes a group of boys who run out of the building. Her son is not among them; she only sees a dimmed image of his face in one of the windows that instantly disappears.

When the mother and the father meet at home, they already seem to know what has happened. She asks her husband, 'Stefan hasn't come back, has he?' as if she wants to confirm her intuition. He confirms it with a mere gesture. She sits next to him in silence. There is no talking about or sharing of anxiety about the son, no giving of hope to each other. Silence serves as an acceptance of inevitability and hopelessness. Again the image of their son against the blue sky appears.

The next scene takes place on the street in a phone booth. The parents phone different hospitals in search of their son. Images from the hospitals they are calling are also presented in parallel. The montage between the scene in the booth and those in the hospitals uses asynchronous sound and distorted chronology, disrupting the effect of the initial realism. The most conspicuous break with codes of realism occurs when the camera follows a young doctor going to check whether Stefan has been admitted. Suddenly the camera leaves him and goes its own way through dark Kafkaesque corridors until complete darkness fills the screen. Just after this visual 'dead end' the parents find out that their son is in a military hospital. Immediately after they get this information the scene is rapidly cut. Again, there is no talk, no assumptions are made about their son's state, no mutual consolations are given and no efforts to hearten each other. There is only an abrupt cut to the hospital where the son has been found.

In the hospital a secret agent identifies them and leads them to the doctor. The mother's question about her son is answered brutally: 'He's dead. They killed him.' She responds to this with complete silence, not one single grimace appears on her face to reveal her emotions. She remains motionless and speechless. Her husband asks the secret agent if they may see their son, but in vain. He is told that they will be notified at the 'proper' time. He protests, again in vain. There is a sharp contrast between the mother's and the father's behaviour. He establishes a kind of dialogue with the representative of the oppressive order. In other words, through his dialogue with the agent he complies with the 'order of things'. Her silence is a clear sign of a refusal to entertain this possibility. Later, they go to the hospital mortuary, but are forbidden entry. She responds to this absurd prohibition by saying, 'I don't understand anything'. Then she turns to another woman, who is apparently in the same situation, asking her whether she understands it, finally directing the same question to a group of silent onlookers.

Clearly, she refuses to accept any kind of 'historical necessity' or 'historical accident'. She simply acts as a mother whose innocent son has been killed. Soon her right to bury the dead body will be violated. Therefore, she, like Antigone, will fight to fulfil this duty. This situation which could have been presented as a psychological drama, is transformed here into an elegiac existential drama. This can be seen in Wójcik's acting in particular, for she does not use methods of psychological realism as proposed by Stanislavski. Therefore there are no visible signs of emotions to signify her psychic state after the son's death. Both her movement and gestures are more than restrained, as if she were an actor in ancient Greek theatre. Her acting may be also perceived as resembling the Brechtian *Verfremdung* effect, as Magda Teresa Wójcik distances herself from the character she plays, Stefa Stawicka. If Stanislavski's precept is to make the protagonist as individualised as possible, Wójcik tries to make her character as universal as possible. She tries to minimise what is specific about Stefa Stawicka and to magnify all that is universal in her as a mother. The viewer is therefore prevented from responding to the heroine through emotional empathy, but rather is kept at a distance.

The style of acting is not the only means of distancing the viewer from the diegetic world. The dialogue is also far from the conventions of psychological realism. It is crude, laconic, and often too universal to be related to the particular situation. The subsequent scenes are frequently a description of a static situation rather than a presentation of an event that will contribute to narrative development. Further, they are separated from one another by means of fades creating discontinuities in the fictional world. Finally, the absence of point of view shots, as well as shot-countershot editing, precludes our subjective inscription into the text. The spectator can only be a distant observer who watches world in which innocent children are killed and in which their mothers and fathers have to fight for their bodies in order to bury them.

In *The Complaint* the religious component of the myth of the Polish Mother is again as significant as the patriotic one. After a second visit to the hospital, when the parents are refused their son's body for a second time, the heroine goes to the church to talk to a priest. She expresses her doubts about God's benevolence and confesses that she is not able to pray any longer. The priest says that the soul leaves the body without any grief and that her son's soul stands in front of the Lord already. This certainty is questioned in one of the last scenes that take place in the mother's room. It is night; she sleeps on the sofa, still in her clothes. Suddenly a disturbing noise wakes her and she sees a white bird, a gull, beating on the window. She tries to open it to let the bird in, but her husband prevents her. When he tries to convince her that it was an ordinary gull, she denies it, insisting that the bird was a tormented soul – the soul of her son. Here the filmmaker uses a familiar image of the soul: that it cannot go to the other world, as it is tied to the unburied body. The father's rationality is strongly contrasted with the mother's certainty of receiving a message from her deceased son. Then there is a knock on the door. Two secret agents come in and ask them to dress as they are being taken to the cemetery for a funeral.

The funeral takes place in complete darkness. There is a false priest who is unable even to read the mourning prayer fluently. Despite this they have a chance to see their son's body. This assures them that they are not taking part in a wholly fake ceremony. The day after, they go to the cemetery to pray in private. The mother prays: 'God, listen to me. If it has to be as it is, that children are taken away from mothers and they are killed, I ask you to stop everything on the Earth, stop time. Give all the lost and killed children back to their mothers and let them bring their complaints to heaven. I ask you, God. Please, forgive me.' While speaking to God on behalf of all mothers who have lost their sons, she eventually transcends the individual experience of her own private pain and suffering and brings a collective complaint to God. Representing the strength of the collective 'maternal body', she dares to complain to God about the order of the world. However, she finishes with a request to be forgiven for this act of questioning the divine order. Indeed, due to the distancing devices used by the filmmaker, the spectator of *The Complaint* is not so much horrified by the individual case, as with the world that allows this to happen. Through this process of 'pity and fear' there is an attempt to relieve the trauma of Polish history. Significantly, as Izabela Kalinowska notes, the figure of a suffering woman appears disconcertingly often in films recreating a traumatic past in order to mark an ideological direction in the present (see Kalinowska 2002).

Both film audience and critics received Wójcik's employment of tragic structures with reserve and reluctance. This highly conventionalised picture of contemporary history and the mythical figure of the Polish Mother were perceived as too anachronistic and this film, along with many others, was considered 'a Mass of Martyrdom' with which Polish viewers were tired. Instead of living in the past, as was the case in Polish culture for so long, the Poles were soon to be teased by Aleksander Kwaśniewski's electoral campaign slogan, 'Choose the Future'. A filmic corollary of this was that the anachronistic figure of the Polish Mother had to be erased from Polish cinema. This actually happens in the film *Kroll* (1991) by Władysław Pasikowski, one of the most prominent representatives of the younger generation of film directors who entered Polish cinema after 1989. A symbolic act of the elimination of this iconic image of Polish femininity occurs in one of the early scenes of the film, when the hero's mother, searching for her son, who is absent without leave from his military unit, appears as a weak and helpless person, finally ending up with a heart attack. The disempowered figure of the mother disappears from the fictional world and his friends undertake the traditional 'maternal' task of protecting her son. Whether they are successful or not, a mother is no longer needed.

Note

1. The full name of the Party was the Polish United Workers' Party (Polska Zjednoczona Partia Robotnicza).

CHAPTER 3

Polish 'Superwoman':
a Liberation or Victimisation?

ELŻBIETA OSTROWSKA

Socialist realism was an aesthetic doctrine imposed upon Polish art in 1949; it was systematically enforced for almost seven years. This period in the history of Poland is referred to as 'Polish Stalinism'.[1] The Constitution of the People's Republic was inaugurated on 22 July 1952. Theoretically, it appeared to introduce a model democracy. However, this democracy was a legal fiction, as the working class, whilst being the official recipients of political power, had no opportunities to execute it. In reality, this ostensibly nascent system was, as Norman Davies puts it: 'a dictatorship of the Party over the people' (Davies 2001: 6), precisely recapitulating a repressive past it presumed to eradicate and replace. '[P]riority was given to heavy industry', whereas 'agriculture was turned over to compulsory collectivisation' (ibid.: 7). The Roman Catholic Church, being the prime cultural agent of tradition, was persecuted. In 1950 all Church properties were confiscated and members of the priesthood were arrested, including the Primate, Cardinal Stefan Wyszyński (ibid.: 7). In addition, in another strategy of repression, Moscow terrorised the entire Soviet Bloc with the prospect of an imperialist American nuclear attack. This resulted in widespread xenophobia and, consequently, any contact with the outside world could result in accusations of espionage. For example, listening to jazz was forbidden, as this kind of music was considered to be decadent and imperialistic. The most bizarre example of this anti-American mind-set was the widely propagated myth that America planned to drop vast numbers of Colorado beetles on Polish fields, in order to deprive the country of a basic foodstuff, thus resulting in a weakening of the Soviet Bloc. All forms and manifestations of individualism were condemned and often persecuted. Totalitarianism proposed that people did not belong to themselves or their families any longer. Instead, they belonged to the various state institutions within which they functioned. 'The Russian system of informers was introduced in factories and schools' (ibid.), with the intent to devastate the natural bonds between people. 'Be careful! The enemy does not sleep!' was the most popular slogan of the times. The regime's propaganda also attempted to undermine familial bonds; children were forced to denounce their parents, who themselves were encouraged to cultivate an attitude of systematic and mutual distrust. The general message was to trust no one, as anyone could be an enemy of the system.

These issues were reflected in the artistic life of the country, which was to be lived, or rather manufactured, according to the rules of 'socialist realism'. The Soviet aesthetic ideology, as formulated by Andrei A. Zhdanov in 1934, required that the artist become 'an engineer of human souls'. It dictated that art should not offer an objective depiction of reality, but instead articulate the revolutionary ideal, and serve as a didactic tool of revolutionary propaganda. The truthfulness and historical accuracy of the artistic portrayal should be combined with the ideological remoulding and education of the labouring classes in the spirit of socialism. A characteristic style in cinema was developed. Its main features were: simple plots, clear-cut conflicts and characters neatly delineated as good or evil. Tractor drivers, steel workers and bricklayers populated the fictional worlds of films. Their respective triumphs were intended to instil an atmosphere of optimism for a glorious communist future.

During this period many women were beginning to be employed in areas of work previously thought of as exclusively male. Their presence in these cannot, however, be regarded as a result of the successful implementation of the communist ideal of gender equality, for it had more to do with the specific economic situation in Poland, as well as other states within the Soviet Bloc. Due to the rapid development of heavy industry and serious labour shortages as a result of war losses, women were forced to enter the job market. This economic necessity was presented to them as a unique opportunity for self-realisation. On the situation of women in Eastern Europe after the Second World War, Chris Corrin notes, 'In the immediate years after the war many households had no men in them. In such situations the women were more or less forced to become "superwomen", heading the household as the main provider as well as the main carer and domestic worker' (Corrin 1992: 8). Even if this new position for women was mainly driven by the necessity for economic and political reconstruction, nonetheless it provided them with new life opportunities and relative independence. However, the price for this was a double burden. Women had to successfully conjoin their roles as public or domestic workers, with the demand to be good wives and mothers. Clearly, the films made according to the formulae of socialist realism chose to highlight these new possibilities. However, the issue of this 'double burden' remained unrepresented. The image of the 'Superwoman' became a principal symbol of the new ideological order to be implemented by the communist state. Consequently, female characters played important roles in almost all of the movies made at this time. Some of them directly addressed the issue of women's emancipation, making it their main theme.

I will analyse a number of Polish cinematic heroines of the early 1950s in order to deconstruct the propagandistic message they were meant to convey. The main issue I wish to address is whether this image of a 'New Woman' presented a model of womanhood that successfully questioned the feminine role, as prescribed by a supposedly defunct patriarchal hegemony. The chapter will conclude with an examination of the figure of the 'Superwoman', which recurs in films made during the 1980s, offering a revisionist perspective on the Stalinist period in both Polish history and cinema.

An exemplary model of the Polish 'Superwoman' appears in Jan Zelnik's documentary, *Kobiety naszych dni* (*Women of Our Days*), made in 1951. This film is characteristic of a cinematic form prevalent in Polish cinema at this time, which manifestly attempts to validate the new ideological order to the audience. Moreover, it exhibits almost all of the textual strategies employed by contemporaneous fiction films in terms of the positioning of female characters within the narrative. The film begins with a panning shot of a group of women taking part in an apparently political meeting. The image is accompanied by a male voice-over announcing the following 'historical truth': 'Yesterday the ruling classes provided women with the "leftovers" of human rights. Today, in the People's Poland, for the first time, a woman feels the warm-hearted care of the state. Yesterday there were lies about the so called "feminine vocation", today unlimited possibilities for learning are open to women.' It is evident that the import of the commentary is based upon a binary opposition between the past and the present, in which the former is equated with 'evil' and the latter with the 'good'. This kind of dichotomy underpins the fictional world in all the films of socialist realism.

In examining the relationship between image and voice commentary in *Women of Our Days* the dominance of the latter becomes increasingly obvious. This was another strategy exploited by filmmakers of the time. An unequivocally propagandistic message is far better served by the word than by the image, which is always open to interpretative ambiguity. Zelnik's film, intended as a revelation of the new possibilities open to women, significantly chooses to articulate its ideological position through the male voice. Women are shown as speechless and therefore passive; in general, they are reduced to the role of an empty sign, illustrating the master discourse of a male ideology. This quiescence is confirmed by the use of the passive mode in the commentary in relation to the feminine. Once, deprived of human rights – by Man – now they are generously provided with these rights, again – by Man! This emphatically demonstrates that within this 'new' ideological discourse, women still function as objects, not subjects.

By and large, the 'revolutionary' message is exposed as significantly complicit with the ostensibly questioned patriarchal order. This complicity is revealed throughout the film. For example, images illustrating the 'unlimited educational possibilities now open to women' frequently depict women as the passive recipients of male teachers' 'lesson'. The most symptomatic example of such a dependency is demonstrated by Zelnik while 'Gabriela Maroszek's case' is presented. Firstly, she is offered an opportunity to be educated as a lathe turner by the Party secretary, a benevolently paternalistic figure (this kind of male character appears in virtually every film concerning the issue of women's emancipation). Secondly, her son becomes her teacher. The son's implicit patriarchal power is also conveyed by the mise-en-scène, for he is physically placed above his mother, dominating her in a conspicuously visible way.

This visual dominance of male power is also noticeable in all images depicting the congress of the Polish Women's League. Although women deliver speeches to women, which could be interpreted as proof of a new-found subjectivity within the state structure, it is evident that this feminine public space is symbolically controlled by male power. Two huge portraits of Josef Stalin and the Polish President, Bolesław Bierut, hang above the tribune and the female orators demonstrate this. The unintentional, yet manifest, complicity of Zelnik's film with patriarchal order reflects the real situation of women living in the Soviet Bloc. As Irene Dölling notes, 'A form of state socialist patriarchy retained control over women's lives by "caring for" them in a paternal way which excluded any autonomous women's activities and any belief that women were capable of making gains for themselves' (Dölling, quoted in Corrin 1992: 19). In fiction films made at that time in Poland, the contradictions between the progressive propagandistic message and the stability of the patriarchal order are also apparent. This is evident in films which take the issue of 'women's emancipation' as their narrative centre, such as *Niedaleko Warszawy* (*Not Far from Warsaw*, 1954), by Maria Kaniewska, *Autobus odjeżdża 6.20* (*The Bus Leaves at 6.20*, 1954), by Jan Rybkowski, *Przygoda na Mariensztacie* (*An Adventure at Marienstadt*, 1954) by Leonard Buczkowski, and *Irena, do domu* (*Irena, Go Home*, 1955) by Jan Fethke.

The predominant theme of all these films is the female character's emancipation through work. The notion of 'work' refers here to employment traditionally regarded as masculine: Wanda Bugajówna (Urszula Modrzyńska) in *Not Far from Warsaw* is a technician controller in a steelworks, Krystyna Poradzka (Aleksandra Śląska) in *The Bus Leaves at 6.20* is a welder, Hanka Ruczajówna (Lidia Korsakówna) in *An Adventure at Marienstadt* is a bricklayer, and Irena Majewska (Lidia Wysocka) in *Irena, Go Home* is a taxi driver. Before any of these female protagonists engage with male activity or 'work', they are singularly occupied with traditionally feminine concerns. At some point in the narrative, they decide to change their lives. Significantly, their choices are often motivated not so much by their affinity for the new ideology, but rather by personal reasons. For example, Hanka in *An Adventure at Marienstadt* leaves her village for Warsaw to become a construction worker, not as an end in itself, but in order to pursue a hoped-for romance with the iconically heroic bricklayer, Janek Szarliński (Tadeusz Szmidt) (see Haltof 2002: 60). In *The Bus Leaves at 6.20* Krystyna appears to be somewhat frustrated by her job as a hairdresser's assistant, yet makes her decision to leave the small town for Silesia only after discovering her husband's (Jerzy Duszyński) infidelity. However, she hopes that he will follow her so that their marriage might be saved. Eventually, she is compelled to choose between her career and her family life, and she is prepared to sacrifice the former in the name of love for her husband. Fortunately, this becomes unnecessary, for, in the meantime, her husband has undergone an ideological conversion and has accepted her professional status. In all these films, the ultimate professional success of the woman is paralleled by the positive resolution of the romantic and heterosexual elements of the narrative. Positive propaganda requires a happy ending at all levels.

The importance of the heterosexual plot in socialist realist cinema was determined to a large extent by the strategies implicit within the authorial agenda. Tadeusz Lubelski identifies a number of strategies employed by postwar Polish filmmakers. Understanding 'strategy' as a set of cinematic conventions used by a group of filmmakers to gain particular objectives, he distinguishes, amongst others, the strategies of the 'professional' and of the 'propagandist', as used in some socialist realist films (Lubelski 1992: 53–74, 93–111). In particular, *An Adventure at Marienstadt* and *Irena, Go Home* represent a mixture of these two. This resulted from the fact that the respective directors, Leonard Buczkowski and Jan Fethke, worked in prewar popular cinema. Although they had to bow to the demands of the socialist realist aesthetic in terms of theme and necessary propagandistic message, they were skilful enough to translate this into a form of popular cinema that would simultaneously entertain its audience. In *An Adventure at Marienstadt* the generic convention of romantic musical comedy is used extensively. The affinity of Fethke's film, *Irena, Go Home*, with prewar comedy, is additionally exposed by the appearance of Adolf Dymsza, the most popular Polish comic actor of the 1930s, as Irena's husband. Consequently, both films present the woman's struggle for independence through the comic convention of an 'eternal battle of the sexes' rather than as the result of an ideologically conscious decision.

Interestingly, the heroine of socialist realist film is never able to overcome the obstacles on her way to emancipation on her own. Usually male adherents of the previous ideological order thwart her aspirations, whether they be her master in work or at home. In *Not Far from Warsaw* Wanda has to struggle with her father, the engineer, and even her boyfriend (Jan Żardecki), who is a respected Stakhanovite worker, but also a brutal macho. In *An Adventure at Marienstadt* Hanka, the female protagonist, is employed on a construction site where her main antagonist is the misogynistic, yet comic, master, Leon Ciepielewski (Adam Mikołajewski). Her boyfriend also criticises her work and treats her neglectfully as a result. Krystyna in *The Bus Leaves at 6.20* is both humiliated by her husband in his attempt to subordinate her to his patriarchal power and simultaneously struggles with the misogynist prejudices of her employer. The main antagonist of the heroine of *Irena, Go Home* is her husband, whose love for home-made food seems to be the main reason for his conservative attitude. All these women are able to overcome these difficulties thanks to the support and help they receive from other men, usually from the party Secretaries (see Lubelski 1992: 102–3).

In *Not Far from Warsaw* (Figure 3.1) in the whole steelworks only the Party secretary, Wielicki (Wiktor Grotowicz), understands Wanda's difficulties and tries to cheer her up whenever she experiences humiliation from her male colleagues. In the beginning of the movie he says to her, 'Here we push women up.' This optimistic and potentially liberating message for

Figure 3.1 Urszula Modrzyńska as Wanda Bugajówna and Jan Żardecki as Józek Wieniarz in *Niedaleko Warszawy* (*Not Far from Warsaw*), 1954, dir. Maria Kaniewska © Studio Filmowe 'Oko'

women is underpinned by a clearly paternalistic attitude. If this phrase is subjected to scrutiny, it reveals its complicity with a traditional conception of women's passivity, for they are treated as an object that could be moved by an external agency rather than act autonomously. Wielicki also functions as a symbolic father for Wanda (see Stachówna 1996: 21–23), whereas her own father (Feliks Żukowski) is shown as attached to the prewar model of life. Not only is he against Wanda's work, but he also unconsciously supports the saboteur who wants to destroy the steelworks and kill his daughter, as she tries to prevent his plans from being realised. At the end of the movie Wanda's father attends a Party meeting in order to make a confession and is told by one of his oldest friends, 'You think that you have brought your daughter up! Wielicki has, the steelworks has, the working class has, not you!' This dialogue echoes the above-mentioned effort to destroy and replace traditional human bonds, especially familial ones, with new ones, generated from within the structure of the Communist Party.

Similarly symbolic father figures are embodied in the characters of Party secretaries in both *An Adventure at Marienstadt* and *The Bus Leaves at 6.20*. The heroines are also provided with symbolic mothers who support them in resolving their romantic problems. In the former this is Alina Rębacz (Barbara Rachwalska), a Stakhanovite worker; in the latter this is Krystyna's roommate at the technical high school, to which the heroine has been 'sent' by her symbolic father. *Irena, Go Home* is an exception to the rule, as the main character is supported mainly by an older female neighbour and by the manager of the transportation company for which she is supposed to work after completing her course. Interestingly, he is shown as a weak man, subordinated to his fiancée, who represents a dominating type of femininity. This structural departure in Fethke's film can be explained through its strong affinity with the generic form of comedy, in which only the theme reflects the demands of the new ideology.

In all these films the same narrative pattern is repeated: a female protagonist overcomes numerous obstacles, forges for herself a professional career and is eventually reunited with her lover. As has been noted by Oksana Bulgakova, there is a deep structural similarity between fairy tales and Soviet films of the socialist realist period, especially in the 'Cinderella' type characters played by Lubov' Orlova (Bulgakova 1993: 158). Many Polish films recapitulate this fairy-tale structure, with one main modification: the Party secretary replaces the good witch. Krystyna Poradzka from *The Bus Leaves at 6.20*, as well as the heroines of *An Adventure at Marienstadt* and *Not Far from Warsaw*, can be seen as archetypical versions of the 'socialist Cinderella'. In the course of the film their metamorphosis from a neglected, miserable and often humiliated woman, into a respected and romantically successful individual is nurtured and mentored by Communist Party representatives. Bruno Bettelheim's analysis of the Cinderella story as symbolising a young girl's maturation and the formation of female sexual identity (see

Figure 3.2 Lidia Korsakówna as Wanda Ruczajówna and Tadeusz Schmidt as Janek Szarliński in *Przygoda na Mariensztacie* (*An Adventure at Marienstadt*), 1954, dir. Leonard Buczkowski © Studio Filmowe 'Oko'

Bettelheim 1977: 236–77) reveals the thematic parallel, in regard to sexuality, between the fairy-tale figure and the heroines of socialist realist films.

An interesting attempt to analyse the issue of female sexuality in socialist realist cinema is offered by Wiesław Godzic. Firstly, he claims that although *An Adventure at Marienstadt* (Figure 3.2) is ostensibly socialist realism, it is closer in structure to a fairy tale rather than to any kind of realism. (Lynn Atwood makes a similar observation regarding Soviet films: 'Despite the stress on "realism", symbols and myths are a strong feature of films of the Stalin era' [Atwood 1993: 68]). Secondly, he maintains that the propagandistic narrative regarding women's emancipation could be psychoanalytically read as a story about repressed desire in which a woman is deprived of her sexuality. These repressed desires had to be sublimated into different realms of women's activity in the form of 'work' (Godzic 1991: 120–28). As Godzic writes,

> From the psychoanalytical point of view the plot of *An Adventure at Marienstadt* presents the story of a young woman who searches for her sexual identity. She meets a man, who plays the symbolic function of a father, to whom she also addresses her erotic desires. Experiencing a failure on this stage moves her to a complex of masculinity and a retreat from the opposite

sex. Finally, through contact with a new symbolic father and the figure of a mother she enters a mature stage of adolescent female sexuality, overcoming fears regarding castration and making the first symbolic father her object of love. (ibid.: 122)

Inspired by Godzic's psychoanalytical interpretation of Buczkowski's film, Grażyna Stachówna claims that Wanda's story in *Not Far from Warsaw* is built upon exactly the same principle of repressed female sexuality (Stachówna 1996: 22).

Godzic's and Stachówna's opinions on the issue of the socialist realist heroine's sexuality are undoubtedly more insightful than those expressed by the majority of film critics, who take for granted desexualisation of women in this kind of film. For example, Marek Haltof writes, 'The communist model propagates the masculinisation of "new women" ... . In the world of ascetic socialist realist films, in which female characters can only be with an ideologically correct man, there is no place for love, not to mention sex' (Haltof 2002: 64; also see Bulgakova 1993: 158; Zwierzchowski 2000: 128, 132). Clearly, the asexuality of socialist realist heroines is usually conjoined with their masculinisation. Rafał Marszałek has interestingly examined this in a comparative analysis of the changes in costume of female characters in Polish prewar and socialist realism cinema (Marszałek 1988: 35–55). In his essay entitled 'Kapelusz i chustka' (A Hat and a Kerchief) he postulates that in the former, women were clothed in a manner that emphasised their feminine sexuality, whereas in the latter, their clothes are intended to transform them into masculine or asexual figures.

Although Marszałek offers an insightful sociocultural analysis of change in the notions of femininity and masculinity in postwar Polish culture, it must be stressed that his interpretation is underpinned by a relatively limited understanding of gender that he identifies only through the conventional usage of external attributes such as clothes and behaviour. It is also worthy of note that even though women engaged in 'masculine' occupations in socialist realist film are dressed in an 'unfeminine' way, that is, in working uniforms and kerchiefs concealing their hair, this occurs only within the working environment. When these women finish work, they are shown, almost exclusively, in evidently feminine garb and, interestingly, all of them have long hair. Indeed, all the working clothes are exceptionally modest, concealing rather than revealing the heroines' sexuality; however, there is no doubt that after hours all of these women are represented as 'truly feminine'. This reveals the multiplicity of the demands made of women: to be a good worker, a good mother, a good wife, and last but not least, to be a beautiful woman. Sometimes, their femininity is shown as something temporarily hidden beneath their 'masculine' working attire. For example, Wanda hides a beaded necklace beneath her working uniform, which she habitually holds in her mouth when she is stressed or experiences disrespect from her male colleagues. Moreover, along with almost all other heroines, she removes her kerchief whilst experiencing doubt as to her ability to successfully perform a 'masculine job'. This gesture, exposing long hair, formerly concealed by masculine attire, at once discloses these heroines' femininity and, if female hair is read in its fetishistic function, also their sexuality. Overall, the usage of costume demonstrates that the Polish Superwoman was supposed to retain her conventionally understood femininity, whilst sexuality was often to be repressed. In offering this type of female heroine, the socialist realist film did not question the gendered order of the precommunist patriarchal world, but once again presented women in a way that was significantly complicit with the position ascribed to woman within it.

The repressed female sexuality of the positive heroines was often displaced onto their negative counterparts. These women are usually presented as deprived of a communist consciousness, and as strongly attached to prewar petit bourgeois feminine aspirations for nice clothes and a handsome partner. The most conspicuous example of this type of heroine is Janeczka (Barbara Drapińska) from *The Bus Leaves at 6.20*. She works as a minor clerk at the steelworks where both the main characters, Krystyna, and her husband are employed (Figure 3.3). Janeczka first appears in a scene that takes place in the steelworks office, when Krystyna comes to apply for a job. The two women are contrasted with each other through multiple signs: modest and

Figure 3.3 Aleksandra Śląska as Krystyna Poradzka and Jerzy Duszyński as Wiktor Poradzki, Krystyna's husband, in *Autobus odjeżdża 6.20* (*The Bus Leaves at 6.20*), 1954, dir. Jan Rybkowski © Studio Filmowe 'Oko'

unfashionable clothes vs. elegant dress exposing the curves of body, the plain, 'natural' beauty vs. intense make-up highlighting sensuous lips, shy yet dignified behaviour vs. arrogance. To complete this image of the 'evil woman' as a reversal of the 'angelic femininity' embodied in Krystyna, Janeczka is equipped with an indispensable accessory of the *femme fatale*: a cigarette.

Interestingly, if the wearing of masculine work clothes on the part of the socialist realist heroine was intended to attenuate or blur gender difference between positive male and female icons, the prop of a cigarette somehow renders this weakened division visible again. There is no instance of a heroic female smoker in any of these films, whereas all of the male heroes partake of the habit. Clearly, male smoking is positively associated with a working lifestyle, whereas female smoking signifies 'a bad woman'. If a cigarette can be read as a phallic fetish, between the lips of a woman it can also signify a predatory and castrating female. No wonder that the positive heroines cannot be seen to indulge in the pleasures of smoke, whereas it is a predominant attribute of their negative counterparts, who are eventually punished or simply eliminated in the course of the narrative. This is the case with Janeczka, who plays the role of *femme fatale* in the story (perhaps it would be better to call her a caricature of this type due to the character's simplification), and who endangers Krystyna's marriage. She seduces Krystyna's husband, convinces him to start working as a clerk, though he is a talented electrician, and finally entices him into a life of crime. Of course, the precepts of socialist realism 'save' the hero from the downfall he would have experienced in *film noir*. Once he realises all the wrongs he has committed under the influence of this 'bad woman', he comes to fully respect his wife's accomplishments and devotion, finally deciding to go back to her.

This pattern, whereby female sexuality is located in and identified with 'bad' female characters, is repeated with greater ostentation in *Pierwsze dni* (*First Days*, 1951) by Jan Rybkowski. This film, unlike those examined above, presents from the outset a very male story, in which 'good guys' fight with 'bad guys', respectively workers and saboteurs. The female characters are also strictly delineated as 'angelic' or 'evil' types, in a manner directly borrowed from the realm of popular cinema. In fact, the female characters appear in an unexpected moment of the action and without any particular motivation. For the significant part of the story the male characters try to address 'masculine conflicts', when suddenly women enter the action, with no apparent narrative justification, and disrupt these strongly depicted homosocial bonds within both groups. It might be hypothesised that these female characters are hastily introduced to the fictional world to diffuse a possible homosexual undertone within the presented 'male world'. In having the function of restoring an endangered heterosexuality in the fictional reality, women are unavoidably represented in a highly stereotypical way, signifying respectively 'proper' and 'improper' femininity as defined by patriarchal ideology. Therefore, an 'angelic' type of womanhood is embodied in the character of a teacher (Celina Klimczakówna) who protects, in an almost maternal way, the main male hero. She is briefly contrasted with an archetypically evil female figure, who is sceptical, if not overtly hostile towards the workers' ideals. The moral contrast between these two female figures is emphatically signalled through the difference in their manner of dress and make-up. Obviously, the 'bad' one smokes a cigarette. A third episodic female character appears as the girlfriend of the head saboteur. He is presented as a grotesque caricature of an American gangster (mostly through his costume and performance, reinforced by setting: a luxurious estate in a wood), and she, correspondingly, caricatures the figure of a gangster's moll. Similarly, as in the case of the two former female characters, her appearance somehow disturbs the development of the narrative. Specifically, a close-up of her, or rather a fragment of her body, clad in bikini, initiates the scene in which the saboteurs meet with their boss. Her role as an 'object to be looked at', which Laura Mulvey identifies with Hollywood classical cinema (Mulvey 1975: 746–57), is confirmed in the dialogue. The boss reprimands his subordinates for looking at her and brutally orders her to go home. She stands up and with silent obedience leaves the men.

By and large, these examples demonstrate that there were two main strategies employed to represent female sexuality in socialist realism. In the case of positive female characters sexuality is first repressed, then displaced into a surrogate form through professional competition with men, to be finally and positively resolved through a narrative pattern of heterosexual romance, complicit with the patriarchal order. In contrast, the 'bad' female figure is provided with all the overt signs of female sexuality/sensuality, but is ultimately punished for this, either literally or by her simple eradication from the fictional reality. It seems evident that the 'good' female, whose sexuality is controlled and subsumed by the needs of society, is to be seen as a proponent of a new communist order and the 'bad', with her overt sexuality and its potential power over men, as an opponent. In this respect these films reproduced exactly the fearful and suppressive myths regarding female sexuality that were inherent within the patriarchal ideology they presumed to question.

There is also a third group of female characters, older women who are not defined in terms of their sexuality; and perhaps this explains their location beyond the binary opposition of 'good' and 'bad' femininity. Leaving aside the problem of constructing these characters according to the stereotypical equation of female sexuality with youth, which reduces it to a reproductive function, it should be said that their asexuality renders them as neutral figures in the world of struggle between the 'old' and the 'new' order. In fact, this neutrality signifies passivity, for they neither oppose nor support either of these two orders. The figure of Wanda's mother (Halina Biling) in *Not Far from Warsaw* demonstrates this passivity in an exemplary way. She is a silent figure who is located in the background of the main plot, and is shown as constantly engaged in domestic work, which she neither enjoys nor resents. Whilst Wanda's father strongly opposes his daughter's professional aspirations, the mother seems to be rather indifferent to them. Apparently, she is ready to accept any social change as she knows that this will not affect the sphere of her own life which is limited to cooking, gardening and cleaning the house until the end of her days. She epitomises women's exclusion from history, which is established by consequently locating her in private space.

Although the marginal position of this type of woman within the fictional world may seem insignificant, they are important, as their engagement in domestic work allows the young women to function within the public space and pursue the path of a professional career. Wanda can fully concentrate on her job and help to unmask the saboteur, as her mother is responsible for maintaining a cosy and friendly home. From time to time Wanda helps her, which is probably intended to demonstrate that she would be able to reproduce this ideal image of domestic life. Krystyna Poradzka in *The Bus Leaves at 6.20* can leave her town for Silesia only because her mother-in-law can take care of her little son. When Krystyna is given a flat, her mother-in-law moves in and continues to do all the domestic work. Generally, it could be said that all these old women bear the burden of domestic work so that their filmic 'daughters' can pursue a professional career. Thus, the double burden of women has been erased from the ideal vision of reality produced by these films. Symptomatically, numerous nice and cosy homes are presented in socialist realist films, but none of them is run by an emancipated woman. The narratives end in a moment of positively resolved heterosexual romance, a fairy-tale message: 'And they all lived happily after.' However, the lives of women who had to successfully combine the roles of worker, wife and mother remain unrepresented.

This lacuna in the representations of women's lives during the Stalinist period could be closed only after the Polish 'thaw' of October 1956, when many directors decided to analyse and rework the propagandistic intentions of Polish cinema under socialist realism. One example is Jerzy Zarzycki's film, *Zagubione uczucia* (*Lost Feelings*), made in 1957. Its heroine, Stańczakowa (Maria Klejdysz), is a typical socialist realist heroine. She is a blacksmith who also attends evening technical school to obtain qualifications. Zarzycki shows what is hidden behind this propagandistic image familiar to a Polish audience. Stańczakowa has been left by her husband so that he can pursue a political career, whilst she brings up their four children. Her job and the classes in the evening school are so time-consuming that all domestic duties must be performed by her fourteen-year-old son, who, unable to cope, runs away from home to join a group of hooligans. Stańczakowa's life shows that all the possibilities and promises for women made by the communist government, were illusory. The heroine cannot achieve economic independence because her job is extremely low paid and she cannot

gain self-fulfilment in motherhood either, as her work and education con-
sume all her time. As a single woman she is also sexually frustrated and
social norms do not allow her to resolve this problem. Disillusion, frustration and a continuous feeling of guilt are the dominant elements of this portrayal. This figure of a mother, in her padded boots and jacket, which serve
to mask her femininity and render her as masculine, is contradicted by her
face, calm, dignified and full of suffering, which transforms her into an
another variant of the figure of the Polish Mother. Although it has lost
something of its traditional dignity, it still has, even in this hybrid form, a
considerable power. Her suffering does not stir admiration, but rather compassion. The image of an unhappy mother in *Lost Feelings* efficiently questioned the communist myth of socialist happiness, which was probably the
reason for the film being banned.

The exclusion of Zarzycki's film from public discourse marks the beginning of an attempt to repress the collective memory of the Stalinist past that
lasted for many years. The heroes of socialist realism only came back to the
screen at the beginning of the 1970s in a small number of documentaries.
Even these were banned until 1981 (see Haltof 2002: 208). Only later, at
the beginning of the1980s, did a wide range of films appear revising the
propagandistic image of the 1950s.

Among the documentaries examining the issue of Stalinist ideology in
Poland, the most significant were made by Wojciech Wiszniewski. He dealt
broadly with the theme of the Stakhanovite idea of work competition. One
of these films, *Wanda Gościmińska – Włókniarka* (*Wanda Gościmińska,
the Textile Worker*, 1975) (Figure 3.4) tells the story of a woman who
worked for forty years in a textile factory in Łódź. Wiszniewski divides the
story of her life into separate episodes, entitled: 'Genealogy', 'Yesterday',
'Generations' and so on. Before the first appears on the screen, we are
shown a motionless close-up of an older woman with a blank, tired face,
accompanied by the monotonous noise of textile machines. The title of the
first part is then displayed, followed by a stylised picture of several people
sitting at a table on which there is a big loaf of bread. Unlike the women
presented in *Women of Our Days*, the heroine of Wiszniewski's film is
allowed to speak with her own voice. However, her monologue lacks a personal tone. She introduces herself using words that reproduce those used in
official state language. We are shown, in a long pan, close-ups of people sitting at the table, with hands destroyed by incessant labour. She speaks of
her family and its miserable life before the Second World War, again in
phrases used by Stalinist propaganda. She describes the end of the war as a
double liberation, from both occupiers and capitalism. Before the war a job
had to be begged for, but after it there was so much to do. Not a single word
is spoken about the issue of women's emancipation through work. Instead
she speaks about the economic demands of the present. When asked by a
group of young people whether her job really was the most important thing

Figure 3.4 Wanda Gościmińska in *Wanda Gościmińska – Włókniarka* (*Wanda Gościmińska, the Textile Worker*), 1975, dir. Wojciech Wiszniewski © Wytwórnia Filmów Oświatowych w Łodzi

in her life, she answers that it was one of many important things in one's life, and that this was so for all of the postwar generation. She adds that young people now ask many questions, but the past 'was not a time for asking questions'. Her prewar history, her forty-year-long working life, is summarised in one sentence, 'After completing technical high school I started working as a forewoman and after forty years I retired.' At one point Wiszniewski places Wanda Gościmińska's silhouette against the monumental picture of her as a Stakhanovite worker. There is a striking contrast between the pompous grandeur of the picture and the small figure of a tired woman. She is still unable to speak her own words. Her use of the platitudes of Stalinist propaganda demonstrates the discrepancy between the propagandistic version of reality and the real people, whose lives it purported to portray and whose minds it sought to change. As Mirosław Przylipiak notices, '[Wiszniewski] filmed the consciousness of the heroine, and even more, he showed the gap between her self-knowledge and her existence determined by ideology' (Przylipiak 2000: 190).

Wanda Różycka employs similar juxtapositions of propagandistic images of the 1950s with images of contemporary life in her documentary *Kobieta z węgla* (*Woman from Coal*, 1982), portraying the life of a female coalminer. The heroine also started her job at the beginning of the 1950s and was seized by the idea of women entering 'masculine' professions. She describes herself working under the earth, loading fifteen tons of coal per day, until the sixth month of pregnancy. Her declarations concerning women's capacity to work as hard as men are juxtaposed with images of her husband, who claims that women should not perform certain jobs as they are too strenuous. He maintains that a woman's place should be at home, but there are times when a man is not able to earn enough money for living expenses, therefore a second income would help. Różycka's heroine, placed in a chair against a heap of coal, mechanically intoning the message of female liberation through masculine work, looks like a kind of living fossil emerging from the Stalinist past. She remains completely indifferent to the long list of various diseases she suffered due to her hard work and she takes for granted that young women should take over her position. This blind acceptance of her situation is contrasted with a young woman's rejection of the necessity for her to take the old woman's place in the workforce. She claims that the work is too hard for women and that she would be paid less than a man for the same activity. The 'woman of coal' responds by repeating once again her strong belief that 'women can do'. Różycka's film, as well as Wiszniewski's, does not question this capability of women, but at the same time the films provoke the question as to what these women gained for themselves through their life-long hard work. Their life stories do not reveal any particular motivation for choosing a certain professional career. Rather, they passively subordinated their lives to the external demands of the communist ideology and the economic situation.

If in documentaries there is a prevalence of passive female victims of Stalinist propaganda and exploitative standards of work, in fiction films one encounters feminine characters that are negative reversals of the ones that dominate socialist realism. Such a figure can be found in Andrzej Wajda's *Człowiek z marmuru* (*Man of Marble*, 1976), which initiated the trend to revise Stalinism. Interestingly, Mateusz Birkut (Jerzy Radziwiłłowicz), the main male hero, is presented as a tragic figure, a victim of Stalinist propaganda, who after discovering the truth undertakes a rebellion, which results in his imprisonment. His wife, Hanka Tomczyk (Krystyna Zachwatowicz), a sportswoman celebrated by communist propaganda, lacks this moral strength and epitomises the worst kind of political opportunism. While he is in prison, which is the price he pays for his faithfulness to ideals of truth and justice, she declares loyalty to the communist authority and publicly denounces her husband as a 'public enemy'. Twenty years later, whilst delving into a 'repressed past', Agnieszka (Krystyna Janda), the main character, makes a film about Birkut, in which he is revealed as the eponymous Man of Marble, representing all the moral virtues, whereas his wife has become a pathetic alcoholic who cannot be reconciled to her nefarious past.

A similarly treacherous wife is cast in Janusz Zaorski's *Matka Królów* (*Mother of the Kings*, 1982, released in 1987), which tells the tragic story of Łucja Król (King) (Magda Teresa Wójcik) and her four sons during the period of the Second World War and then Stalinism (see Chapter 2). Similarly to *Man of Marble*, the wife of one of Łucja's sons, who is imprisoned by the totalitarian regime, declares her loyalty to the Party and believes in her husband's guilt. When asked by his mother to contact some influential colleagues within the Party in order to obtain help, she refuses to comply, mechanically repeating propagandistic slogans concerning the people's weakness and susceptibility to enemy's forces. There is a strong contrast between the character of Łucja Król, who is presented as an embodiment of the icon of the Polish Mother, for whom family ties are the most important human relationship, and this young woman who chooses to be loyal to the Party, not to her husband. Another example of a woman who betrays the 'sacred' family tie is presented in Jerzy Domaradzki's film *Wielki bieg* (*The Big Run*, 1981, released in 1987). As in *Man of Marble* and *Mother of the Kings*, there is the character of an 'honest communist' who is imprisoned by the Stalinist regime. Whilst his son is fully convinced of the innocence of his father, his daughter doubts it, saying, 'The party does not make errors.' Overall, we can see that female characters are frequently presented as blind zealots of a 'new ideology', incapable of critical and independent thinking.

One of the most symptomatic examples of the female communist zealot can be found in Wojciech Marczewski's *Dreszcze* (*Shivers*, 1981) (Figure 3.5). Marczewski's film goes far beyond a mere description of the times of political terror, being rather an attempt to explain the mechanisms by which the Polish mind was seized by communist ideology. To put it crudely, Marczewski asks a question: How was it possible that so many people became ardent advocates of the totalitarian order? Unlike Wajda, who in *Man of Marble* undertook a broad political and social perspective in examining the issue, the author of *Shivers* decided to explore the problem from an individual perspective, with the main focus put on psychological mechanisms of engagement with Stalinist ideas. To expedite this objective he decided to use the form of a coming-of-age story, as it enabled him to touch upon the issue of the acquisition of identity. The main hero, a teenage Tomek (Tomasz Chudziec), comes from a family which is not embroiled in Stalinist ideology and tries as far as possible to survive the times beyond its grasp. As a consequence, the father is eventually arrested and the familial sanctuary from a hostile world is destroyed. Moreover, Tomek is sent to a scouts' camp which is conceived as a training ground for future Party activists. Here, unprotected by his family, which no longer exists, he is open to the impact of communist ideology. Symptomatically, this ideology does not reach him in the form of abstract slogans or simple propagandistic text. It is instead conveyed by a female figure, the activist (Teresa Marczewska), who is presented as a surrogate mother to whom he addresses his primal erotic desire. In this respect she treats him with a maternal tenderness,

Figure 3.5 Teresa Marczewska in *Dreszcze* (*Shivers*), 1981, dir. Wojciech Marczewski © Studio Filmowe 'Tor'

which also contains an erotic undertone. It could be said that Tomek's engagement with communist ideology is presented as a result of seduction. He is neither forced, nor does he uncritically accept this ideology (in fact, he also befriends two 'dissidents' of the camp). He simply and emphatically shares with his object of desire her emotional engagement with the ideas of communism. This emotional attachment to the ideology on the part of the female activist is contrasted with the rational attitude of her boyfriend who visits her at the camp. All his efforts to 'open her eyes' are in vain and she hysterically tries to save the 'object of her love'. Overall, a man is presented as capable of maintaining his objectivity within the ideological system in which he functions, whilst a woman's subjectivity could only be formed by assimilation and identification with it.

Filip Bajon explores much the same problem in his film *Wahadełko* (*Shilly, Shally*, 1981, released in 1984). However, he concentrates more on the relationship between the Stalinist past and the present, as the main line of action takes place in the 1970s. The main hero, Michał (Janusz Gajos), who lives with his mother (Halina Gryglaszewska) and his sister (Mirosława Marcheluk), suffers from depression or a kind of neurosis. His sickness clearly results from childhood trauma, as suggested by flashbacks from his past which often take the form of recurrent nightmares. All the memories from his solitary childhood come from the time spent in a sanatorium, whilst his mother was engaged in her professional career and her participation in work competition. The motif of an 'absent mother' dominates all these flashbacks and continues in the contemporary part of the narrative. Michał and his sister talk about the mother and look at her through a window as she is busy with gardening. Later, in the siblings' conversations she is presented as a symbolic incarnation of the 'castrating mother', who disturbed the proper psychosexual development of her children (see Nurczyńska-Fidelska 2003: 168). This is expressed in one of the dialogues between the brother and the sister which reveals the sadomasochist relationship between them. He mockingly says that she is 'the best sister in Middle Europe but unfortunately nobody wants to pull out a dick for her'. When she advises him 'to worry about his own', he says that 'there is nothing to worry about as he is an eunuch'. This impotence in a literal and figurative sense is presented as having its source in the Stalinist past which is incarnated in his mother. At the end of the film the mother appears for a while only to demonstrate that she has not changed since the times that are recollected in the flashbacks and the siblings' conversations. She says that she does not understand her son's sickness and she does not want to. Michał bitterly concludes that in her world, which is based on the principle of mimicry, there is no space for his sickness, as it represents his inability to adjust to external circumstances. Michał's character lends itself to a metaphoric evocation of the dilemma of Polish masculinity. His psychic sickness signifies his disagreement with surrounding reality, but it also means a retreat from it and as such it has to result in impotence. Symptomatically, the mother is to be blamed for it.

To conclude, in many of the films realised in the 1970s and 1980s, which recollect the Stalinist past in order to heal the audience from this collective historical trauma, the male and female characters are poignantly contrasted, mostly in terms of their contribution to the establishment of the Stalinist order in Poland during the 1950s. By and large, the flawless heroines of the socialist realist films are reversed into blind zealots of the totalitarian doctrine who stubbornly maintain their beliefs long after the collapse of the system. While male characters are capable of discovering the truth hidden beneath the propagandistic slogans, the female heroines are shown as perfect products of political indoctrination. Paradoxically, the women who were previously shown as actively entering the realm of the public, as subjects producing history, are in later films located outside it. This is demonstrated by their blind attachment to ideas that were discredited and shamefully abandoned a long time ago. Consequently, their previous activity in revisionist films of the 1970s and 1980s is compromised as an actual passivity. Moreover, if male characters are constructed as multidimensional protagonists and undergo an internal metamorphosis, their female counterparts are usually presented as static figures who do not develop throughout the narratives. *Man of Marble* offers the most

symptomatic example of the gendering of history, in which the male socialist hero is elevated to the position of national hero, whereas the socialist
heroine, in the form of his wife, ends as a pathetic alcoholic who is unable
to acknowledge and pay for her 'youthful sins'.

Overall, the cinematic figure of the Polish Superwoman exemplifies an
objectifying use of women within the signifying practices of a culture determined by the demands of an imposed ideology. The seemingly emancipated
and independent female characters of socialist realism actually work in
complicity with patriarchal ideology. In turn, later films that were conceived to relieve 'repressed memory', in fact also expressed a barely hidden
misogyny. The Polish Superwoman, a token of totalitarian ideology, now
appears as the Other in the revisionist films of the 1980s and, as such, has
to be punished for entering the male world.

Note

1. The characteristic of Stalinism in Poland is based on Norman Davies's book,
   Heart of Europe: The Past in Poland's Present (2001: 6–8).

CHAPTER 4

Caught between Activity and Passivity: Women in the Polish School

ELŻBIETA OSTROWSKA

The emergence of the Polish School in the late 1950s initiated a break in Polish cinema, distinctly opposed to the schemata of the previously dominant forms of socialist realism. That impersonal model of cinematic propaganda was replaced by films offering an individualised vision of reality, whether it was in Andrzej Wajda's romanticism and expressionism, Andrzej Munk's grotesquerie and irony, or Kazimierz Kutz's realism. Yet, all of these dealt with the same theme: the need to revise a certain type of experience of the Second World War that had been either suppressed, or distorted in socialist realism. According to Tadeusz Lubelski, the films of the Polish School represent the strategy of a psychotherapist (see Chapter 3). A director using this strategy tries to 'restore his audience to health' by providing a self-knowledge that can be gained through an analysis of the recent past. Lubelski claims that Andrzej Wajda's *Popiół i diament* (*Ashes and Diamonds*, 1958) is the best example of this strategy as this film managed to reunite the Polish nation, which had been fractured by the demands of the totalitarian doctrine of communism. This reunification was made possible through representing the war experience of those who had been members of the Home Army, the resistance movement, led by the Polish government in exile and opposed to the communist takeover (Lubelski 1992: 143–84).

In this chapter I will reassess the portrayals of women in these films, in order to see whether they reflect with some equality the war experience of both sexes. Male directors made all the films of the Polish School that deal with the theme of war, traditionally considered a male subject. However, it is not my intention to examine the correctness or incorrectness of images of women in these films, but rather to discuss the specific uses of these descriptions of Polish women in relation to broader issues of nation and history in the mid- to late 1950s and the beginning of the 1960s. In order to achieve this goal I will trace out exemplary variants of female experience during the Second World War as they are portrayed in the films. In other words, I intend to reconstruct a model biography of Polish woman as it is represented in the Polish School. Therefore, the film analyses will parallel the course of history from the beginning of the Polish–German war in September 1939 to the end of the Nazi occupation.

The beginning of the Second World War is the subject of Wajda's film *Lotna* (1959), showing the fight of the Polish cavalry against the Nazis in September 1939. The focus of attention is a group of three men whose fates are bound up with the beautiful white mare, Lotna. Clearly, this is a male world and the absence of women is marked in one of the first scenes, when the three men enter a desolate, deserted palace. Their conversation uses a conditional mode of speech: 'If there were women here, you would get something to eat', and later, when they see the overflowing bathtub, one says 'You could have washed her back.' This hypothetical female object of desire is soon replaced by the white horse they encounter standing by the bed of an old nobleman. Later, one of them, Witek (Adam Pawlikowski), says that no girl can compete with her. His friend, Jerzy (Jerzy Moes), replies that they have the same taste. Indeed, no woman can compete with Lotna, even Ewa (Bożena Kurowska), Jerzy's future wife. She became an object of desire for Jerzy only when he already knew that he would inherit Lotna after his captain's death.

The first time Jerzy sees Ewa is at the school where she lives as a country schoolteacher. Their flirtatious conversation is abruptly broken by an air raid. Horrified, Ewa falls into Jerzy's arms and from then on it is clear that their relationship cannot be developed in a 'proper' temporality. Within two days, Ewa plays almost all of the social roles prescribed to woman: girlfriend, fiancée, wife and widow. Unlike Jerzy, she knows the real reason for this haste. She says to Witek on the wedding night, 'Be happy for us. Tomorrow may be too late', and later, when her husband says, 'Let's go. Time drags when you are impatient', she adds, 'For death'. She senses its imminence and decides to accompany her husband when his squadron goes to battle. When they stop on their way, she prepares a picnic meal to which her husband responds with annoyance. He rebukes her that this is a war, not a trip. 'I know. That's why I want you to sit here next to me', she answers, and tells him that as a little girl she used to play house and held receptions. Then she invites, in somewhat theatrical way, her husband: 'Let me invite you to our new home.' She knows that there will be no home for them and so, instead, she tries to stage a performance of it to let him know how it would be. Her behaviour may be seen as an attempt to understand a male world of battles, horses and lancers, but it is rather more about his inability to accept her 'feminine' values. He abruptly leaves the picnic table to follow a scared Lotna who is escaping because of an explosion. This chase means death for him. Earlier Witek's statement that no woman can compete with Lotna is confirmed in this scene and, according to Christopher Caes, may be interpreted as 'the disengaging of masculine desire from women and its firm relocation within the homosocial group of the cavalry riders' (Caes 2003: 120).

Indeed, the male bonds seem to be of primary importance in Wajda's film, which results in his abandoning the character of Ewa almost immediately after her husband dies, allowing Lotna to dominate the plot again, until she breaks her leg and has to be shot. Witnessing Lotna's death, Witek breaks his sabre as a symbolic gesture of submission and the end of his war. If one sees a sabre as a fetish of masculinity, the gesture acquires the additional meaning of his abandoning of masculinity. This seems inevitable, if all objects of desire have disappeared. Such an endangered, or weakened, notion of masculinity dominates almost all the films belonging to the Polish School and this factor significantly determines its representation of women.

The organising of resistance almost immediately followed the defeat of the Poles in the Polish–German war. This is depicted in Andrzej Wajda's directorial début *Pokolenie* (*A Generation*, 1955). Polish film historians consider the film a hybrid, belonging partly to the paradigm of socialist realism, but also foretelling the change in Polish cinema (see Miczka 1996/97: 28–29). Based on the purely propagandist novel by Bohdan Czeszko, *A Generation* (Figure 4.1) tells the story of a group of young communists during the Nazi occupation of Poland. A young woman nicknamed Dorota (Urszula Modrzyńska), an experienced member of the Communist Party, leads this group of four young men. She is a strange combination, stemming from the Romantic tradition of a heroic woman-knight type, and the figure of 'Superwoman' that emerged within communist propaganda. This contradiction is noticeable in the first scene in which she appears on the screen, when she comes to an evening school to encourage young people to join the resistance. Among them is Stach (Tadeusz Łomnicki), the main male character. At first, she appears in a distant low-angle shot that significantly monumentalises her figure. This effect is reinforced by her gesture, the rebelliously held-up hand, familiar from the figure of Marianne from Eugene Delacroix's painting, as well as from propaganda posters or socialist realist painting. This ambiguity is maintained in her speech as she addresses the issues of communism, but also the dignity of the Polish nation that is being devastated by the Nazis (see Kozioł 1992: 229). On finishing her mission, she vanishes instantly, adding a mystery that goes well beyond necessary secrecy. Stach suddenly wants to join the Fighting Youth. Apparently, he cares more about this mysteriously powerful young woman than the leaflets she has left. He jumps out into the dark street to pursue her. In vain: she has vanished in the rainy gloom. However, from then on he tries to track her, acquiring a gun to impress her, rather than, as he claims,

Figure 4.1 A scene from *Pokolenie* (*A Generation*), 1955, dir. Andrzej Wajda ©
Studio Filmowe 'Oko'

to enable him to enter the resistance. Though Dorota is apparently conceived as a type of a 'new woman', endowed with an ideological consciousness, Wajda gives her in this scene a specific aura of mystery that
makes her an object of desire.

Later Dorota maintains this doubled status. Stach respects her as the
leader of their unit and is in love with her, but unable to admit it. This difficulty in expressing his love cannot be explained simply by the war that
demands an individual sacrifice of his individual needs for the collective
cause. In the course of their conspiratorial work, situations arise that lend
opportunities for intimacy. However, Stach is usually embarrassed rather
than pleased by them. Dorota observes his 'internal struggles' with patience
and the slight amusement that mothers usually have for their small boys. It
is worth mentioning that Stach still lives with his mother, whereas Dorota
has a small apartment and there is no reference to her parents. Apparently,
these circumstances reinforce the difference between them in terms of
'maturity' and 'immaturity'. Dorota is undoubtedly presented as a
'woman', whereas Stach and his three fellows appear to be 'boys'. Another
member of the group, Mundek, played by a very young Roman Polański,
wears shorts that are the most conspicuous and hilarious visual detail in
relation to this characteristic.

Dorota's 'womanliness' and Stach's 'boyishness' are confronted and then renegotiated in the scene of their last meeting, which is also the first and only love scene in the film. This scene takes place at Dorota's apartment. They talk about the necessity for Stach to hide, as he is known to the Gestapo. She offers her apartment and says that he will be the leader of a new unit. Hearing this, Stach responds with astonishment, looking at Dorota with enormous gratitude. Gently smiling, she says, 'The others say you are tough, but I think you are a kid.' Stach's reply confirms his vulnerability and for the first time he discloses his feelings for Dorota, admitting that he is scared of being shot and not being able to see her again. Then, in medium close-up we see Dorota in front to the camera and Stach putting his head on her arm, in a way that is usually associated with femininity, searching for protection, or consolation from a supposedly strong masculine figure. The distortion of the roles traditionally prescribed to the sexes is complemented with a line of dialogue, spoken by Dorota, who says that perhaps it is easier to die than to live for the cause, which refers to a general problem rather than to the current intimate situation. The composition of the next shot uses a *mise-en-scène* that is traditionally more typical of love scenes. Stach holds Dorota in his arms, then bends over her and this is the very first time in the film that he dominates the frame in terms of space. Finally, she reveals to him her real name: Ewa. Thus, she also reveals her true femininity hidden behind the conspiratorial posture. Yet, this disclosure of vulnerability turns out to be temporary as the next morning, when Stach goes to a shop to get some food for breakfast, Nazis come to Dorota's place to arrest her. One could assume that this tragic event prevented not only love but also erased femininity from the male arena of the war. The last scene of the film conveys, however, a different message. When Stach goes to meet the members of his new unit, he sees a group of four young boys and one girl, almost a replica of his previous group and Dorota. Soon they also will be initiated into the world of love and death, as he has experienced it. Knowing this, Stach silently cries in front of the camera and the viewer.

The group of young people who appear in the end of *A Generation* may well be assumed to take part in the Warsaw Uprising of August 1944, the subject of Wajda's next film, *Kanał* (*Canal*, 1957) (Figure 4.2). Most of the insurgents presented by the director are young boys and girls, for example, Halinka (Teresa Berezowska), who 'leaving home ... promised her mother to wear warm underwear'. Another young girl we can see, covered with a blanket, lies on a stretcher. A young man approaches her, as he recognises in her somebody whom he met before the uprising. He asks jokingly: 'I see that you joined the uprising. What's your mother say to that?' The girl answers calmly that she is dead. Confused, the man asks whether her wound is bad. Her equally calm voice replies: 'Nothing much', and after a while he sees her amputated leg. This scene from the very beginning of the film introduces the kind of silent heroism that seems to be the main feature

Figure 4.2 From the left: Władysław Sheybal (composer Michał), Tadeusz Janczar (Korab), and Teresa Iżewska (Daisy) in *Kanał* (*Kanal*), 1957, dir. Andrzej Wajda
© Studio Filmowe 'Kadr'

of the women characters in *Canal*, and is contrasted with the expressive and somewhat histrionic bravery of men. The latter is epitomised in the scene in which Korab (Tadeusz Janczar) undertakes a spectacular solitary attack on a German tank that results in his being badly wounded.

Korab and Daisy (Teresa Iżewska) are the main characters in the film. Their first meeting takes place just before Korab's spectacular heroism. Daisy is a messenger girl who operates mainly in the sewers. She appears in Korab's quarters after one of her missions; we can see her entering the door in the mirror, in front of which Korab stands, as he is shaving. This device is maintained almost throughout the whole scene until its end, when we see them together in the frame. What should be stressed is that both of them are the subjects of the look into the mirror and therefore the scene cannot be interpreted as a familiar subject-and-object-of-desire structure. This device gives an effect of mutual separateness and distance, reinforced through the dialogue that becomes a cynical play on words. Daisy may well seem an 'experienced' girl who tries to get as much pleasure as it is possible in these hard times. Korab, in turn, seems not to be bothered much about this and explicitly shows her that she is not important to him (see Stachówna 1998b: 56). At last, an openly loving gesture from Daisy brings about a genuine intimacy between the couple that, however, is abruptly disrupted by a bomb explosion. Korab hastily grabs his white shirt and runs out of the building to undertake his near suicidal attack on the Nazi tank.

Korab's performance is the final point of insurgent heroism, as the platoon is ordered to evacuate through sewers to another part of the town, for this is the only way to save their lives. They are not happy with this solution as it seemingly puts them in the position of rats escaping a sinking ship, far from their idea of themselves as Polish Davids, fighting a powerful Nazi Goliath. Yet, the whole platoon enters the sewers where soon, due to the turmoil underground, its members are separated into smaller groups whose varying plights are presented in parallel lines of action. The wanderings of Daisy and the wounded Korab become one of these.

In the sewers a reversal of gender roles and a questioning of a conventional masculine heroism occurs. It is Daisy who is strong, protective, down to earth, and competent. When, delirious because of his wound, Korab says, 'It's calm and misty. We're walking through a dark and fragrant forest', Daisy brutally answers, 'We are stumbling through stinking crud.' Korab concludes her brutally true words with a statement that she could not fall in love. She does not answer but only puts her head on his arm for a while, a gesture, that is, however, unnoticed by him in his feverish state. Here Korab is continuing his previous role. A while before he was a romantic fighter, now he tries to be a romantic lover. This locates him within a domain of lofty ideas, whereas Daisy as a messenger girl, who has operated in the sewers from the very beginning, belongs to the material side of existence, as evoked by Korab's remark in the earlier scene in his quarters: 'Wash up. You stink.' Now they both stink and it is she who knows how to get them out of it. She undertakes the role of a guide as well as of a mother. At one point she even says to him that he is a child. This role of a nurturer is also evoked by the *mise-en-scène*; her body usually dominates his, as she holds him up for almost the whole time, and just before their tragic end he lies on her lap, which resembles familiar paintings with the *pieta* figure.

What is striking here is Daisy's reluctance to verbally admit her love for Korab, which might conventionally be expected from her in this situation where they are balancing between life and death. During a rest Korab notices a message on the wall that says 'I love Jacek', but he can only read the first part of it: 'I love …' and so asks Daisy to finish it. Reading it, she changes the name of Jacek, which is Korab's real name, to Janek, and then she says that she also used to write on the walls, but somewhat different messages, like 'Kiss my ass!' Standing behind Korab's back she bends over him tenderly and adds with a soft voice that someone who wrote these words loved Jacek 'very, very much'. This scene echoes the previous one in Korab's quarters, when 'behind his back' she expressed with a gesture her love for him. Her attitude signifies both her willingness for self-sacrifice, a constant self-denial that is expressed by her constant favouring of 'you' at the expense of 'I', and her rational understanding of the situation in which there is no space for any kind of individual relationship.

Finally, they reach a point that seems to offer a chance of rescue, but it turns out to be a deadly trap. The entrance to the river Vistula is barred. Daisy decides to keep Korab in an illusion of a world of beauty and calmness. Looking at the river's shore beyond the bars she says to the almost unconscious Korab: 'I see water, Jacek … and green grass … we'll come out soon onto the green grass. No, no, don't open your eyes because the sun's come out.' And then the camera moves slowly above her arm to show the bars. As in *Lotna*, a woman is doing a kind of performance that is aimed at saving a man from directly facing death. Yet, she is capable of openly contemplating the bars that now permanently separate them from the world of life.

These tragic and lofty themes do not appear in all films of the Polish School that deal with the issue of the Warsaw Uprising. Andrzej Munk's *Eroica* (1957) serves as an opposition counterpoint to Wajda's films. In comparing the films of these two directors one encounters a set of oppositions: tragedy vs. buffoonery, loftiness vs. triviality, expressionism vs. the grotesque. The characters of *Eroica* seem to be a negation of all the features that characterise Wajda's protagonists. The main male hero, Dzidziuś Górkiewicz (Edward Dziewoński), represents everything but heroism, as he tries to keep himself apart from all manifestations of the national romantic martyrology, even poking fun at it (see Nurczyńska-Fidelska 1982: 82–4). However, when a genuine chance of helping the uprising arises in the form of military support from a Hungarian squadron that is staying in his neighbourhood, he commits strongly to the cause, while still pretending his indifference to it. Though his wife, Zosia (Barbara Połomska), is in the background of the story, she can also be seen as a similarly contradictory figure. Initially she appears as an almost ideal incarnation of the figure of the 'dumb blonde', a very rare phenomenon in Polish postwar cinema, and in addition she is not entirely faithful to her husband. When Dzidziuś comes back to their home after leaving the Warsaw Uprising, which is doomed to failure, he finds Zosia in an excellent mood, deeply involved in flirtatious conversation with a handsome Hungarian officer (Leon Niemczyk). Instead of a dramatic reaction of pain and disappointment, or an enraged scene of jealousy, he cynically notices that she is managing quite well and asks her whether she sleeps with him. Zosia reacts with an exaggerated, theatrical gesture of resentment of vulgar straightforwardness, but at the same time she exchanges a look of understanding with the Hungarian officer, who suggests a walk to Dzidziuś. When they are outside, still drinking liquor, the Hungarian presents him with an offer of military support for the insurgents, in return for official confirmation of it to the Allies.

Apparently, this offer had been discussed earlier with Zosia, as their mute exchange of looks had clearly indicated, even if this happened between one kiss and another. To bring this up is by no means to show that in Polish cinema the figure of 'dumb blonde' can be transformed into a politically conscious person. Also it is not my aim here to question gender roles, but to indicate that Munk plays with the schematas and stereotypes of heroism and cowardice, as well as images of masculinity and femininity. Therefore, in his film a man is neither as heroic as one would like him to be, nor is a woman as stupid as she may seem to be. A small episode, when a simple old woman, doing her washing in the river, gives a minutely detailed answer, when asked by Górkiewicz about the battle positions of the Nazis, confirms Munk's sceptical attitude to accepted stereotypes.

In *Pasażerka* (*The Passenger*, 1962), Munk shifts his female characters from their relatively marginalised position in *Eroica* to the very centre. This film represents the concentration camp experience of Polish women, recollected by Liza (Aleksandra Śląska), a former Nazi camp officer, who travels with her husband on a liner to Europe from the United States. During the crossing she notices a woman who is very like Marta (Anna Ciepielewska), a former prisoner of the Auschwitz camp. This unexpected and shocking encounter triggers the memories that she had tried to suppress. There are three flashbacks that bring the past into the present.

The first one consists of brief images of a naked woman desperately trying to break out from a circle in which she is imprisoned by Kapos. Interestingly, the female body, publicly exposed and humiliated, becomes a key sign of the camp's horror. A Polish film critic, Konrad Eberhardt, claims that the recurrent motifs of naked female bodies in this first flashback, structured like a cinematic 'stream of consciousness', may be interpreted as an expression of the repressed homoerotic desires of Liza (Eberhardt 1974: 149–64). A similar interpretation is offered by Elizabeth Nazarian: 'The images express what is most abject for Liza in her experience as a camp overseer: her homoerotic desire ... The physicality of these bodies can be read as evidence of Liza's deeply repressed homoerotic fascination, a fascination which manifests itself through Liza's transgressive attachment to Marta' (Nazarian 2002). Whether we agree or not with this interpretation, there is no doubt that this part of the film exposes the ruthless reduction of a human being to a humiliated corporeality.

Regaining her composure after the first distracting recollection of memories, Liza starts telling this story from the past to her husband. In so doing she tries to regain some sense of humanity during her Auschwitz experience. She begins the story with the words, 'I just did my duty', and tries to present herself as a person who did not have anything to do with the 'death industry', as she was in charge of a warehouse. Moreover, she recounts that she had tried to save Marta's life and yet she was ungrateful for this. She says, 'I saved her life. I didn't ask for thanks, but at least I deserved her trust. She didn't want to show it.' As Nazarian notices, 'As a narrative, then, this second flashback is unreliable and incomplete, because Liza is unable to make public and shareable that which haunts her in the first flashback. In the version that Liza is able to tell another person, there is nothing abject: no naked bodies, no transgressive games' (Nazarian 2002).

The truth is revealed in the third flashback, in which Liza tells the story to herself once again. Her motivation to save Marta's life appears now more complex and ambiguous. Instead of mercy or compassion for the prisoner, one can observe an apparent fascination with her that sometimes takes the shape of an obsession, an unreciprocated love. Indeed, when Liza sees Marta for the first time she notices in her 'something vulnerable and child-like', therefore something needing protection and care that ought to be responded to with gratefulness, trust, and love. She gives her a job in the warehouse unit and observes with pleasure Marta's transformation back into a 'real woman'. She even makes plans for the future, to take Marta with her to the Reich when she gets promotion. These internal comments, along with a series of Liza's point of view shots of Marta, reveal a homo-erotic desire hidden within the feeling of human compassion. To her disap-pointment, Marta reveals a psychic resistance and, moreover, already has someone to be loved and longed for, as her fiancé is in a camp as well.

Though the expected gratefulness does not come from Marta, Liza is unable to change her attitude to her. It is as if she is masochistically addicted to her. She continues the struggle 'for' and 'with' Marta even when the lat-ter admits to writing an illegal letter concerning the camp to be smuggled outside Auschwitz. This represents Marta's ultimate refusal to accept any-thing from Liza. Though she condemns herself to the death, she demon-strates her internal freedom. Thus, Munk radically questions the relationship between a victim and a victimiser. As Ewelina Nurczyńska-Fidelska notes, 'Marta remains free in her internal world, Liza is a slave to her duty, and even more, to the system she believes in. ... Liza has to become a tormentor in an open way. In a collectively committed genocide an individual cannot keep her own hands clean' (Nurczyńska-Fidelska 1982: 163). This collective guilt has been repressed by Liza for years, to return because of the acciden-tal encounter with 'a passenger'. Nazarian claims that,

> the narrativisation of Liza's memories functions as a therapeutic process which allows her to recover speech and positions her at the threshold of the realm of the Symbolic, that of language and memory. By verbalising the unnamable states of fear, which make up what is most unapproachable in the unconscious (Kristeva 1982: 37) Liza is able to domesticate, even rationalise, them. As the disconnected images of the first flashback are contextualised and planted within a causal, narrative discourse, Liza's suffering, fear, and disgust 'quiet down, concatenated into a story' (ibid.:145). However, this third, lin-ear and coherent flashback is one Liza can only reveal to herself. Thus, there is a discrepancy between Liza's ability to make her memories communicable and her ability to communicate them to someone else. This discrepancy reveals that Liza's narrated identity remains challenged and unstable. (Nazarian 2002)

However, as other Polish films show, some of the female prisoners of the concentration camps were able to reestablish their lives as a coherent narrative. Their way back to life is the subject of Stanisław Różewicz's *Trzy kobiety* (*Three Women*, 1956). Its action begins in Germany after the liberation of the camps and then continues in Poland, where the three women try to build a new life for themselves. However, only the youngest, Celina (Anna Ciepielewska), is successful in this. What helps her to recover from the trauma of the camp, and regain her identity as a woman, is the love she receives from a young man, who also sees in her a chance to overcome the horror of his own war experience. He says to her, 'When I look at you, I think that there was no war, no torture. Your eyes are those that did not see any evil.'

The idea of love as giving the possibility to renew life after war is a regular motif in the Polish School. Wajda's film *Ashes and Diamonds* (Figure 4.3), adapted from Jerzy Andrzejewski's novel, is located in the political-historical context of Poland's liberation. However, the new communist order was bent on the persecution of Home Army survivors. This turning point in the history of the Polish nation is captured in this film. The hero, Maciek Chełmicki (Zbigniew Cybulski), is a member of Home Army. He has taken part in the Warsaw Uprising and is now under orders to assassinate the local chief of the communist party, Szczuka (Wacław Zastrzeżyński), to prevent the success of the new political system. An

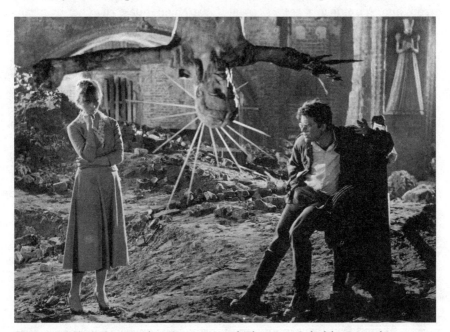

Figure 4.3 Ewa Krzyżewska (Krystyna) and Zbigniew Cybulski (Maciek Chełmicki) in *Popiół i diament* (*Ashes and Diamonds*), 1958, dir. Andrzej Wajda © Studio Filmowe 'Kadr'

accidental meeting occurs with Krystyna (Ewa Krzyżewska), a barmaid working in the hotel where Maciek and his target are staying. This chance event brings about his internal metamorphosis; from then on he experiences an irresolvable moral dilemma (see Lubelski 1992: 171; Stachówna 1998b: 56–57). The character of Krystyna is the factor that triggers Maciek's dilemma. When she first appears, Maciek and his friend and superior officer, Andrzej (Adam Pawlikowski), sit at a bar. Maciek talks to his friend, but also is staring at a mirror reflecting the image of the girl working behind the bar. Not only is she presented as an object of the male gaze, but she is deprived of her material substance through being presented as a mirror reflection. Clearly this device creates a certain distance between Maciek and Krystyna. As Maciek approaches the bar a flirtation begins between them. He orders two vodkas and when she tries to pour the liquor into the glasses, Maciek turns this into a game. He rapidly moves the glass from one place to another and finally takes from his pocket a wartime souvenir, a tin mug. Krystyna observes his histrionic gestures with calmness. He neither annoys her, nor is she captured by his charm. Andrzej briefly leaves Maciek, yet soon his off-screen voice calls with a tone of authority and Maciek instantly submits to this request. This situation establishes a mould for many later scenes throughout the film, namely Maciek's position between his object of desire, Krystyna, and the principle of authority that demands full loyalty from him. A number of scenes repeat this triangular pattern either by means of frame composition, or in the organisation of the soundtrack.

Krystyna seems to be well aware of her 'in-between' position in this triangular configuration. When Maciek again appears in the bar where he is supposed to meet Andrzej, she asks him ironically, 'Have you got a date?', and when Andrzej eventually shows up, she reiterates 'Your date is coming.' Of course, one can interpret these words as an example of a convention, often used in flirtatious conversation. Yet, the specificity of these jokes reveals Krystyna's awareness of Maciek's involvement. She knows that she cannot break up, to again use Christopher Caes's notion, the 'homosocial bonds' that bind him to his male friend and the collective cause, like Ewa in *Lotna*, who knew that she could not compete with the white mare.

Krystyna's consciousness of the difficulty of any genuine relationship between Maciek and herself is evident when she goes to Maciek's room. She says that she came to him because she knows that she could not fall in love with him. Apparently, she also knows that he would not be able to fall in love with her. However, quite unexpectedly, things take a different direction. Somehow, this accidental erotic encounter between these two people leads them to the experience of love. Wajda marks the act of entering into a new realm of existential experience through a stylistic 'alienation' of the scene. While deep-focus photography, which Bazin considered crucial to achieve the effect of realism, is the stylistic dominant in the film, spatial realism is done away with in this sequence. Shown almost entirely in close-ups and using a diffusion effect, a distance from reality is built. What is striking here is the avoidance of shot-countershot editing. The close-ups of Krystyna or Maciek dissolve into one another and the camera consecutively slowly pans across their faces. Therefore, in terms of the visual, neither character is privileged, and they seem to be equally the point of reference for each other. This 'democratic' cinematography creates a gender equality that may well be perceived as the visual expression of true love. However, at some point they have to leave this abstract space and return to the realm of deep-focus photography, evoking the real world, ruled by processes of History.

In the next scene, when Maciek and Krystyna leave the room, the couple is positioned again in a triangular composition, this time with Szczuka as the third element. When Krystyna leaves the frame, her place is occupied by Szczuka, who moves to the right side of Maciek, who is still looking to the left after her. Through the organisation of the characters' movement and their position within the frame, the moral dilemma of the main male hero is visualised. Clearly Maciek is torn between Krystyna, who serves as a metaphor of love and normal life, and Szczuka, who signifies duty and war. More directly, he faces a choice between life and death. The female character appears therefore as an empty sign to be filled with abstract connotations like love, life or hope. The male hero can choose all these values, even if this choice is limited by the romantic code of behaviour which he has inherited from the past, the main demand of which is to put collective duty over individual needs and desires. Maciek's tragic dilemma and internal struggle is thus contrasted with Krystyna's passivity. This is particularly evident in the penultimate scene of the film when we see her motionless, watching a Polish group dance a polonaise that visualises a state of emotional paralysis, from which it will be difficult to recover.

The paralysing nature of the war experience is also explored by Wojciech Jerzy Has in his 1963 film, *Jak być kochaną? (How to be Loved?)*, particularly worth discussing here, as it presents the story from the perspective of the heroine. She is a radio actress, the main female character of a popular radio show, who recollects her past life while flying to Paris, where she has been invited by one of her fans.

The film opens with a close-up of a woman who is being photographed from behind at a forty-five degree angle. She holds a small mirror and is putting on some lipstick. This image of anonymous femininity is accompanied by voice-over, 'I am a sister of the lonely and a wife of widowers. If I ever write memoirs, I will entitle it "From Ofelia to Felicja, or how to be loved?"' Then the camera tracks out and we can see the woman sitting at a bar while the monologue continues, 'All this was as if I was in the wrong play in which I played the role of a comical tragedienne.' The comparison she makes between her life and theatre has a double meaning. First, it is a reference to her profession: her acting career had begun with the role of

Ofelia, but was disrupted due to the outbreak of the Second World War. Secondly, it displays her awareness that the theatre was not the only space where she was supposed to perform a role. For she knows that her whole life could be seen as a spectacle in which all the parts were written well before. Her part as 'a woman' was supposed to actualise such values as love, fidelity and sacrifice. The fact that her life could be perceived as playing a role is additionally confirmed by the fact that her real name remains unknown until the end of the film. The viewer can identify her only as Felicja, the role she plays in the radio show 'Dinners at Konopkas' (Obiady u państwa Konopków). If her life is compared to theatre, it is seen as a re-creation rather than creation, and as such demands a passive adjustment to the precepts of a role, instead of actively creating it from the beginning.

To be loved by a particular man had been the linchpin on which her life had turned. Everything she did was because of him: a renowned, but foolish actor who had an immature expectation that life should be 'bigger than theatre'. No wonder that the war seemed to him a great opportunity for transforming his life into a spectacular performance of bravery and heroism. However, the only thing he was able to do was to conduct a petty argument with a former theatre colleague whom he suspected of collaboration with the Nazis. This pathetic spectacle had occurred in the presence of the heroine who watched this with forbearance and patience. As a result of further accidental circumstances the Nazis issued a warrant of arrest and consequently the underground movement organised a hiding-place for him. The heroine, asked to transfer him to the designated place, instead decided to take him to her own place. What is interesting in her attitude is her disguising her love for him behind the curtain of patriotic duty. In helping him as a war hero she hides her actual motive – her love for him and her desire to be with him. The parallel with Daisy's behaviour in Wajda's *Canal* can be noted here, as she also pretended to other people that she was taking care of Korab as a wounded insurgent rather than her beloved man. It can be said that Polish cultural norms allow a woman to love a man as 'a brave son of the Motherland' only. This further demonstrates the ways that gender relationships are related and subordinated to broader national causes.

The foolish heroism of the man is contrasted with the silent heroism of Felicja, who sacrifices virtually everything in saving his life, expecting 'to be loved' for it in the end. She even allows herself to be raped by Gestapo soldiers in her flat to protect him and, further, decides to work in the German theatre in order to acquire better documents that would guarantee their safety. Her decision results in ostracism from her colleagues and friends and, after the end of the war, she is forbidden her profession by the arbitration of her fellow workers. What is striking in her attitude is a complete passivity and reluctance to defend herself. Her willingness to sacrifice herself continues the cultural demand on feminine pride and dignity. Again, as with Daisy from *Canal*, who did not care about her bad reputation, Felicja neglects the opinion of an external world. She displays a strength and independence in her ability to ignore the expectation of a 'proper' Polish femininity. However, at the same time, she conforms to the pattern of an ideal femininity in which sacrifice is the only way to make one's life meaningful. Therefore, in this heroine there is a peculiar kind of intertwining of activity and passivity, in which activity means the conscious act of exposing the self to suffering and sacrifice.

Similar contradictions characterise the male hero of the film. His foolish act of heroism is contrasted with his helplessness, especially stressed in the scene of Felicja's rape. Paradoxically, the only way to save both of them is for him to be a hidden witness of the horror that is occurring beyond the wall. His inability to perform the traditional masculine task of protecting a woman first brings about frustration and then aggression. No wonder that when the war is over he flees the shelter in which he had lost his 'masculine power'. Now he tries to recover it by means of restaging the spectacle of his legendary war heroism with the warrant for his arrest as the main prop. These drunken pathetic spectacles deprive him of the last remnants of dignity. Again Felicja tries to save him, again in vain. He decides to commit suicide, to take away the life that she had wanted to save at any price. This flashback scene provides the narrative framework for the story of Felicja's life, as recollected by her during her flight to Paris. The subjective narration, an internal monologue, combined with other flashbacks, builds up a distance in relation to the events of the main story. The result of this, however, is not an understanding of the past in terms of seeing it as an unconscious self-victimisation, but a bitter acceptance of everything that had happened.

The heroine of *Wdowa* (*A Widow*), the third part of Kazimierz Kutz's film *Krzyż Walecznych* (*Cross of Valour*, 1958) (Figure 4.4), refuses the passive acceptance of fate so often shared by the majority of female characters of the Polish School. Kutz belongs to the so-called 'plebeian trend' of the Polish School, as opposed to the romantic, represented mainly by Andrzej Wajda. Małgorzata (Grażyna Staniszewska), the main female protagonist, is an attractive young woman, the widow of Captain Joczys who had died during the war. Yet, unlike other female characters in the Polish School, she does not want to live in the past and also refuses to play the role of a symbol of national martyrdom.

Kutz's ironic attitude to the national mythology that had petrified into a set of empty stereotypes is strongly expressed in the first scene, in which a big crowd is awaiting for somebody at the rail station of a little town. It is apparent from the overheard conversations that they are waiting for Joczys's widow. Everybody is in a sombre mood, except for one drunkard who provocatively says, 'One more old female will come, another mourning widow.' Everybody tries to hush him up and eventually the train arrives. Among the passengers who step down onto the platform are two women. One, an old woman dressed in black, is the perfect icon of 'a hero's widow'.

Figure 4.4 Adolf Chronicki (Ołdak) and Grażyna Staniszewska (Joczys's widow) in *Krzyż Walecznych* (*Cross of Valour*), 1958, dir. Kazimierz Kutz © Studio Filmowe 'Kadr'

Additional mythic overtones, drawing upon the iconography of the Polish Mother, make further contribution to a developing misrecognition, because, following her, is a younger woman, her daughter, the real widow. The leader of the welcoming committee approaches the older woman without hesitation, but after realising the misunderstanding, he takes her daughter by the arm, and leads her to the house donated by the people of the town, who follow in procession.

The scene of the widow's arrival establishes the pattern of her further life in the town. She is constantly used as a live symbol, a remnant of her perished husband, after whom everything is named, from the school to the fruit-processing factory. Not only is she invited to all the ceremonies naming these places after her husband, but she is also constantly watched by local children, who are obliged to make reports on her to the officials in the town. These reports say that she 'laughs, turns somersaults on the grass, sings', etc. Although this behaviour is confusing and irritating for the local community, still it can be tolerated. What cannot be tolerated by any means is her acceptance of the courtship of a young veterinarian (Zbigniew Cybulski). The local people treat the young man's interest as a kind of sacrilege, as if he wanted to seduce the Holy Virgin, and finally they make him leave the town. To their disappointment, she leaves the town as well, shortly thereafter. Interestingly, just before leaving she protests against being called Mrs Joczys and insists on her own name, Małgorzata, thus conspicuously contrasting her perception of herself from the nameless, anonymous heroine of *How to be Loved?* Stressing her own subjectivity and leaving the anachronistic realm of the national museum of martyrdom, she refuses to fulfil the pattern of suffering femininity in which the majority of the heroines of the Polish School were complicit. Instead of putting on the spurious dignity of a national symbol, she chooses to live her own life. However, most likely, she will now pursue the precepts of another social role, this time one imposed by the system of communist ideology, the role of a 'Superwoman', analysed in the previous chapter.

CHAPTER 5

Agnieszka and Other Solidarity Heroines of Polish Cinema

EWA MAZIERSKA

It is widely accepted that Agnieszka, the heroine of two of Andrzej Wajda's films, *Człowiek z marmuru* (*Man of Marble*, 1976) and *Człowiek z żelaza* (*Man of Iron*, 1981), is the most important female character in the Polish cinema of the 1970s – or, more precisely – prior to the introduction of martial law in 1981. Her significance is at least twofold. Firstly, she is the most widely discussed Polish film character of this period, even exceeding the fame of her male contemporaries, as represented on the silver screen. Secondly, Agnieszka, at least in her first incarnation, became a role model for 'young women on the street' to an extent that is unknown for cinema after 1945. Agnieszka in *Man of Marble* is also an anomaly amongst female characters, depicted by both male and female directors, in the sense that she is an unassailable victor, successfully combining the quest for personal fulfilment with a desire to serve her country.

It is worth talking not about Agnieszka, but about the two Agnieszkas, because in *Man of Iron* she has quite a different personality and fulfils a different narrative function than in *Man of Marble*. What particularly concerns me in this chapter is the nature and sociopolitical background of Agnieszka's creation and her transformation from heroine of *Man of Marble* to *Man of Iron*, and subsequently her 'post-Wajda incarnations' in later Polish films about the Solidarity movement. Considering Agnieszka also provides an opportunity to reflect on the phenomenon of the actress who played her part, Krystyna Janda, the greatest star of Polish postwar cinema.

'Iron Agnieszka'

In *Man of Marble* (Figure 5.1), which is set in the mid-1970s, Agnieszka (Krystyna Janda) is a final-year film college student. She is completing her diploma film, financed by state television, which also provides her with crew and equipment. Agnieszka decides to make a documentary, entitled *Gwiazdy jednego sezonu* (*Falling Stars*), about a bricklayer named Mateusz Birkut (Jerzy Radziwiłłowicz), who took part in building the city of Nowa Huta, which was regarded as the greatest enterprise of the first decade of postwar Poland. Birkut enjoyed a short career in the 1950s as a champion of socialist work of the 1950s, known as Stakhanovite, when he served as an example to be followed by ordinary workers and was even immortalised in marble sculptures. After that he disappeared virtually without trace from Polish politics and social life. The mystery of his downfall is the main reason for Agnieszka's decision to make a film based on his life. There are, however, deeper motives for her interest in the forgotten socialist hero. At one point Agnieszka claims, 'this is the history of my parents', which suggests that she tries to discover her own roots through the story of Birkut. Maria Kornatowska suggests that her feverish activity and idealism results from belonging to the generation born in the 1950s, who struggle to find a place in the world and to have a distinctive identity (Kornatowska 1990:

Figure 5.1 Krystyna Janda as Agnieszka in *Człowiek z marmuru* (*Man of Marble*), 1976, dir. Andrzej Wajda © Studio Filmowe 'Perspektywa'

98). Instead, they must find something to fill their inner void, to help them deal with their lack of history. Agnieszka shares with the twenty-something generation of the 1970s a certain individualism and urge to be successful, to make a career, which was lacking amongst earlier generations, particularly women. These values can be associated with the political and social climate of the 1970s, when Edward Gierek was leader of the Polish Communist Party, described as times of 'real socialism', characterised by openness to the West, consumerism and a relative neglect of ideology. In *Man of Marble* these values are conveyed largely by *mise-en-scène*, showing the affluence and Westernisation of some sections of society, as well as by music, encapsulating the nervous rhythm of the time.

In the history of Polish cinema the 1970s are characterised primarily by the Cinema of Moral Concern, regarded as the most distinctive paradigm in Polish cinematography, alongside the Polish School. The Cinema of Moral Concern was created by directors such as Krzysztof Kieślowski, Krzysztof Zanussi, Feliks Falk, Agnieszka Holland, Janusz Kijowski, Barbara Sass and Andrzej Wajda himself, who was the most senior member of this group. Thematically, their films concentrated on the pathologies of 'real socialism': widespread bureaucracy and corruption, materialism and greed, as well as people's double moral standards: one for home, one for work. The films often articulated the frustration of the younger generation, whose ambitions were thwarted by their seniors. It can also be argued that in comparison with the films made in previous decades, the Cinema of Moral Concern gave more prominent roles to women, which is largely the result of an input into this movement of the work of the female directors Holland and Sass (which will be discussed in the following part of this book). At the same time the bulk of them were openly sexist (see Kornatowska 1990: 189–91).

Stylistically, the filmmakers belonging to this paradigm, many of whom had considerable experience in documentary, draw on realist-documentary tradition. At the same time, there was a strong element of self-reflexivity in their films; the characters represented professionals such as journalists, filmmakers, actors, which allowed the authors to question the role of the filmmaker/artist in a world where moral values, such as honesty and selflessness, are marginalised. By choosing a filmmaker as the main character and utilising realist-documentary tradition, Wajda made a film that firmly belongs to the Cinema of Moral Concern. Due to its emphasis on the Polish 1950s, *Man of Marble* can also be regarded as a bridge between the Cinema of Moral Concern and the earlier cinematic schools, such as socialist realism and the Polish School.

The very process of filmmaking reveals that Agnieszka has the temperament suitable for investigative journalism; she appears to have no initial political or ideological agenda, but is driven by curiosity about the fate of her character, as well as a desire to make an interesting, successful film. In line with her method of working, Wajda's film takes the shape of an 'investigative film', resembling the structure of *Citizen Kane* (1941) by Orson Welles and *The Third Man* (1949) by Carol Reed. It also bears affinity with one of the most important films of the Cinema of Moral Concern, *Amator* (*Camera Buff*, 1979) by Krzysztof Kieślowski, which was made three years after Wajda's film. It is narrated partly by flashbacks, presenting Birkut at various stages of his life, partly by interviews, which Agnieszka conducts with people who knew him in person, including a director, whose films established Birkut as a national symbol, a Man of Marble. Finding these people and persuading them to talk about Birkut proves difficult, as they regard the 1950s as a painful or shameful period of their lives. In order to succeed Agnieszka has to be cunning, even abusing interviewees' trust. Many people submit to her charisma, others give in to avoid her continuous harassment. In this respect she is very different from those whom she interviews and who are shown in the flashbacks; all of them, including Birkut, sooner or later failed, either by being imprisoned, forced to renounce their privileged positions in society or by being persuaded to compromise their high ideals. This unusual strength of character also makes Agnieszka a rarity amongst Wajda's characters, who are often (particularly in the Polish School period) heroic, but at the same time doomed to failure. According to the Romantic tradition they fight not so much to win, as to prove their love and loyalty to their country (see Walicki 1982). Wajda's heroine, on the other hand, does not carry the heavy baggage of Romanticism, she is not even particularly patriotic. Moreover, she wants her film to resemble an American movie, not a Polish School classic. Agnieszka's professional credentials are demonstrated not only by her attitude, but also by her technical skill. Her handheld camera, used for filming marble statues, arouses the admiration of her cameraman, and her ability to find footage, hidden deep in the television archive, secures the respect of her editor. Their high opinion of Agnieszka is particularly significant, as the cameraman and the editor are both highly experienced.

Another of Agnieszka's important characteristics is her authority over men. Firstly, she is a female director with an all male-crew. Although her cameraman, Mr Leonard, calls her 'my daughter', it is Agnieszka who assumes the role of mentor, persuading him to shoot according to her style, and she treats her assistants like dogsbodies. One scene, which demonstrates most poignantly her dominant position over her male crew, is shot in the television archive, where Agnieszka watches documentary footage of Birkut. When her two co-workers sit near the screen, obscuring her view, she asks them to move behind her, and they obey her instantly, virtually disappearing into the darkness, as if completely insignificant. Agnieszka is also commanding in her relationship with the television producer (Bogusław Sobczuk). He is very wary of touching on subjects which might upset the authorities and therefore does not like Agnieszka's idea of rediscovering the

Stalinist past. She, on the other hand, constantly challenges him, accusing him of opportunism and cowardice, especially shameful in the light of his young age of twenty-eight years. They are always shown walking together along the corridors of the television building. The producer walks quickly, as if trying to run away from her, but is unsuccessful: she has no difficulty keeping up with him. On another occasion we see him hiding in the men's toilet when he glimpses Agnieszka walking down the corridor towards him. (In fact, this scene features in *Man of Iron*, but is included in the flashbacks, referring to the same period as *Man of Marble*.)

Another man whom Agnieszka manages to dominate, although in a different sense, is Mateusz Birkut himself, the eponymous 'fallen star' of her own film. In contrast to the scenario (which Laura Mulvey applies to the classic Hollywood period), according to which woman is the image and man the bearer of the look, in Wajda's film it is Agnieszka, who bears the look, while Birkut is only an image. Moreover, by using footage that was hidden for many years in film archives and by discovering his marble statues in the cellar of the National Museum, and by filming them, as well as by talking about him with his old friends, she recreates Birkut, transforming him into a man whom nobody knew and would not know if she had not embarked on her project. Her almost god-like power of resurrecting Birkut is made even more apparent when we learn that at the time Agnieszka made *Falling Stars*, Birkut had already been dead for several years. Tadeusz Sobolewski compares her to a knight from a fairy tale who revives people turned to stone (Sobolewski 1989: 22).

The documentary footage that Agnieszka views in the television archive shows its protagonists in a bad light, either by revealing their past acts of political opportunism and malice, or by demonstrating that over the years they lost their honesty and idealism. This is the case of Burski (Tadeusz Łomnicki and Jacek Łomnicki), the director who 'created' Birkut in the 1950s. Agnieszka discovers that Burski first wanted to make an honest film about Nowa Huta, showing the extremely difficult conditions in which the workers lived and worked. Soon afterwards Burski made *Oni budują nasze szczęście* (*They Build Our Happiness*), glorifying the workers' conditions and praising their bricklaying skills. Agnieszka learns that this was not done by the technique of *cinéma vérité*, but by carefully arranging events that were subsequently filmed. In the 1970s Burski is celebrated as the most acclaimed Polish director. Agnieszka meets him after his return from an international festival, where he sat on the jury. There is a parallel between the careers of Burski and Andrzej Wajda. The success of both of them was at least partially a consequence of their ability to adjust to political circumstances, giving up their desire to depict truth, when it could jeopardise their professional prospects. The connection between Wajda and Burski is reinforced by including Andrzej Wajda's name in the credits of Burski's *They Build Our Happiness* as his assistant. Discovering Burski's dubious route to success, Agnieszka in a sense calls into question the moral credentials of the most celebrated Polish director. It is worth adding that hardly any real Polish filmmaker, film critic or investigative journalist ever had the courage to question Wajda's moral credentials. This in itself elevates Agnieszka to the status of a 'super-journalist' and 'super-filmmaker'. Moreover, by showing that she cannot be silenced by any authority, Wajda confirms her moral superiority over artists from the earlier generation, like Burski and himself. Accordingly, critics drew parallels between Wajda's Agnieszka and one of the most distinguished directors of the Cinema of Moral Concern: Agnieszka Holland (see Lis 1985: 88; Sobolewski 1989: 15).

Agnieszka is constantly on the move, travelling from Warsaw to the most distant parts of Poland, such as Nowa Huta, Katowice and Zakopane in the south, and Gdańsk in the north. Sometimes she sleeps in the television studio or in a van; she does not worry about where she will spend the next night. All her belongings are in a large, sack-like bag, which she carries slung over her shoulder. The bag symbolises her freedom and contempt for material possessions. In comparison with her, everyone she meets, the majority of whom are middle-aged men, are static. They seem to have very little control over their lives, being imprisoned in their jobs, homes and family responsibilities. All of them have achieved much in terms of material success, having vast villas and houses with gardens, but feel emotionally dead. There is even a kind of sadness about them, resulting from their realisation of having betrayed the ideals and people of their youth.

Physical appearance connotes Agnieszka's contempt for middle-class values and disregard for the traditional Polish ideal of femininity. She always wears the same denim uniform, consisting of bootleg trousers and a long jacket, platform shoes, a long shawl and a large, man's umbrella. She wears no make-up and her fair hair is conveniently put in a bun. Her father, concerned about her marriage prospects, even gives her some money to buy 'better clothes', claiming that no decent man will find her attractive in her jeans. In reality, however, her simple clothes accentuate, rather than hide, her well-shaped body. In spite of her apparent indifference towards her looks, men around her recognise her charm which she sometimes uses to achieve her professional objectives. For example, when she gets into Burski's car, straight after his return from a foreign trip, he initially wants to get rid of her, but after noticing her long legs and charming smile, lets her stay and drives her to his home. Although this episode, and some others included by Wajda, nominally adjust to Mulvey's scheme of 'woman as image, man as bearer of the look', Agnieszka is by no means reduced to a passive image. Firstly, she allows men to look at her in an erotic way only when she is in full control of their look and uses it to her own, professional advantage. Secondly, she is not afraid to return their look and always notices more than them, who are somehow disarmed and 'blinded' by her seductiveness.

The kind of femininity and sexuality that Agnieszka epitomised was new to Polish cinema. It was more reminiscent of (or even influenced by) the way young women looked and behaved in the West, than of the traditional standards of Polish femininity. Agnieszka could be compared to the roles of independent women that Jane Fonda or Sally Field created in the 1960s and 1970s. The novelty of her femininity led Polish critics of both sexes to treat her not really as a woman, but as a 'man in disguise'. For example, Maria Kornatowska and Maciej Kozioł describe Agnieszka respectively as 'masculine' and 'bisexual' (Kornatowska 1986: 178–79; Kozioł 1992: 240), and Wiktor Woroszylski sums her up as a 'female Don Quixote' (Woroszylski 1977: 187). Similarly, Dorota Roszkowska claims that 'Agnieszka has very few specifically female features', that she is more masculine than feminine or 'sexually ambivalent' (Roszkowska 1992: 79–80). These views totally mislead us about the type and strength of sexual appeal Agnieszka represents. There was nothing sexually ambivalent in her look or behaviour, as demonstrated by the fact that she strongly influenced the appearance of large numbers of straight young Polish women in the 1970s (while failing to become a lesbian icon in Poland), and by the subsequent career of Janda, who was cast in the roles of heterosexual women, often with a significant erotic dimension. However, the common classification of Agnieszka by Polish critics as 'unfeminine' is in itself worthy of attention, as it indicates how strongly Polish culture was influenced by a particular image of femininity: that of the Polish Mother. Even Kornatowska and Roszkowska seem to regard it as a standard against which all other models of femininity should be judged.

The last scene in *Man of Marble* shows Agnieszka walking the long corridor of the television studio with Birkut's son, Maciek Tomczyk (Jerzy Radziwiłłowicz), as she used to walk with the producer. Although it is Agnieszka who brought him to Warsaw and introduced him to television, he is walking ahead, as if leading her. At times he walks slower, in order to put his hand on her back, in a gesture of support and perhaps tenderness. This is the only scene in the film where Agnieszka is shown being led and supported by a man. She welcomes the gesture, which reveals her vulnerability and femininity. This episode is particularly important, as in it Wajda (perhaps unconsciously) prepares us for an encounter with another incarnation of Agnieszka: the one who will be the heroine of *Man of Iron*.

Agnieszka as a Polish Mother

In *Man of Iron* (Figure 5.2) the part of Agnieszka is smaller than in *Man of Marble*. In contrast to the first chapter of Wajda's diptych, where her role was to establish the truth about the title character, in *Man of Iron* the function of the investigative journalist is taken by someone else: a man called

Figure 5.2 Krystyna Janda as Agnieszka and Jerzy Radziwiłłowicz as Maciek Tomczyk in *Człowiek z żelaza* (*Man of Iron*), 1981, dir. Andrzej Wajda © Studio Filmowe 'Perspektywa'

Winkiel (Marian Opania). He is a radio journalist, sent to Gdańsk in the summer of 1980, during the time of the shipyard strike that established Solidarity as the dominant political force for change in Eastern Europe. Winkiel's task is to collect material which will discredit Maciek Tomczyk, one of the organisers of the strike. He meets various people to learn about Tomczyk's illegal activities. Agnieszka, who by then is Tomczyk's wife, is one of his interviewees. Winkiel meets her in jail; she was imprisoned by the authorities to halt her involvement in the strike. Agnieszka tells Winkiel what had happened to her since she brought Tomczyk to Warsaw in 1976. Her story takes the form of flashbacks (which was also used in *Man of Marble* to present Birkut's history). We learn that she invited Tomczyk to visit the television studio in Warsaw, because at the time she was making her film, Birkut was already dead. He died in 1970, when tanks were used to crush workers' protests. As Tomczyk was the one who told her about the fate of his father, Agnieszka hoped that including him in her film about the last years of Birkut would provide a powerful conclusion to her documentary. For the producer, however, her film was unacceptable, and thus she lost the chance to work in the media and returned with Maciek Tomczyk to Gdańsk. The initial purpose was to finish her *Falling Stars* documentary. Soon, however, she fell in love with Tomczyk and became involved in the

anti-communist movement. The two events are presented as closely connected: she fell in love with Tomczyk partly because she admired him for
his involvement in the conspiracy against communist authority, and she
engaged in the Solidarity movement because she loved him. From that time
Agnieszka's biography conforms to the previously described tendency of
private and public being intertwined in the lives of Polish women.

Once Tomczyk enters Agnieszka's life, she changes her behaviour and
values. In her conversation with Winkiel she admits that in Warsaw she was
driven by ambition, she wanted success more than anything else. In Gdańsk
she lost this aspiration and discovered other values worth fighting for, such
as improving the lives of the workers and replacing totalitarian rule with
democracy. Although Agnieszka embraced these ideas with an open heart,
she did not discover them independently – they were instilled in her by
Maciek. Equally important was her discovery of the 'feminine' side of her
personality, which surfaced in her desire to have a husband and a child.
Their wedding is a powerful sign of her subordination to Maciek's way of
life. She tells Winkiel that she was never religious, but realised that they
must have a church wedding because all Maciek's friends (that is, everyone
involved in Solidarity) were very religious, and the Catholic Church itself
was part of the pro-democracy movement. Moreover, the only guests who
attend the ceremony are Solidarity activists, including the leader of the
movement, Lech Wałęsa (played by Wałęsa himself), who is the groom's
best man. In contrast, Agnieszka's family and friends are absent, even her
own father does not come.

The main impression one has from seeing Agnieszka in Gdańsk is one of
claustrophobia and extreme hardship. Firstly Agnieszka, who in *Man of
Marble* was a creature of open space, moving freely between apartments
and towns, shares a room with Maciek. The place is filled with old furniture, dark and grim, confining and suffocating. After Agnieszka and
Maciek decide to organise an exhibition about the events of 1970, the place
is visited by various officials, representing the communist authorities, who
try to dissuade the Tomczyks from their anti-state activities. Consequently,
Maciek loses his job and is imprisoned. At the time Agnieszka, who is heavily pregnant, finds work in a shop, moving heavy boxes in noisy rooms,
pushed by people who seem to show no respect for her condition as an
expectant mother. Living in Gdańsk, which in contrast to metropolitan
Warsaw feels very provincial, completes her isolation.

Even when Maciek is in prison, he dominates Agnieszka's existence. At
this stage she lives in the flat of old Mrs Hulewicz, who was Maciek's close
friend. His colleagues from the shipyard visit the young woman, bringing
her some money. Initially she refuses to take it, but eventually accepts,
touched, but also humiliated by the shipworkers' generosity. This is a further testimony to her loss of independence and transformation into a
woman who must be supported by men in order to survive. The final stage

of Agnieszka's literal and metaphorical confinement is her imprisonment at the start of the shipyard strikes. At this time she can participate neither in ordinary life by working and earning her living, nor in the anti-government conspiracy. The fact that she is interviewed by Winkiel not in reference to her own involvement in Solidarity, but to Maciek's, emphasises her political marginalisation. In the story she gives Winkiel, Agnieszka constantly undermines herself in relation to pre-Gdańsk times, in order to present Maciek as wise and heroic. She uses expressions such as 'I was mad', 'I was a complete idiot'. In her opinion Maciek was the man who showed her what was important in life and changed her from an ambition freak into a true woman and a patriot. At the same time, perhaps to avoid the accusation of constructing Maciek as an old-fashioned patriarch, Wajda makes Agnieszka say things which suggest that he is also a 'new man'. For example, she claims that at various stages of their life together, he encouraged her to return to her career as a filmmaker.

On the whole, the story that Agnieszka recounts to Winkiel presents a metamorphosis of Wajda's heroine from an independent woman into a Polish Mother (see Roszkowska 1992; Falkowska 1996; Ostrowska 1998). As a Polish Mother, Agnieszka in *Man of Iron* is selfless and has no life of her own, but serves the men of her family: her son and husband. She is confined to her home, leaving politics and breadwinning largely to Maciek. However, I will also argue that in *Man of Iron* she does not even have the famous strength of the archetypal Polish Mother, not to mention her old determination. Her weakness is most clearly demonstrated in a scene when the shipyard personnel officer visits Maciek to discourage him from organising a photographic exhibition in his flat. After the visit Agnieszka takes the pictures off the wall, bursts into tears and must be comforted by Maciek.

The shift from a Westernised, independent woman into a Polish Mother is signified visually, by changes in Agnieszka's costume and general appearance, as well as by camera positions and movements. Initially, once Agnieszka starts to share the flat with Maciek, her denim trousers and jacket are replaced by a denim dress. Afterwards we see her in a wedding dress and later in a wide, long, shapeless maternity dress. Once she becomes a mother, she is never shown in trousers, but in long dresses and coats. On one occasion we even see her with a scarf on her head, of the kind old Russian women wear. In prison she wears a narrow skirt, which, as Dorota Roszkowska suggests, symbolises her loss of freedom (Roszkowska 1992: 80–81). Agnieszka's clothes in *Man of Iron* hide the attractiveness and sexual power which she commanded in *Man of Marble*, instead furnishing her with maternal femininity. They also make her look much older than in the first part of Wajda's diptych. Although there is only five years between Wajda's shooting of *Man of Marble* and *Man of Iron*, the heroine's appearance suggests that many more years have passed. In her accelerated aging she is also reminiscent of the archetypal Polish Mother, who signifies maturity. After her pregnancy Agnieszka also loses the power of the look. Unlike the time when she made her documentary about Birkut, she now avoids looking at people and often walks with her eyes lowered to the floor. This attitude makes her virtually invisible; people whom she passes ignore her, even push her, as if she was an inanimate object.

Janina Falkowska draws attention to the fact that in the scene previously mentioned, when Maciek's comrades from the shipyard visit Agnieszka at home, she is stylised to look like a Madonna and a socialist realist monument. 'The construction of the mise-en-scène places Agnieszka, the Madonna with unborn child who is looked up to by Birkut's fellow workers with pious adoration, in the centre of the picture. However, Agnieszka looks monumental, statuesque, presented without any ironical comment' (Falkowska 1996: 146). Falkowska also quotes Gilbert Adair, who notes that the way Agnieszka is photographed bears associations with both Catholicism and socialist realism. 'In *Man of Iron* Agnieszka and Birkut's son was apotheosised – statufied, so to speak – as pious, forward-straining hero out of a tradition that can be described only as Stalinist' (ibid.: 146). I agree with Falkowska that the origins of Agnieszka in *Man of Iron* are both Stalinist and Catholic. Paradoxically, the two ideologies have much in common in their approach to women, as they tend to idealise and sanctify them. In the real world, however, they offer women only secondary positions, while expecting more from them than from men. The fact that Agnieszka in pregnancy is monumentalised suggests that the film's author approves of the transformation of his heroine from an independent young woman into a prematurely aged Polish Mother. On the whole, *Man of Iron* is a very masculine film, where men initiate and take the main parts in the events portrayed, as well as carrying the film's ideological baggage. Women only support the men, and this fate is not restricted to Agnieszka, but also includes the previously mentioned Mrs Hulewicz, an old friend of Mateusz Birkut and Maciek Tomczyk. Characteristically, there are also no women of importance in the documentary footage which Wajda included in his film. The Solidarity opposition, the communist authorities and the media are all represented by men, although the director shows that the masses of Solidarity members and supporters consist largely of women.

Myths, as has been demonstrated earlier in this book, often express dominant ideologies. In the nineteenth century the myth of the Polish Mother served the rule of patriarchy by expecting the woman to stand by her man (or the memory of him, if he died in battle), and by claiming that a woman's place at home determines her position in society. Consequently, the revival of the myth of the Polish Mother in Wajda's film conveyed and promoted the new attitudes to women, which took place about the time *Man of Iron* was made. One can find analogies between the situation of Agnieszka and the attitude to the roles of women in Polish society, as expressed by

Solidarity, as well as the position of the real Solidarity heroines during and after the famous shipyard strikes in 1980. As Hauser et al. note, 'in the 1980 Gdańsk Agreements, Solidarity created a number of special benefits for women, including generous leave for childbirth and childrearing. These policies met women's real needs but also helped maintain them in traditionally subordinate positions, reinforcing the image of woman as secondary wage earners focused on family and home' (Hauser et al. 1993: 262). The view that a woman should devote herself primarily to homemaking was supported by the increasingly anti-liberal attitude of Solidarity to abortion. As Hauser et al. note, 'Solidarity's 1981 program did not call for the banning of abortion outright, but expressed a hope that with an improving economic situation the economic reasons for terminating pregnancy would be eased. After 1990, it became clear that the economic situation would not improve quickly. Consequently, the Solidarity position on abortion evolved to endorsing, in March 1990, a total ban on abortion, irrespective of economic or even health considerations' (ibid.: 262).

Solidarity's position towards women, which can be described metaphorically as a desire to transform the ethos of the Polish Mother into a formal system of rights and duties, governed by the law, was accompanied by the marginalisation of women in the Solidarity movement and in the wider political and social life. As the previously quoted authors claim, 'Less than eight percent of delegates to the first Solidarity Congress in 1981 were women, although female workers constituted almost one-half of the union membership' (ibid.: 262). In the 1990s women constituted only a tiny minority in the leadership of Solidarity and in the AWS (Solidarity Election Action), a right-wing political alliance, dominated by Solidarity politicians. Moreover, their stance in parliament was often identical to that of their male colleagues, or even more extreme in advocating that women submit to their traditional roles of mothers and homemakers. Some of the handful of women who played prominent roles in the early Solidarity movement, such as Barbara Labuda, left Solidarity altogether in protest against its increasingly anti-liberal stance. Anna Walentynowicz, another prominent figure in the Solidarity movement, a shipyard worker whose dismissal was the immediate cause of the strike in the 1980s (and whose name is mentioned in *Man of Iron*) disappeared into complete obscurity.[1]

It could be argued that in the twenty or so years since the shipyard strikes, the Solidarity movement has had no distinctive female politicians. As in Wajda's *Man of Iron* the women in Solidarity are mute, invisible and confined to their homes. The fact that Wajda and his scriptwriter, Aleksander Ścibor-Rylski, created Agnieszka in *Man of Iron* as a Polish Mother is testimony to their political intuition, something for which Wajda was praised for most of his artistic career. However, Wajda's acceptance, even welcoming, of Agnieszka's change into the Polish right wing's female role model is much less comforting. At the same time it confirms my conviction that the most famous Polish director is a political opportunist, hardly challenging his audience's deepest views or values.

Agnieszka and Krystyna Janda

In Europe, in contrast to America, we are accustomed to regard film characters as the sole creation of the director, at the expense of appreciating the input of scriptwriters, and even to a larger extent, of the actors. In many cases, however, the actors play such a significant part in shaping the role that it is almost impossible to say whether they 'play' their character, or simply reveal their own personality. This is reflected in the attitude of the audience, who are unable to distinguish between the actor and their character, and endow the actor with the same feelings which they hold for the person they play, which was the case of Krystyna Janda who played Agnieszka. Janda was born in 1951 and *Man of Marble* was her film début. Her role was regarded as a tremendous success and instantly elevated her to the status of great star and idol of her generation. The audience attributed to the actress many of the characteristics of her heroine, simply perceiving her as Agnieszka.

In the light of Agnieszka's 'prior history' and Janda's own experiences, the identification was to a large extent justified. The character moved through a series of metamorphoses, before appearing on screen. In the first version of the script for *Man of Marble*, written by Aleksander Ścibor-Rylski in 1962, Agnieszka represented the generation of those born at the end of the 1930s, and her role in the narrative was relatively small. She was described as looking no more than twenty years old, wearing a dark, tweed jacket, dark stockings and dark, high heels. Her clothes were rather old, but in good taste. The first Agnieszka was shy, lacking in self-confidence and silent. Ścibor-Rylski's script was eventually accepted by the political authorities in 1975. At this stage she transformed into a person born in the 1950s. However, her basic characteristics hardly changed: she was still meant to be shy and restrained (Roszkowska 1992: 79). The final shape of Wajda's heroine was given by the actress Wajda chose for the role. Janda says that when Wajda was looking for someone to play Agnieszka, he did not wish to employ someone with excellent acting technique, but rather a young woman with a strong personality and little acting experience (see Metzel 1978: 16). She had considerable freedom to shape Agnieszka, to instil her with her own opinions and mannerisms. Janda also claims that as a student in the theatre school she was interested in Polish screen 'idols', particularly Zbigniew Cybulski, the actor who played the main part in Wajda's *Ashes and Diamonds* (ibid.: 16). She completely identified with Cybulski's opinion that 'to be an actor means to be able to smell his time, to be able to express the emotions of one's own generation' (Roszkowska 1992: 79). The young actress was fully aware of Agnieszka's uniqueness. She noticed that in contrast to the majority of the most memorable heroes of Polish cinema – particularly in films of the Polish School – who were doomed to failure, her heroine was destined to win. Janda was also proud to play a character who did not suit the female stereotype in Polish cinema as being subservient to men (Metzel 1978: 16–17). According to her own words, she also identified completely with the second incarnation of Agnieszka in *Man of Iron* and was even able to detect an affinity between Agnieszka's evolution and her own personal development. There is no resentment at her heroine being reduced to a secondary character and inscribed into patriarchal order. Janda commented:

> *Man of Iron* completed my education as a citizen. It confirmed my way of thinking about my country and its tragic history. Sometimes I think with horror that if I had not read certain books and met certain people, I would remain a complete idiot. In the film there is a similar motif: thanks to Birkut, Agnieszka meets many wise people, who change her completely ... Revolutions are made by men, a woman must be his support, take care of their home. In this film I played a mature, wise Agnieszka and a national symbol. (Janicka and Janda 1999: 58)

After her roles in *Man of Marble* and *Man of Iron*, amongst other films, Janda played in two later movies directed by Wajda, *Bez znieczulenia* (*Rough Treatment*, 1978) and *Dyrygent* (*Conductor*, 1979), and in a stream of films in which she portrayed characters who rebel against communist authority, such as *Stan wewnętrzny* (*Inner State*, 1983), which will be discussed later, and *Przesłuchanie* (*Interrogation*, 1982) by Ryszard Bugajski. For the latter film she received many awards in Poland and abroad, including an award for best actress at the 1989 Cannes Festival. These roles confirmed Janda's status as a 'national actress', understood as someone whose motive for acting is less about earning money or gaining popularity, but rather of conveying the ideals and interests of the whole nation. In the years that followed she tried to live up to this image both in the cinema and in her off-screen life. Apart from playing in many popular films both in Poland and abroad, she expressed her political views in numerous interviews, worked for children's charities, wrote magazine articles and made a record. On the other hand, on the rare occasions when she revealed that she liked money and the luxurious life, she was scorned by her admirers, as if they were unable to forgive Janda that she was not the selfless Agnieszka, but an 'ordinary' celebrity. In 1995 Janda made her début as a film director, adapting for the screen *Pestka* (*Stone*), a bestseller written by Anka Kowalska in the 1960s about a tragic love affair between a married man and a single woman, played by Janda herself. Agata, Janda's character in the film, in spite of being at least ten years older than the heroine in *Man of Iron*, still reveals the same intensity of feelings as Agnieszka. However, the energy is directed entirely to her private life: Agata's love and

suffering caused by her guilt at destroying her lover's family. There is no reference to politics in Janda's film; her character, although middle class and
sophisticated (she works as a radio journalist and has a Ph.D. degree),
seems not to care about anything apart from her romance. Agata's total
preoccupation with the private sphere might be regarded as symptomatic of
the role prescribed for women by respective postcommunist governments,
as well as of Janda's own change of opinion about women's role in society.

In the 1990s Janda was still regarded as the greatest female star of postwar Polish cinema and a role model for a new generation of Polish actresses.
Yet, her status as a political actress and national symbol weakened significantly after the collapse of communism. Her most memorable roles in the
last fifteen years or so have been in theatre plays, which she has frequently
directed. Amongst other roles, she played Maria Callas and Marlene
Dietrich. Janda herself is sceptical about her future in Polish cinema. In an
interview given in March 2000, she said '[Polish] cinema is now made by the
young generation. They have their own subjects, their own actors, their own
problems. As for me, I can possibly play the mother of a thief or a gangster'
(Gałązka 2000: 4). In another interview Janda admits that while she was a
symbol of the 1970s, the 1990s belonged to Katarzyna Figura, an actress of
immense sex appeal, regarded as a Polish Marilyn Monroe, who specialised
in contemporary comedies (Piasecka 1998: 22). At the same time, she yearns
to repeat her early successes and believes that her chance to play someone in
the same league as Agnieszka depends on Wajda's willingness to employ her
again. In an interview she noted, 'I do not know Andrzej Wajda's intentions,
but whatever they are, I will be happy to respond to them' (Gałązka 2000:
4). Interestingly, after Agnieszka, Wajda was unable to create any interesting
and memorable female characters, in spite of the fact that women were cast
in the principal roles in two of his later films: *Wielki Tydzień* (*Holy Week*,
1995) and *Panna Nikt* (*Miss Nobody*, 1996).

Other Solidarity Heroines

The impact of *Man of Marble* and *Man of Iron* in the history of Polish cinema was so great that they initiated a wider phenomenon of films, depicting the history of Solidarity with a female heroine at the centre of the
narrative. Two films are of particular interest to me – *Stan wewnętrzny*
(*Inner State*, 1983) by Krzysztof Tchórzewski and *Człowiek z...* (*Man of...*,
1993) by Konrad Szołajski – as in a sense they provide new versions or con-
tinuations of the stories of Wajda's characters.

The character of Ewa in *Inner State* especially resonates with memories
of Agnieszka, as she is played by Krystyna Janda herself. Ewa is a sailor and
Solidarity activist, who in 1981 embarked from Gdańsk on a single-handed
round-the-world yacht race, with the ambition of breaking the world

record. When martial law was introduced in December 1981, many of her friends (including those working in the Gdańsk shipyard), who helped her to realise her sailing ambitions, lose their jobs or are interned by the communist government. Ewa encounters a complex moral dilemma: to finish her race, as the military authorities want her to do and to return home as an 'official hero', or to remain in exile somewhere in the West, or to return to Poland without finishing the race. In spite of having very limited information about the situation in Poland, she chooses the last option and returns to Poland, risking persecution by the military authorities.

If we assume that Ewa is an 'older Agnieszka in disguise', *Inner State* confirms the image of Agnieszka as somebody who remained faithful to the ideals of Solidarity. In this respect, Ewa is similar to both Agnieszkas in *Man of Marble* and *Man of Iron*. Her ambition to achieve something unusual and 'masculine' (there are very few women who embark on long, single-handed races), as well as her unusual energy and mobility, surpassing both men and women around her, place her closer to the first incarnation of Wajda's heroine. Moreover, although she fails to complete the race, she breaks the world sailing record. On the other hand, in common with Agnieszka in *Man of Iron*, Ewa relies heavily on men, in this case on her ex-husband, her boss and lover, thanks to whom her yacht is of world-class quality, and her friend, who works in television. There is also some uncertainty about her main motive in interrupting the race, as she returns to Poland knowing that she is pregnant by her ex-husband. Ewa's future remains open; we do not learn if she will suspend her career as a professional sailor and devote herself to motherhood completely, or if she will try to reconcile the various aspects of her life. On the whole, the author of *Inner State* tries somehow to reconcile Agnieszka in *Man of Marble* with Agnieszka in *Man of Iron*, imbuing her with features of Wajda's heroine from the two stages of her life. Sadly, the film fails to enrich the portrayal of the Solidarity heroine, created by Wajda, because Ewa is comprised entirely of various clichés Wajda used in the two films.

Another film that reworks the story presented in *Man of Marble* and *Man of Iron*, albeit in a very different way, is *Man of...*. Szolajski's film, being one of the handful of successful comedies of the 1990s, is a caricature of Wajda's epics. Its heroine, Anna (Agata Kulesza), a young film-school graduate, is mistaken by the military police for an anti-communist conspirator during the martial law of 1982. She emigrates to the West and returns in 1989 as a celebrity to a democratic Poland, to make a film about the activist of the anti-communist opposition, Marek Mirkut (Sławomir Pacek). In common with Agnieszka, who tried to discover the past of Mateusz Birkut by watching newsreels made in the 1950s, Anna spends long hours in the archives, watching documentary footage about Mirkut's work in the Solidarity underground. Most importantly, she learns that he joined Solidarity not so much to fight against the communist oppressors, as to win the heart of a girl called Maria (Ewa Gawryluk), who suffered 'neurosa eroica': being unable to fall in love with anybody except a hero. Marek's story consists of many events typical of Solidarity figures, which were included in Wajda's films and recycled by other directors. For example, Marek organised the escape of a member of the opposition. He was also interned during martial law and eventually won the heart of Maria. However, none of the events in Szołajski's film looks as they did when immortalised in the 'Solidarity myth'. The general impression is that martial law was not particularly harsh, and that many people joined the anti-communist opposition for reasons that were less than noble, and after the collapse of communism cynically used it as a passport to a career in politics and business.

In *Man of...* two women bear similarities to Agnieszka: Anna resembles Agnieszka in *Man of Marble* and Maria resembles the heroine of *Man of Iron*. However, the connection between Anna and Agnieszka is rather superficial, referring only to their roles in the narrative structures, not to their personalities. Phlegmatic and slightly naïve, Anna is less than a shadow of her cinematic predecessor. Moreover, her career in cinema and politics is a result of a series of lucky coincidences, not her own determination, as it was in the case of Agnieszka. Her warm prettiness and feminine clothing further account for the gap between Wajda's and Szołajski's heroines. We can find more meaningful similarities between Agnieszka and Maria. Maria, as Wajda's heroine, yearns to do something important and patriotic. Moreover, in tune with the tradition of the Polish Mother, Maria gives up her independence and takes the role of supporter of the man whom she loves. She encourages him to take part in the most dangerous and heroic acts of anti-communist conspiracy, and supports him during martial law by visiting him in a camp for interned conspirators, disguised as a man. Unfortunately, she tries so hard not to be recognised by the camp guards that she virtually changes into a man. Consequently, Marek, who cannot give up his love for Maria (who became Marian), changes his gender too, becoming a woman called Maria. The sex change of the main characters might be treated simply as farcical, adding to the postmodern style of the film by creating associations with such classics as *Some Like It Hot* (1959) by Billy Wilder, or the Polish popular comedy *Poszukiwany, poszukiwana* (*Searching For*, 1972) by Stanisław Bareja. The director himself, in an interview which I conducted in 1999, played down the importance of gender issues in his film, claiming that it was simply a comedy device. However, it can also be read in the context of the 'gender politics' of Wajda's films, as Szołajski's mockery of Wajda's decision to highlight the men and marginalise the women in *Man of Iron*. Szołajski does this by portraying Maria as being much braver than the weak and effeminate men engaged in the Solidarity conspiracy. *Man of...* might also be regarded as a rewriting or deconstruction of the Polish Mother myth. By showing Maria as fulfilling her Polish Mother's duties of patriotism with extreme seriousness and determination, Szołajski demonstrates that she not only outshines her man, but changes him into a passive tool of her own plans, and thus makes him unimportant.

In common with Ewa, Anna and Maria do not come across as real women, but only as re-presentations, or variations of Wajda's heroine – and they are not meaningful alternatives to Wajda's Agnieszka. This can be regarded as being as much a testimony to the talent of Andrzej Wajda and Krystyna Janda to create a convincing and memorable character, as to the inability of Polish filmmakers to portray Polish women as co-creators of the Solidarity movement, or at least as politically active. Tchórzewski, Szołajski and some others, such as Feliks Falk, the director of *Koniec gry* (*The End of the Game*, 1991) (about a female politician-kleptomaniac), try to give women more prominent parts, but fail to make them convincing. In the next chapter I will argue that in the majority of Polish films in the 1990s women are either marginalised in the narratives, or portrayed as enemies of male protagonists and the common good. Thus, to put it metaphorically, Agnieszka had some less talented sisters, but no daughters, and her beloved son grew to be a more patriarchal man than his father.

Note

1. The erasure of women from Polish history of the 1980s was also recognised by literature depicting this period from the perspective of an anti-communist fighter. For example, in Cezary Michalski's novel, *Siła odpychania* (*The Force of Repulsion*) the main female character, in a part of her diary describing her past experiences of struggle for Polish independence, appropriates a male voice because, as the narrator informs us: 'In the 1980s true victims were Polish men' (Michalski 2002: 68).

CHAPTER 6

Witches, Bitches and Other Victims of the Crisis of Masculinity: Women in Polish Postcommunist Cinema

EWA MAZIERSKA

The transition from communism to democracy and a free market economy in 1989 is regarded as the most important factor to shape Polish cinema in the last one-and-a-half-decades. Most critics suggest that the shift resulted in its depoliticisation. For example, Marek Haltof writes, in his article about Polish cinema after 1989, that: 'Filmmaking has ceased to be a national and social mission. It has once again become a strictly professional endeavour. Rather than being "more than cinema" it has now shrunk (without negative connotation) to "simply cinema" and exists somewhere on the margin of Polish life. It entertains, reflects life and is free from political pressures and commitments' (Haltof 1997: 137). In my view, this opinion is grossly simplified, if not overtly false; Polish cinema indeed changed, but did not lose its connections with politics and ideology. Firstly, the state did not abandon its function as a major sponsor of Polish culture. A large proportion of film production and distribution in Poland is still financed by the state, or institutions using state money, such as public television, and political pressure is still exerted on filmmakers, only more subtly. Consequently, those who aspire to receive state funds feel obliged to conform to and even promote the dominant ideology, articulated, for instance, by government, parliament and the Catholic Church. Those who rebel against it, favouring more controversial issues and points of view, must typically content themselves with a much longer road to filmmaking, significantly smaller budgets and less exposure in the media than their more conforming colleagues. Secondly, Polish cinema after 1989 remained an important source of meaning, engaging in such debates as the role of various strands of Polish cultural heritage in creating a new cultural identity for the country, the status and future of Polish intelligentsia, as well as the role of the state in regulating citizens' private lives (the films about abortion law, discussed in the chapter about Dorota Kędzierzawska, testify to that). It could even be argued that its role increased due to the changes in the structure of audiences and channels of distribution. Unlike previous periods, when the bulk of viewers consisted of representatives of the intelligentsia with a mature outlook on life, after 1989 the audience of all films shown in cinemas consisted largely of teenagers and people in their twenties. The convictions of this group of viewers are still in the process of forming, therefore they are particularly prone to ideas and opinions directed at them from the screen. Moreover, due to the proliferation of video, cable and satellite television, as well as a relatively short gap between the premiere of the film in the cinema and its showing on television, Polish cinema has wider exposure to a more heterogeneous audience than ever before in its history. The purpose of this chapter is to discuss one aspect of Polish postcommunist cinema: the representation of women in feature films. I will attempt to establish the main tendencies in the way women are portrayed, arguing that they are by no means ideologically neutral. However, before discussing these issues it is worth saying something about the political, social and economic situation of women and men in postcommunist Poland. Men can not be ignored in this context because gender operates dialectically: the position of women must be measured in relation to the situation of men.

Women and Men in Poland after 1989

The collapse of 'really existing socialism' and the shift to postcommunism which took place in Poland in 1989 affected the citizens of this country in a profound way. For men and women there were both gains and losses in virtually all spheres of social life. In economic terms women were the first to lose their jobs when rationalisation of employment was introduced in the early 1990s. Many women became unemployed due to a decline of some of the traditionally female industries, particularly the production of textiles (largely relocated to poorer countries of the old Eastern Bloc, such as Ukraine or Belorussia), which affected some large towns, such as Łódź. However, restructuring the economy had an even more negative impact on male employment, as more masculine than feminine branches of industry were slimmed down or axed in postcommunist Poland. As a consequence of the communist system privileging heavy industry over other branches of the economy, men employed in coalmining, shipbuilding and steel production used to earn significantly more than the national average wage; losing their job, therefore, resulted in a dramatic decrease in living standard. Moreover, workers in those branches played a pivotal role in overthrowing the communist system, therefore their morale suffered particularly badly. Many of them turned against the political forces of Solidarity origin, which promised them a better life, and started to support extremely right-wing or postcommunist parties (see Klein 2002: 2). At the same time, following the shift from heavy industry to a service economy, the need for female employment in Poland increased. In regions where a large proportion of men had been employed in male industries, there are now more women working than men, although their jobs are relatively poorly paid and of low status. On the whole, women earn at least 20 percent less than men in Poland.

Women who during communism were underrepresented in positions of power, such as senior managerial posts, parliament, local and central government, remain underrepresented. There are now even fewer of them in parliament than before 1989. The opinion was even voiced that the Polish parliament after 1989 resembled an English gentlemen's club (see Watson 1996: 218). There is a widespread opinion that politics in Eastern Europe after the fall of the Berlin Wall generally, and in Poland in particular, is marked by the rise of masculinism and the marginalisation of women (see Watson 1996; 1997; Graff 2001). However, there is also a significant difference between communist and postcommunist times regarding real female participation in politics and access to power. Before 1989 women were chosen to join political institutions, such as parliament, mainly to conform to the Marxist idea of gender equality but they had relatively low positions and little real authority (see Molyneux 1994). For example, before 1989 Poland had no female prime minister and very few female ministers or members of the central committee of the Communist Party. By contrast, after 1989 some women achieved positions of real power; examples are Hanna Suchocka, who was prime minister in the years 1992–93 or Hanna Gronkiewicz-Waltz, who in the years 1992–2000 was the director of the central bank and a candidate in the 1995 presidential election. Yet, the majority of women of political power do not have a pro-women's agenda. On the contrary, Suchocka and Gronkiewicz-Waltz distanced themselves from, or even criticised, feminism (see Graff 2001: 63–64).

At the same time, we observe a mushrooming of feminist organisations in Poland. Unlike their predecessors in the communist epoch, which were encouraged or even imposed by the political authorities, they are bottom-up movements, which articulate the true interests and concerns of women. Although both in terms of the number of women participating in the pro-women's movement, and in their political and cultural presence, they are much weaker and less radical than their Western counterparts (see Limanowska 1996; Umińska 1996), the male backlash against them, as well as the hostility amongst the majority of traditionally minded women, is significant. Feminists and all women who do not fit the right-wing, Roman Catholic ideal of a woman (for whom, as the Polish representative on the Council of Europe, Marcin Libicki said 'pregnancy is a blessing'

[Watson 1996: 218]), stand accused by politicians and Church officials (not unlike Jews in some earlier periods of Polish history) of causing the various real problems and imaginary calamities falling on Poland after 1989. Amongst them are falling birth rate, proliferation of prostitution and pornography, bad behaviour of children and decline of morality as a whole (see Watson 1996; 1997; Graff 2001).

In the official political discourse 'family', understood in conservative terms (as a household consisting of a husband and wife and their children), gained unusual prominence after 1989. Solidarity and subsequent governments deriving from this movement proclaimed that the state should support family life and the natural role of a woman as a mother and homemaker. Such a stance can be read partly as a way for the new authorities to distance themselves from the previous official opinions concerning the role of a 'family'. It must be said that in a large part of Marxist discourse the family had negative connotations, being associated with the exploitation of women, a 'bourgeois mental framework', and putting private interests over the welfare of society as a whole (see Bronfenbrenner 1972). Yet, governments in socialist Poland hardly followed any coherent anti-family agenda. It could be even argued that numerous attempts were made to reconcile the traditional outlook on the family, rooted in Roman Catholicism, with socialist principles. Nevertheless, in popular consciousness an opinion prevailed that the communist state did not value the family as highly as it should.

The opinion that family and family life should be given priority over other types of households and lifestyles was promoted even more forcefully by the Catholic Church, which was always the buttress of traditionalism in Polish society, particularly in matters of sexuality. After the collapse of communism it exerted maximum pressure to secure full protection for the 'unborn child'. The main consequence of this approach was a new abortion law, introduced in 1993, after almost four years of parliamentary discussion, making abortion illegal in most circumstances (see Fuszara 1993). It replaced the liberal legislation of the 1950s, which allowed a woman to terminate her pregnancy virtually on demand and free of charge. Women were also initially given longer maternity leave to help them to fulfil their maternal role. At the same time, we observe a decrease in state provision for childcare, which made it more difficult, particularly for women – as they typically are the main carers for children – to combine employment with parenting. Judging by statistics, Polish women did not fulfil the expectation to put their maternal role first. Poland (in common with the ex-Soviet Union and many other countries of the Eastern Bloc) has one of the lowest birth rates in Europe: in 2000 it reached 1.38 children per woman. Paradoxically, although understandably, conservatism in sexual matters, advocated and imposed by the main social institutions in Poland has been accompanied by an explosion of commercialised sexuality in the form of numerous sex-shops and pornographic magazines, obtainable even in small, provincial towns, and soft-porn films saturating private television stations. Hence, it appears that in contemporary Poland two contrasting models of female sexuality prevail: one extremely restrained and subordinated to the needs of family, the other, hedonistic, but commodified. Both models have a tangible impact on the real situation of women and the way they are perceived, significantly reducing their life choices and constraining their subjectivities.

These measurable changes were accompanied by certain shifts in the sphere of common consciousness and even subconsciousness, referring to the way men and women perceive their roles in society. These shifts are conceptualised by two apparently contrasting paradigms: the rise of masculinism, which dominates feminist discourses of the state of Polish society after 1989, and the less widespread idea that Polish men are in a state of crisis, which also negatively affects women. The first paradigm, to which I have already referred, can be summarised and explained by the words of Peggy Watson:

> Traditional views of what 'normal' men and women are have acted as a vehicle for change in Eastern Europe, 'freedom' being associated with the freedom to more fully enact a traditional feminine or masculine identity, untrammelled by the constrictions of the socialist state. However, the changes which have been wrought now offer systematic advantage to men ... Civil society means the empowerment of men and the enactment of masculinity on a grand scale. (Watson 1996: 217)

The second paradigm is rooted in the idea that the end of communism, which can be regarded as the last stage of over two hundred years of different kinds of colonisation and many wars, brought men some drawbacks. They include the loss of status resulting from shrinking opportunities to be heroic, which for Polish males was regarded as the most noble destiny, promoted in Polish literature, art and mythology, especially of Romantic origin. As renowned literary critic Maria Janion observes, with the victory of Solidarity, Romanticism declined in Poland (see Janion 1996a; Wyka 1996) and Polish men risk feeling or even becoming redundant.

It is possible to reconcile these two paradigms; the rise of masculinism and the hostility to women that accompanies it, can be interpreted as a reaction to, or a by-product of, the impossibility on the part of Polish men to fulfil the traditional masculine role of hero and the defender of the country. In such an interpretation, the woman – or at least a certain type of woman – who dares not agree with the secondary position allocated to her by men (who might therefore be labelled a feminist), is given the thankless task of becoming the replacement for the old enemies, such as the communist state. Peggy Watson supports this view by arguing that the legacy of communism – or more precisely, a certain way of interpreting the communist past – and the rise of nationalism in postcommunist countries allowed the association of feminism with socialism: 'To the extent that women are seen as having benefited from socialism or as having had the socialist state as their ally, feminist becomes socialist and can be attacked as anti-national' (Watson 1997: 154).

The bottom line of my argument is that irrespective of regarding the period after 1989 as being marked by the rise of masculinism or a crisis of masculinity, it results in hostility towards women and a desire to contain the 'female element' by prescribing women the traditional female roles of mothers and homemakers. Films made in the last fifteen years or so perfectly testify to it.

Genre and Gender

One factor that cannot be omitted in discussion of the representation of women in Polish postcommunist cinema is that, in contrast to previous periods, it is dominated by generic films. Hence, the images of women in these films are partly shaped by the rules governing respective genres. On the other hand, the very choice of a particular genre is not ideology free. Some genres are more concerned with men, others with women, and different genres tend to represent gender relations in a particular way, thus reflecting the real or postulated position of women and men within the society.

In terms of quantity and size of budget, Polish postcommunist cinema is eclipsed by two genres: police/gangster films, prominent in the first half of the 1990s, and 'heritage cinema', which dominated the cinematic landscape in the second half of the decade and the beginning of the new century. We also observe an upsurge in production and popularity of criminal comedies. Films of the first genre were created largely by the generation of 'Young Wolves': those born between the late 1950s and the early 1970s who made their first films after the collapse of communism. The name came from the film *Młode wilki* (*Young Wolves*, 1995), directed by Jarosław Żamojda, including Władysław Pasikowski, who can be regarded as the father of the movement, Żamojda, Maciej Ślesicki and Bogusław Linda. These directors overtly express their admiration for Hollywood cinema, especially films made by their most famous American contemporary, Quentin Tarantino. Hence, the opinions and criticisms voiced by feminist critics in reference to American films of the 1980s and 1990s – such as Alison Butler's claim that

As the 1980s gave way to the 1990s, redefinitions of masculinity in cinema seemed to give way to reinstatements of masculinity. *Reservoir Dogs* (Quentin Tarantino, 1991) initiated a new cycle in US cinema, in which extreme violence, narcissism and misogyny became the stock-in-trade for young filmmakers. Ironically, young male cinema might have rescued low and medium budgets as a possibility, at least for first films, but in the process it has redefined independent cinema as an outsider's cinema only in the sense that its values are regressive. (Butler 2000: 76)

– can also be applied to Polish gangster films. Their films are masculine both in terms of giving men the role of the agents and bearers of the film's ideology, and in their uncritical affirmation of macho masculinity and misogyny. Women in these films, as Haltof observes, are 'voiceless figures in a male-dominated landscape' (Haltof 1997: 151). However, I will disagree with Haltof's claim that their 'task is no longer to "stand by their man" as in Hollywood cinema, but to find a place for themselves in a ruthless world where only their sexuality matters' (ibid.). The very fact that in this universe 'only their sexuality matters' suggests that this is a world where men create and enforce the rules. Moreover, as will be demonstrated in due course, women are punished if they do not stand by their men and choose independence instead.

While the gangster film of the type proposed by Pasikowski and his younger colleagues can be regarded as a new phenomenon, 'heritage cinema', including *Ogniem i mieczem* (*With Fire and Sword*, 1999), directed by Jerzy Hoffman, *Pan Tadeusz* (1999) and *Zemsta* (*Revenge*, 2002), directed by Andrzej Wajda, *Przedwiośnie* (*Early Spring*, 2001), directed by Filip Bajon and *Quo Vadis* (2001), directed by Jerzy Kawalerowicz, has many predecessors. Adaptations of literary masterpieces, especially those forming the school canon, were popular amongst Polish directors and constituted an important part of national cinema after 1945. Consequently, comparing the representation of women in the new heritage films with those from earlier periods can serve as a litmus test for detecting changing attitudes to the nature of women and their place in Polish society.

Absent Women, Witches and Bitches

Lack of interest in women, leading to their marginalisation or even absence from the narrative, is the most commonly observed feature of the part of postcommunist cinema which conforms to generic rules, especially gangster films and criminal comedies (see Jankun-Dopartowa 1998; Stachówna 2001; Sadowska 2002). Władysław Pasikowski, who was also the first of the new generation of filmmakers to be accused of sexism, summarises this approach by claiming that woman's role in cinema is 'to look good' (Bergel 1998: 77). In order to conform to his idea of the role of a woman in film – and by extension, in society – the majority of gangster movies are set in a masculine environment, such as the mafia, the army, the secret police, to which women do not normally have access. This microcosm is usually depicted as a masculine paradise, which crumbles and disintegrates when females penetrate it, or when men abandon it to join a more heterogeneous society. Consequently, misogyny is another defining trait of generic films (see Szczuka-Lipszyc 1994; Jankun-Dopartowa 1998; Stachówna 2001). Equally symptomatic is the fact that male hatred in these films is usually directed towards those women who are either absent from the screen, or only partially represented, being mute or seen solely on a photograph or on a television screen, or somehow weakened, as if the directors were unwilling to put women on an equal footing with men and risk that men will be defeated.

The group of bad and invisible women is dominated by ex-wives who after divorce take their children away from their fathers, as did Franz's wife in *Psy* (*Dogs*, 1992), directed by Władysław Pasikowski, and Cezary's wife in *Tato* (*Dad*, 1995), directed by Maciej Ślesicki. Little explanation is given as to why these women abandoned their families. Asked by his new lover why his wife left him, Franz says simply 'because she was a bad woman'. These 'bad women' have no chance to present their point of view as they are only talked about by men, rather than being characters in their own right. Much hostility in the films is also directed to abstract women, women in general and to certain models of femininity, previously accepted or even exhalted in Polish culture. In *Dogs* and *Kroll* (1991), directed by Władysław Pasikowski, Ślesicki's *Dad* and *Gnoje* (*Dung*, 1995), directed by Jerzy Zalewski, we find statements such as that women conspire to destroy manhood, that all are selfish or stupid, or that all are hookers. We also find criticism, often in the form of mockery, of the Polish Mother, who, as stated on many occasions in this book, is the dominant and exclusively positive model of femininity in Polish culture. A widely quoted example is provided by *Dad*, whose male characters sneer that only in Poland are mothers rewarded with monuments; in other countries maternity is taken for granted. Little more respect is given to the women who took part in the Solidarity struggle for democracy and women who possess political power. The fact that even such noble models of femininity are undermined clearly testifies to the depth of men's resentment of women, as well as to male fear of confronting women face to face, when arguments can be presented and discussed in a rational and balanced way.

The second group of females hated by male film directors and characters is composed of women who are marginalised in society by such factors as illness (especially madness), poverty, being foreign or working as prostitutes. Particularly striking in post-1989 Polish cinema is the multitude of 'witches': women who possess extra-human power, or are simply mad or strange and un-Polish (see Mazierska 2002); and 'bitches': prostitutes or women who are promiscuous and behave in a sexually provocative manner (see Stachówna 2001). We find the first type in, amongst other films, *Dad*, *With Fire and Sword*, *Rozmowa z człowiekiem z szafy* (*Conversation with a Cupboard Man*, 1993), directed by Mariusz Grzegorzek, *Szamanka* (*Shaman*, 1996), directed by Andrzej Żuławski, *Demony wojny* (*Demons of War*, 1998), directed by Władysław Pasikowski and *Ciemna strona Wenus* (*The Dark Side of Venus*, 1997), directed by Radosław Piwowarski. The second type is in virtually every second film of this period, directed by men. The two categories are not mutually exclusive: 'witches' are often 'bitches'; they are hungry for sex and use their sexuality as a weapon of male destruction. The plots of the films about 'witches' and 'bitches' often revolve around a power struggle between a woman and a man, ending with the man's victory and punishment of the dangerous Other. Moreover, destroying a dangerous woman typically coincides with the main character accomplishing some noble objective, such as winning a war or saving a child.

Dad is a model example of a film with a 'witch'. It depicts the bitter custody battle for a child between, on the one hand, a father, and on the other, his wife and his mother-in-law. The father, named Michał (Bogusław Linda), comes across as a devoted family man, who works hard as a cinematographer to secure a happy and prosperous life for his wife, Ewa (Dorota Segda) and daughter Kasia (Ola Maliszewska), and rejects any opportunity for extramarital romance. Ewa, who is a housewife, not only does not appreciate her husband's efforts, but treats him with the greatest and most inexplicable wickedness and aggression and tries to corrupt Kasia. As time passes, Ewa's condition deteriorates. Suffering from delusions, she attacks people at random and even kills Michał's friend, Cezary (Cezary Pazura), before being locked up in a psychiatric ward.

Michał's mother-in-law (Teresa Lipowska) is an even more potent adversary than his wife and she is also cast by Ślesicki as an evil woman, who steals, imprisons and harms someone else's child. An indication of her possessiveness and cruelty is her refusal to send Kasia, for whom she received custody from the court, to school and the bruises Michał notices on his daughter's body. Ewa's mother hates her son-in-law and is ruthless in her fight against him. When he 'steals' his daughter back from his mother-in-law, in order to provide her with a safe environment, she hires two hitmen to beat Michał up and to return Kasia to her home.

The costume and iconography reinforce the witch-like qualities of Kasia's mother and grandmother. Ewa has dark shadows under her eyes and long, straggled hair and prefers darkness over light. Her mother has a puritanical, harsh demeanour, dressed mostly in black with an old-fashioned hat. The door chain, which is meant to prevent Michał from touching and perhaps stealing his daughter, reminds us of the chains used by witches in fairy tales to prevent children from running away. The most poignant scene is one where, after hearing about the court's decision to take her away from her father, Kasia climbs to the top of the court and stands on the window-sill, pretending that she wants to kill herself. Her grandmother, who tries to rescue her, uses a broomstick to bring her to safety and falls herself, with the broomstick between her legs. This event marks the happy, fairy-tale-like ending: with his mother-in-law dead and his wife locked in a mental asylum, Michał is eventually able to resume his role as Kasia's single parent.

The most distinctive 'witch' in heritage cinema is Horpyna in *With Fire and Sword*. This film is based on one part of Henryk Sienkiewicz's *Trilogy*, which depicts Polish military successes in the seventeenth century and represents the fight between Poland and Ukrainian (Cossack) insurrectionists. Horpyna is of Gypsy Ukrainian descent and lives in a remote grotto, hung with skeletons and skulls. Being a friend of a Cossack, Bohun (Alexander Domogorov), and secretly in love with him, she helps him on numerous occasions, tending his wounds and providing shelter for his beloved Polish aristocratic beauty, Helena (Isabella Scorupco). Moreover, using her supernatural power of clairvoyance, she is able to read people's futures and she tells Bohun than he will fight and be defeated by the Polish nobleman, Michał Wołodyjowski (Zbigniew Zamachowski). Although Horpyna uses her powers to do good, and Poles, in common with Bohun, should be grateful to her for caring for Helena, she is the object of their utter hatred. The sole reasons for this aversion seem to be her un-Christian power and her ugliness, which together constitute her 'otherness' (the impression of which is strengthened by her being played by a Ukrainian actress, Ruslana Pysanka). In the end she is shot dead by a group of Polish noblemen, including Wołodyjowski. After her death Wołodyjowski drives a wooden stake into her heart to ensure that she will not be reborn. This act, traditionally committed on vampires and devils, symbolises the triumph of the Christian order and, by the same token, of the rule of patriarchy and Polish culture over paganism and the influence of women. Horpyna's demise coincides with the Poles being able to turn the wheel of fortune in their favour; soon afterwards they defeat the Cossacks and capture Bohun.

In *Pan Tadeusz* the role of the enemy of decent Polish folk, if not of a straightforward witch, is filled by Telimena (Grażyna Szapołowska), an impoverished spinster, who lives in the house of her rich, aristocratic relatives. She is cunning and selfish, which is revealed in her attitude to a younger woman who was left in her care, the young, beautiful and rich Zosia (Alicja Bachleda Curuś). Telimena does not use her position to further Zosia's welfare, but for her own advantage, trying to seduce two attractive men who are both interested in Zosia: Hrabia (the Earl) (Marek Kondrat) and the eponymous Pan Tadeusz (Michał Żebrowski). Not unlike Horpyna, she also signifies cultural otherness and a threat to genuine Polish culture, being an uncritical follower of Russian fashion (Petersburg is for her the peak of civilisation). Her punishment in the narrative, like Horpyna's downfall, coincides with the happy ending of the film: Tadeusz and Zosia are betrothed and Poland has a chance of regaining her independence thanks to Napoleon's war with Russia.

'Witches' can also be found in films that are less clear-cut generic productions, like *Shaman* (Figure 6.1). The film, set in contemporary times, starts with an encounter between two strangers. She, Włoszka (Iwona Petry), is a student; he, Michał (Bogusław Linda), is a lecturer in anthro-

Figure 6.1 Iwona Petry as Włoszka and Bogusław Linda as Michał in *Szamanka* (*Shaman*), 1996, dir. Andrzej Żuławski. © Canal+

pology. She moves into his flat and they almost immediately become lovers. Their first sexual encounter starts as a rape, when he throws her violently onto the bed, face down. Yet, after some time of suffering pain, her face expresses ecstasy. He, on the other hand, turns up the whites of his eyes, as if losing control of his senses and his whole body. The first lovemaking establishes a pattern: he initiates the intercourse, but she always welcomes his brutal advances. Michał's infatuation with Włoszka, which distances him from reality, is paralleled by his fascination with a shaman, whose perfectly preserved, three-thousand-years-old corpse was discovered at an archaeological excavation and transported to the university laboratory where Michał works. The archaeologist believes that the shaman died an unnatural death, as part of his brain is missing. Eventually, when drunk and hallucinating, he learns from the mummy that he was killed by a young woman, who was a more powerful shaman than he. This precipitates his decision to leave his lover and to become a Catholic priest. When he is about to leave, Włoszka kills him and then eats his brain.

As with the women in *Dad* and *With Fire and Sword*, demeanour, appearance and costume mark Włoszka out as a dangerous other. She never walks, but runs and jumps, making uncontrollable gestures with her hands. More often than speaking, she emits inarticulate, animal-like noises. When she eats, she constantly salivates, spits and vomits; she eats cat food, lying on the floor, and swallows raw meat, including dead rats, minced by a machine in the meat factory. In the end, as mentioned above, she eats the brains of her dead lover. Somehow ironically, this is the only meal which Włoszka consumes with a spoon. Otherwise, she only uses her fingers or her mouth. She clearly enjoys filth: after each meal she tries to spread the food remains all over her body and makes a mess in the house of Michał's boss.

Żuławski's heroine proves her credentials as a witch particularly strongly by her attitude to sex:[1] therefore she can be also classified as a bitch. She is never tired of lovemaking; when she does not have a partner, she masturbates. Neither is she ashamed to make love in public places: in trains, on the streets, in the hospital. There is even a scene of her making love in front of two frightened nuns, suggesting Włoszka's pagan hostility to Christian order. Michał is not her only sexual partner; she also makes love to her old boyfriend and to a colleague from the university. However, the anthropologist is the only one able to fulfil her sexual hunger. His superiority over her other lovers seems to result from his brutality and perversity. When he wants to reach her body, he usually tears off her clothes; he also forces her to perform oral sex and commits buggery on her. She reciprocates by inserting a piece of raw meat into her vagina and asking Michał to eat it. Włoszka uses her external beauty to attract men, and later she uses her sexual power to destroy them. One of her lovers, a shy student, who wanted to marry her, is killed by a tram when he pursues her on his motorcycle.

While the narrative demonstrates that Włoszka is a victor over Michał and men in general, other aspects of the film, especially *mise-en-scène*, point of view and casting suggests otherwise: that she is a victim. Włoszka spends most of the time in her rented apartment, which is ugly and cramped. Some of the furniture is covered with dust sheets, suggesting that she is not allowed to use them, that she does not control her own space. Being confined, she is condemned to passivity. Włoszka is energetic, but her activity is constrained and futile, like the movements of a lion, locked in his cage. There is also a difference of levels between the characters: Włoszka is usually positioned lower than Michał, crouching on the floor, lying on a bed, sitting on the toilet. She looks at Michał from below, he looks at her from above. Jan Olszewski compares it to a dog–master relationship (Olszewski 1996: 63). Bogusław Linda, the most charismatic Polish actor of his generation (who also took the main part in *Dad*), plays Michał. 'He brings to the film his myth of a physically and emotionally strong man, who always gets what he wants,' writes Olszewski. 'Włoszka, on the other hand, is played by a young person with no acting experience' (ibid.). Moreover, Linda's acting is very narcisstic and on the verge of camp. He parodies his roles as a man whom women cannot resist but who finds them boring.

Still, Włoszka is atypical of Polish 'witches' and 'bitches' because she possesses some power over men. Other women of these kinds in Polish postcommunist films are devoid of any authority. If they are young and attractive, they happily submit to the desires of men who are often much older than them, as do female characters in *Dogs*, *Słodko gorzki* (*Bittersweet*, 1996), directed by Władysław Pasikowski, *Chłopaki nie płaczą* (*Boys Don't Cry*, 2000), directed by Olaf Lubaszenko, *Sara* (1997), directed by Maciej Ślesicki, and Kasia's teacher (Renata Dancewicz) in *Dad*, becoming nothing more than men's dispensable, erotic toys. In the best case their function is to ease men's tensions that result from performing dangerous or responsible jobs. Their inferior status is often conveyed by their nicknames, such as Suczka, meaning Little Bitch in *The Dark Side of Venus*, or Cycofon – Large Breasts – in *Boys Don't Cry*. Sometimes they are rewarded for their erotic service to men with money, free lodging and consumer goods; Michał in *Dad* buys a foreign bra for his daughter's teacher, who agrees to spend a night with him. However, it is up to the men to decide if and how they will reward their lovers. If the 'bitches' are older, like Rysia (Katarzyna Figura) in *Kiler* (1997), directed by Juliusz Machulski, Telimena in *Pan Tadeusz*, Ewa (Agnieszka Wagner) in *The Dark Side of Venus* and Diana (Katarzyna Figura) in *Autoportret z kochanką* (*Self-portrait with a Lover*, 1997), directed by Radosław Piwowarski (Figure 6.2), they struggle to seduce men simply by using their looks. Sometimes they even beg them or bribe them with money to 'take them', ending as undignified or ridiculous figures and parodies of their younger selves. Apart from 'bitches' who go to bed with men for free, we find a large number of prostitutes in Polish postcommunist narratives. Examples are *Prostytutki* (*Prostitutes*, 1998), directed by Eugeniusz Priwiezencew, *Billboard* (1998), directed by Łukasz Zadrzyński and *Reich* (2000), directed by Władysław Pasikowski. Their proliferation does not mean, however, that men who use paid services cannot find women who will have sex with them for free, but rather signifies the male desire to separate sex from their proper lives, which is led in a masculine environment. Prostitutes allow heterosexual men to fulfil those needs which only women can meet without a requirement to show their partners any real gratitude. To put it another way, thanks to prostitutes men achieve two objectives at once: sexual gratification and moral authority to keep the women who served them in contempt.

In Polish postcommunist films we find no equivalent of Sharon Stone's Catherine Trammel in *Basic Instinct* (1992), directed by Paul Verhoeven, or Bridget in *The Last Seduction* (1993), directed by John Dahl – namely, a woman who consciously uses her charms to her advantage and has control

Figure 6.2 Katarzyna Figura as Diana and Waldemar
Błaszczyk as Kuba in *Autoportret z kochanką* (*Self-
portrait with a Lover*), 1997, dir. Radosław
Piwowarski © Wojciech Staroń

over her lovers and the narrative (see Stables 1998). Eroticism in the new
Polish cinema tends to disgrace and disempower women, placing them at
the margin of society. There is also little chance of finding in this paradigm
any women who combine sex appeal with brains: for Polish male directors
these two characteristics are mutually exclusive.

Imprisoned Princesses and Ignorant Wives

In many films, both contemporary and those set in the distant past,
'witches' and 'bitches' are juxtaposed either with virginal or with nurturing
women. Typically the virgins are at least as attractive as the 'bitches', but

their sexuality is subdued, playing only a minimal role in the film's narrative and ideology. The virgins tend to be much younger than their erotic or dangerous rivals. In *With Fire and Sword*, for example, Horpyna, who is depicted as an old witch, is contrasted with the young and beautiful Helena Kurcewiczówna, who is the object of the erotic desire of the Cossack, Bohun and the Polish nobleman, Jan Skrzetuski. In *Pan Tadeusz* Telimena, who desperately tries to find a husband before middle age exposes her wrinkles, meticulously hidden under her make-up, competes for the heart of the eponymous Pan Tadeusz with Zosia, who has barely reached womanhood. Women of the second type, consisting of wives and mothers, are usually significantly older, but there is little real difference between the virgins and the nurturing women, as all live for and through men, having almost no independence or control over their own fate. The virginal women can be described as 'nurturing women in waiting', as it is suggested that in the near future they will get married and have children. Their subordination to men is often conveyed by their physical confinement and their muteness. Hence, Helena rarely leaves her bedroom where she dreams about her beloved Skrzetuski. Moreover, she often faints and spends long days in bed, weak, sick, exhausted and completely mute. Zosia, who is depicted as an unsophisticated 'child of nature', hardly ventures outside her garden.

Similarly, wives and mothers rarely venture beyond the domestic sphere; they tend to have no other occupation than looking after home and children. This rule governs the lives of the wives of decent men as much as those of criminals. Michael Stevenson observes that the family of the high-ranking gangster Gross (Janusz Gajos) in Pasikowski's *Dogs* is

> no ordinary family. In seven shots and thirty seconds we are shown the 'perfect' family (at least for a certain type of masculinity). It is entirely female. The blond and elegant young mother has three highly feminised daughters, intelligent, but certainly aware of themselves in the role of Daddy's girls. This marks a radical separation in the text between public and private spheres ... Male and female are strictly demarcated. In Gross' ideal family there is both a sense of the privatised bourgeois life but also something more disturbing. I am particularly reminded (given the brutal certainties of Gross' character) of the radical separation within Fascism between '*Kinder, Kuche, Kirche*' and external male activity, definitely not for women. (Stevenson 2000: 143)

Such a separation between home and male external activity is the norm in Polish films made after 1989. Sometimes men tend to keep their partners and wives in ignorance about their lives as a way of protecting them from possible dangers and anxieties. This is the case in *Dług* (*Debt*, 1999), directed by Krzysztof Krauze, in which two entrepreneurial protagonists, who fall prey to a loan shark, keep their respective wife and girlfriend in ignorance about their situation because they believe it will spare them unnecessary worry and disappointment. This assumption, however, proves false. Male secrecy precipitates a serious crisis in their families. Moreover, the men cannot keep their affairs secret for ever: the truth is eventually revealed, causing recriminations on the part of the women and almost leading to the break-up of their relationships. Krauze even suggests that if the women were better informed and more involved in the professional lives of their partners, they could help them to avoid disaster.

In the majority of postcommunist films the separation of wives and girlfriends from the lives of their partners is not discussed, but taken for granted, as if it is the natural order of things. Such separation allows male characters to lead a double life, including having mistresses and one-night stands, without risking being criticised or divorced by one's partner. Take, for example, Paweł Mayer (Radosław Pazura) in Władysław Pasikowski's *Operacja Samum* (*Samum Operation*, 1999), who while working in Iraq has an affair with a female Mossad agent and ends up in prison. Once his problems are solved and the affair is finished, his father advises him not to mention anything to his wife back in Poland, as if nothing had happened. Wives and girlfriends who accept being kept in the dark about their husbands' and partners' activities, are typically rewarded with life in material comfort and idleness. In common with 'bitches', but to an even greater extent, wives in Polish postcommunist films are represented as ardent consumers.

It is worth drawing attention to the fact that while men usually succeed in having a double life, women are punished if they attempt the same. Take, for example, Agata (Ewa Bukowska), the wife of Kroll in the film of the same title (1991), directed by Władysław Pasikowski, who has an affair with her husband's friend when Kroll does his military service. Her unfaithfulness is not only exposed, but results in multiple tragedies, involving her husband, her lover and herself. The obvious lesson to be drawn from the respective films is that there are two moral and sexual codes in Poland: one for men and another for women.

Men do not always choose a pure woman over an erotic one. As was previously mentioned, Michał in *Shaman* abandons his well-mannered and faithful fiancée to devote his time completely to the wild and promiscuous Włoszka. A similar situation occurs in *The Early Spring*, whose protagonist, Cezary Baryka (Mateusz Damięcki), gives up on virginal Karusia (Urszula Grabowska), who is his best friend's orphaned cousin, to pursue a romance with Laura (Małgorzata Lewińska), a widow engaged to another man. However, choosing a 'bitch' over a virgin is always perilous for the man. Not only does he lose a woman who would be an excellent wife and mother, but he finds no happiness living with a 'bitch' or a 'witch'. Such an outcome suggests that in no circumstances should men discard their patriarchal role; however, they are allowed to combine it with pursuing more dangerous pleasures.

In heritage films the narrative role and ideological function of the older, witch-like women increased in comparison with the literary originals and earlier films, based on classics of Polish literature, while the role of young and noble women decreased. Helena Kurcewiczówna in *With Fire and Sword*, whom her sinister aunt (Ewa Wiśniewska) tries to deprive of her estate, does not have any opinion in this matter. Neither does she mind what happens to her family or her country. The only thing she seems to care about is who her future husband will be. In her passivity and lack of wider interests Helena provides a striking contrast to the heroines of the two remaining parts of Sienkiewicz's *Trilogy* and their screen adaptations, which were also made by Jerzy Hoffman: Basia (Magdalena Zawadzka) in *Pan Wołodyjowski* (1968) and Oleńka (Małgorzata Braunek) in *Potop* (*Flood*, 1974). The first was represented as good at horse-riding, knowing how to use a sword and having a good sense of humour, almost a tomboy. Moreover, Basia, unlike most of the women of her generation, was not passive in love, but fought for the heart of the man whom she found attractive. She even declared her love for him first. Oleńka in *Flood* was very serious and patriotic; for her marriage was not a question of romance, but of choosing an honourable man who would serve his country perfectly.

At the end of this section it is worth adding that in a significant number of films made after 1989 we find the type of woman who does not fit the standards of either a passive and silly bimbo or an active, but dangerous, 'witch'. This type is the famous Polish Mother. She can be found both in historical and, albeit more rarely, in contemporary films, but, as argued in Chapter 2, she was either regarded by the audience as utterly anachronistic, as in Zaorski's *Panny i wdowy* (*Maidens and Widows*, 1991), or relegated to the margin of the narrative, as in Pasikowski's *Kroll*, demonstrating, that, as Ostrowska put it, 'a mother is not needed any longer'.

Looking in Vain for a Partner and Father for One's Child

In the films that reject generic rules, particularly those made by first-time directors, sexism and gender stereotyping, which is regarded as a staple diet for the audiences of gangster and heritage films, is much less widespread. The most interesting of them adopt a female point of view, asking the question how Polish women imagine their relationship with men and what they expect from life. Examples are *Przystań* (*Haven*, 1997), directed by Jan Hryniak (Figure 6.3), *Patrzę na ciebie Marysiu* (*I Look at You, Mary*, 1999), directed by Łukasz Barczyk and *Portret podwójny* (*Double Portrait*, 2001), directed by Mariusz Front. All these films draw attention to male inadequacy and women's disappointments with men.

Karolina (Maja Ostaszewska) in Hryniak's film is a young woman who is working as a teacher in an after-school club in a provincial part of Poland. She regards her life as grey and empty, and dreams about living somewhere else. Such a chance appears when she meets Jan (Rafał Królikowski), a young businessman from Warsaw who comes to her town

Figure 6.3 Rafał Królikowski as Jan and Maja Ostaszewska as Karolina in *Przystań* (*Haven*), 1997, dir. Jan Hryniak © TVP, photo: Witold Płóciennik

on a training course for young entrepreneurs. They fall in love and soon Karolina leaves for Warsaw, followed by her twelve-year-old pupil, Szymek (Tomasz Popławski), who is in love with her. There, however, Karolina discovers that Jan has no interests apart from making and spending money. She leaves him, disgusted by his materialistic attitude, by which Jan hoped to impress her, and the colourful but soulless Warsaw, and returns with Szymek to her home town and unglamorous job.

The eponymous Mary (Marysia) (Maja Ostaszewska) in Barczyk's film is a geology student; her boyfriend Michał (Michał Bukowski) works as a junior hospital psychiatrist. Despite being a couple for seven years, they started to live together only two years previously, presumably in rented accommodation. Moreover, they admit that they are still supported financially by their parents. There is no doubt that for Michał this dependence creates a significant problem, affecting his self-confidence and the way he thinks about the future. He prefers to avoid commitments, especially having a family. When asked whether he would like to have children, he answers 'yes, but not yet' and admits that despite being twenty-nine years old he feels immature. No wonder he is unhappy to learn that Mary has become pregnant. He tries to persuade her to arrange an abortion, but she refuses. There follows a series of unfortunate events, such as Michał's increasing difficulties at work and a speedily arranged wedding, at which he has a mental breakdown and decides to quit his job as a psychiatrist. Of course, Marysia is very disappointed and feels betrayed by Michał. In one of the most memorable moments of the film she says, 'I love you and you torment me.'

In Hryniak and Barczyk's films, unlike those previously discussed, women are no longer associated with consumerism. For both Marysia and Karolina love and having a family are the highest values, and they are prepared to live on a modest income to achieve them. By contrast, men are very susceptible to the temptations of 'Western life' and they measure their success by the amount of money they earn. Hence, paradoxically, patriarchy is in crisis not because of selfish women who give up on children in order to pursue careers and consumerist pleasures, but due to men who refuse to be husbands and fathers. Marysia and Karolina are played by the same actress, Maja Ostaszewska, who despite her young age (b. 1972) and the modest number of films in which she has played, is regarded as one of the most distinguished Polish actresses to emerge after the collapse of the communist regime and epitomises the new generation of Polish women (as did Krystyna Janda in the previous period).[2] Ostaszewska's stardom conveys the idea that the majority of contemporary Polish women do not regard themselves either as primitive bimbos or dangerous praying mantises.

Elżbieta (Elżbieta Piekacz) in *Double Portrait* (Figure 6.4) appears to have more professional ambitions than Karolina and Marysia. She trained as an actress and intends to pursue her career in this field (the film is filled largely with scenes of auditions for films and television programmes), while supporting herself financially by working in a supermarket. Nevertheless, she also wants to have a family and a child, and in common with Marysia and Karolina encounters male resistance in this matter. Her boyfriend, Mariusz (Maciej Adamczyk), like Michał in *I Look at You, Mary*, admits to feeling immature – which primarily means refusal to take responsibility for another person. The signs of Mariusz's immaturity are also similar to that of Michał: uncertainty about his professional prospects, little money and lack of one's own place to live. He only recently graduated from film school and tries unsuccessfully to make his first film; he rents a small flat with Elżbieta and earns his living working in a supermarket. There is an additional factor why he does not want a child: a previous disappointing relationship and a small son with whom he has little contact.

Haven, and to an even greater extent *I Look at You, Mary* and *Double Portrait*, have an 'unpolished' style, marked by extensive use of video footage, fragmented narrative and improvised dialogue, reminiscent of the Dogme 95 films. Unlike the gangster and heritage movies of Pasikowski and Ślesicki, they come across as being true to reality, helping viewers' identification with represented characters and situations.

Unlike the three films made by the young directors, all films by Marek Koterski, including those made after the collapse of communism, such as *Ajlawju* (1999) and *Dzień świra* (*The Day of a Nutter*, 2000), concentrate

Figure 6.4 Elżbieta Piekacz as Ewa and Maciej Adamczyk as Michał in *Portret podwójny* (*Double Portrait*), 2001, dir. Mariusz Front © Wytwórnia Filmowa 'Czołówka', photo: Janusz Sus

on male subjects and present the male point of view. Moreover, Koterski's work, in common with the films made by the 'Young Wolves', is awash with deep-seated misogyny: most women in his films are intrusive, nagging, gossipy, rude, noisy, stupid, self-centred and physically unattractive. However, unlike Pasikowski or Ślesicki, Koterski does not represent Polish men as macho, nor celebrates macho masculinity. On the contrary, his main character, named either Adam or Michał Miauczyński (played respectively by Cezary Pazura and Marek Kondrat) and largely modelled on Koterski's own real life and persona, is portrayed as being insecure about their maleness, introverted and self-centred to the extent that they do not even want to risk life with a woman, however attractive she might be. In *The Day of a Nutter* this feature is presented in the imaginary episode in which Adam meets a woman from his dreams, who proposes to him that they live together. Instead of seizing this opportunity with joy and gratefulness, he rejects it, saying, 'There is no place for a woman in my life.' The symbol of both his yearning for perfect love and his inability to face its challenge is his evening ritual of masturbation, which he describes as 'barren'. Koterski's male also feels that he is unable to be a proper father. As a result of divorce he is reduced to being a 'visiting father' who does not even try to be a role model for his child. The message of Koterski's films is that Polish men prefer to perceive women as one-dimensional witches and bitches, because they are not up to the challenge of living with attractive, intelligent and altruistic women; they will inevitably squander such a chance.

The decline of patriarchy – understood as the power exercised by a man over a woman and children through being their defender and breadwinner – to which films discussed in this section refer, is, as Barbara Ehrenreich maintains, widespread in Western societies, particularly American (see Ehrenreich 1995), but there is an important difference between the situation described by Ehrenreich and that depicted in Polish films. In the latter, a man's agreement to take care of his family appears to be a conditio sine qua non of a woman's decision to have a child. Young Polish women feel too weak economically and emotionally to have them on their own. Paradoxically, the more strongly patriarchy is promoted by the law and other institutions in Poland, and the more 'the family' is edified in official discourse, the less patriarchy and the weaker families we find in real life.

It is worth emphasising that *Haven*, *I Look at You*, *Mary* and *Double Portrait* (and several others of similar ideology) were made at the end of the first decade of the new political order, when audiences started to be bored with the macho films of Pasikowski and his younger colleagues. Despite limited distribution they gained notable recognition and even inspired a discussion about the state and direction of Polish cinema. In the light of their success one can risk the statement that perhaps the future of Polish cinema will be more gender-balanced than appeared after the collapse of communism.

Note

1. There are many perceptive studies of the witch as a sexual predator. See, for instance, Kristeva 1982; Creed 1993.
2. The high status of Ostaszewska is testified by several important awards which she received in Poland, including awards for best actress at the 1998 and 2000 Polish Film Festival in Gdynia.

CHAPTER 7

Between Fear and Attraction: Images of 'Other' Women

ELŻBIETA OSTROWSKA

Conceptualising woman as Other is widely regarded as an element constituting patriarchal discourse. As Simone de Beauvoir noticed a long time ago, man considers himself as a norm that is to be inevitably violated by woman. This presumes not only the inferior status of woman, but also, when cinematic images of femininity are at stake, provides the very basis for a metaphorical construction of women's representations in cultural signifying practices. Teresa de Lauretis writes: '*Woman*, the other-from-man (nature and Mother, site of sexuality and masculine desire, sign and object of men's exchange), is the term that designates at once the vanishing point of our culture's fictions of itself and the condition of the discourses in which the fictions are represented' (de Lauretis 1984: 5). It is clear that the notion of woman as Other is based almost exclusively on the notion of sexual difference which was crucial to the feminist critique of representations in 1960s and 1970s. Nowadays this approach is widely criticised as leading to an essentialist notion of femininity. Almost every piece of contemporary feminist writing emphasises that gender cannot be regarded as the sole factor constructing woman's identity, since such components as race, ethnicity, religion, class, nationality, etc. also play an important role in this process (see, for example, Davis 1981). This shift in feminist theory by no means undermines the concept of woman as Other, but rather allows an analysis of its complexity and heterogeneity.

My intention here is to consider woman as Other in relation to Polish postwar cinema. There are few Polish films made during the period of communism representing ethnic, racial or national minorities in Polish society. This absence reflects to a significant extent the demographic changes resulting from the Second World War. Prewar Poland was a multinational and multicultural country with large communities of Jews, Lithuanians, Ukrainians, Germans and Belorussians, and with a diversity of religions. As a result of the Holocaust and, in 1945, the politics of the Yalta Treaty it was transformed into a relatively homogeneous state. Despite all these political transformations and the compulsory displacement of people representing different minorities, some of them decided to stay in Poland even if life there was supposed to be hard and dominated by the mainstream Polish culture. However, the presence of minorities was mostly silenced in public discourses, because it was felt that the exposing national, ethnic and religious differences could undermine the desired unity of communist society. The collective as well as individual identity had to be defined through social class whilst other factors were dismissed as much as possible. Minorities became part of the 'unrepresented world' in Polish cinema. Although the figures of Jew, Ukrainian and Gypsy functioned as images of the Other in Polish collective consciousness, and open acts of hostility towards those remaining took place, none of these conflicts were articulated in contemporaneous Polish films. In Poland the new political occupation replaced the binary opposition We/They usually built upon ethnic, gender or racial difference. The position of 'They' was ascribed to the communist authorities, who were seen as the Other against whom the collective hostility was to be directed. No doubt, this meant a double oppression for all the remaining minorities who inhabited Poland at the time as, firstly, they were subjected to communist power and, secondly, they were marginalised by the dominant society. However, it should be noted that representatives of some minorities, mostly Jewish, as members of the communist regime occupied a position of political power. Clearly, being both Jew and communist (żydokomuna) doubled their Otherness (see Bilewicz and Pawlisz 2000).

The communists' attempts to erase diversity was supposed to create a homogeneous entity of unity of proletarians all over the world. Filmmakers colluded with this and always populated their fictional worlds with Polish characters when contemporary reality was to be depicted. The remaining diversity of Polish society was represented only in films concerning historical issues, or whose action took place in the prewar period. Interestingly, the Jewish community was represented most often. This was due to the fact that the Jewish minority, at three million persons, was the largest in prewar Poland and also due to the fact that the figure of a Jew was an archetypal image of the Other in Polish national culture. As Bożena Umińska writes:

> It seems that almost always the figure of a Jewish man or woman in Polish literature bears the stamp of distinctiveness. The power of the stereotype was very strong and it is difficult to imagine an author who, in introducing a character of a Jew, would treat it in a neutral way, that it would not relate – in any way – to the common horizon of knowledge shared with the readers. (Umińska 2001: 5)

It is worth noting that these images of Jews in Polish culture often function as a contrast to the primary and privileged self-image of Polish society. Jewish female characters are doubly estranged, both in reference to their ethnic background and their gender. These aspects strengthen and justify the fear of Otherness in the Polish collective consciousness. In order to approach this issue I will focus on those films that depict Jewish women as being in opposition to the construction of femininity created and developed in the Polish national discourse, which has its perfect embodiment in the myth of the Polish Mother (see Chapter 1).

If the myth of the Polish Mother is capable of supporting dominant notions of Polishness, it was made possible through a series of overlapping binary oppositions. The masculine/feminine opposition is only one of them. The sub-opposition of Polish femininity/Other femininity also often appears. Jewish femininity has been employed as a particularly significant contrast to Polish femininity in order to emphasise its supposedly positive features. It is also clear that both images of femininity are to be related to notions of Polish masculinity. The question: 'Who is the Other woman and what is she like?' is an indispensable element in defining both dominant constructions of femininity and masculinity in any culture. Therefore, an analysis of Jewish women's representations in Polish cinema will shed light on broader aspects of national gender construction.

In examining appropriate films, two basic critical strategies will be employed. First, I will focus on the methods, visual as well as narrative, that are used to stigmatise Jewish women as Other. Second, I will examine the ideological dimensions of this construction of femininity. I have decided to focus my analysis on Andrzej Wajda's *Ziemia obiecana* (*The Promised Land*, 1974), referring also, when necessary, to other films, such as *Wielki Tydzień* (*Holy Week*, 1995) also by Wajda, *Jeszcze tylko ten las* (*Just Beyond this Forest*, 1991) by Jan Łomnicki, *Pożegnanie z Marią* (*Farewell to Maria*, 1993) by Filip Zylber and *Deborah* (1995) by Ryszard Brylski. The chapter will conclude with an analysis of Jan Jakub Kolski's film, *Daleko od okna* (*Far From the Window*, 2000), which examines the relationship between Polish and Jewish femininity dominant in Polish cinema.

Visibility of 'Otherness'

The Promised Land (Figure 7.1), based on Władysław Stanisław Reymont's novel, presents a conflict between personalities of women of three nationalities: Polish, Jewish and German, against the background of the rapid growth of capitalism in Poland in the nineteenth century. Its action takes place in Łódź – the main area of German and Jewish economic expansion. The principal character, an impoverished nobleman, Karol Borowiecki (Daniel Olbrychski), cooperates with his friends, a Jew, Moryc Welt

Figure 7.1 Daniel Olbrychski as Karol Borowiecki and Kalina Jędrusik as Lucy Zucker in *Ziemia obiecana* (*The Promised Land*), 1974, dir. Andrzej Wajda © Studio Filmowe 'Perspektywa'

(Wojciech Pszoniak) and a German, Maks Baum (Andrzej Seweryn). They decide to build a factory that, it is hoped, will overcome the monopoly of foreign capital. Borowiecki has close relationships with three women. His fiancée Anka (Anna Nehrebecka), also from the impoverished nobility, lives with Karol's father in Kurów, the family manor-house. Lucy Zucker (Kalina Jędrusik), the wife of one of the richest Jewish factory owners, is his mistress. Finally, there is Mada Müller (Bożena Dykiel), daughter of a German factory owner, whom he finally marries for the sake of her immense dowry. Both the novel and the film use the main character to represent the destruction of values typical of the ethos of the Polish nobility. The female characters are used as metaphors, representing the stages of this process.

Wajda employs an expressionist style, which, through its excessiveness, endows his cinematic images with the traits of caricature. The female characters are introduced in such a way that at the very beginning they are fully characterised and fixed in a specific semantic area, which does not change till the end of the story. Subsequent scenes merely confirm those features of a character's personality, attributed to them when they first appear.

It is clear, in comparing the scenes when Anka and Lucy appear, that they are in striking opposition to one another. It is worth mentioning that Wajda significantly alters the literary original by changing the order of introducing the female characters. In the film Anka appears in the first scene, in the background for the credits. In the novel this scene is found later on, in the second volume. As a result of the director's decision, Anka is positioned as a primary and stable reference point for all the later female representations. The opening shots of Anka and Karol are not logically linked to later episodes. They are rather a series of sentimental and nostalgic pictures of a quiet life in the countryside, in harmony with a benign natural world. Without dialogue, with the lyrical motif of waltz on the soundtrack, they symbolise all those values that in the national mythology stand for a perfect and noble Poland. The first shot of Anka shows her running out of the house to meet Karol, the house that in the Polish system of representation functions as part of the myth of the Motherland. This visual message is verbalised in the subsequent scene, when Maks Baum says, 'Since I began to visit this place I understand Karol and Poles better.' Not Łódź and its Polish inhabitants, but a manor-house, evoking the gentry tradition, are, in the German young man's eyes, the 'real Poland'.

Anka's blonde hair (in the novel the character has dark hair), blue eyes, modest buttoned-up dress with a white lace collar perfectly fit the national icon of femininity. This iconic aspect of the heroine's character is to be understood both literally and figuratively, as she is mute throughout the opening sequence. This contrasts her to the male characters whose voices are audible, although their conversation is rather banal and has no significance in terms of plot development. One can hear dogs barking, making the scene appear realistic. Anka's silent image rather belongs to the realm of myth. Anka becomes a nurturing woman, who, as Janey Place notes, is 'linked to the pastoral environment of open spaces, light and safety characterised by even, flat high-key lighting. Often this is an idealised dream of the past and she exists only in memory, but sometimes this idealisation exists as a real alternative' (Place 1998: 60–61).

Paul Coates writes that, 'The shifting ... of the idyllic opening of volume 2 to the film's beginning makes the subsequent passage to Łódź seem like an expulsion from Eden...' (Coates 1997: 224). Indeed, these apocalyptic images of urban life develop into a vision of a modern inferno, the world of Lucy Zucker. She appears on the screen for the first time when she telephones from her boudoir to the factory where Karol works. She is shown in two shots alternated with dark images of grey and gloomy factory halls lit with a cool blue light. Whereas Anka is associated with nature and tranquillity, Lucy remains in a dehumanised industrial world dominated by ruthless greed for money. What is more, her appearance is also in strong contrast to Anka. In the first shot she is seen at a distance lying in her underwear on the sofa in her boudoir. A track in to medium close-up allows the viewer a closer look. We see long dark flowing hair, naked arms, the clear shape of breasts under her lace dressing gown, the intensive make-up of her sensual lips and dark brown eyes. What mostly attracts the viewer's attention, however, is her body, or rather its abundance; one has an impression that it overflows the laces of her dressing gown, a sharp contrast to

Anka's buttoned-up dress. Apparently, Lucy connotes an eroticism impossible to restrain. Her passionate first sentence: 'Karl, I love you', makes her eroticism expansive and rapacious.

Lucy's second appearance on the screen places her sexuality in a troubling context. The action of the scene takes place in a theatre, where all the textile moguls gather with their families. The women's luxurious clothes and rich jewels create a spectacle to rival that on the stage, equally to be objectified and looked at. Karol scornfully scans through his opera-glass this exhibition of male possessions, signified by diamonds ornamenting women's necks, foreheads, ears and wrists. Lucy particularly catches his attention. She notices Karol's gaze and responds to it with vehement pleasure, leaning out of the box to make her body more visible to him. Finally, they exchange a passionate smile. His voyeuristic gaze and her exhibitionist pleasure in being the object of the former seem to be an element of an erotic game. Her role as a sexual object is confirmed by Maks: 'What a pretty piece of a woman is this Lucy Zucker.' 'What a beautiful diamond!', Moryc, Karol's Jewish friend, adds with admiration, slipping smoothly from sexuality to commodity. The discursive intertwining of these two areas soon develops when secret business news reaches the theatre, disrupting the pleasant atmosphere of the evening. Karol and his friends, not belonging to the inner circle of the cotton establishment, have no access to this knowledge. The secret telegram conveying this information is inadvertently left by Lucy's husband, who has hastily quit the theatre. With the telegram she now has unquestionable power, which she uses to seduce Karol. During the following erotic scene, which takes place in a cab, the sexual fulfilment gained by the hero is juxtaposed with his joy in the hope of future material benefits.

The visual contrasting of Polish and Jewish women can also be observed in the other films. In *Holy Week*, where the action takes place in Warsaw in 1944, during the ghetto's liquidation, Irena Lilien (Beata Fudalej), a young Jewish woman, meets her former acquaintance (or possibly her lover), Jan Malecki (Wojciech Malajkat), who decides to give her a hand. Irena is a dark-haired young woman dressed in smart clothes (her silk stockings are signs of both her sex appeal and previous wealth). Her neat hairstyle and make-up complete the image of an elegant and attractive young woman. The appearance of Malecki's wife (Magdalena Warzecha) seems to be in visual opposition. She has long blonde hair in a simple plait, blue eyes, no make-up, and a simple dress that covers her pregnant body. At the meeting of these two women the contrast of clothes is striking. Malecki notices it as well, as he asks his wife: 'Why have you put on this dress? You look awful in it.' Again, costume and make-up connote either sexual attractiveness or lack of it, and this differentiation will turn out to be an essential factor determining plot development. In Zylber's *Farewell to Maria* the characters of Polish and Jewish women are similarly visually contrasted.

By and large, in these films elements of *mise-en-scène* are used as signifiers of a woman's sexuality, respectively drawing upon two different mythologised images of femininity originating from a long cultural tradition: the archetypes of Lilith from the Bible, the symbol of animal sexuality, and the Virgin Mary, whose body is sublime due to the Immaculate Conception.

In *The Promised Land* the visual contrast is the more conspicuous as it has its equivalent in the narrative structure, intensified through editing. The scenes of Anka and Lucy are montaged in parallel to make deliberate comparisons. The recurrence of these contrasted images of Lucy and Anka build a tension leading to a climax. This comes when Karol decides to accompany Lucy on a train journey to Berlin. By turns there are orgiastic erotic scenes between Karol and Lucy and shots showing Anka attempting to part two copulating dogs and, later, as she engages in the role of a true lady, in playing the piano. It is worth noting that none of these scenes comes from the novel: they were added by the director. Their introduction results in a stronger antinomial positioning of women characters than in Reymont's novel. I deliberately described the scene between Lucy and Karol as orgiastic. The erotic behaviour of the female character (Karol is relatively passive) is particularly stressed during the sensual feast they enjoy. One can find many examples of this phenomenon in cinema, and the result is nearly always the same, leading to exposing the physiological aspect of these human acts. Thus female eroticism in *The Promised Land* is reduced to the sexual instinct, which, not subordinate to reason, becomes a destructive force, endangering masculinity. In the parallel scene with the dogs, Anka acts as a super-ego of femininity, controlling her own sexuality, as well as trying to tame it in the world of nature. Metaphorically, she acts in judgement on Lucy's abandonment to illicit pleasure.

The comparison of the filmic images of Jewish and Polish women in *The Promised Land* and other films enables an opposition through the range and kind of sexuality they represent. In the cinematic representations of Jewish women there is an excess of sexuality that condemns them to play the role of a sexual object in the narrative. Showing their sexuality as primitive and expansive motivates and excuses the sexual violence and contempt of men against them.

What is interesting is that Jewish male characters in Wajda's film, in contrast to their female counterparts, are almost entirely deprived of sexual power. Lucy's husband has been unable to impregnate her after several years of marriage, yet this appears a relatively easy 'task' for Karol. Moryc Welt is, in turn, provided with explicit stereotypical homosexual features signifying his 'impotence'. Other Jewish male characters are more or less ridiculed figures, diminishing their sexuality. Karol is the only one able to face Jewish woman's sexual desire and fulfil it.

Polish women in these films are characterised by a lack of sexuality. They are reduced solely to procreativity. Here an analogy with *film noir* comes to mind, namely the two models of femininity represented in the genre, in which, as Janey Place claims: 'woman ... is defined by her sexuality: the dark lady has access to it and the virgin does not' (Place 1998: 47). Reference to this generic convention is also noticeable in plot development, which I will examine later.

It is a common practice in many cultural discourses to metaphorise the Other woman as a repository of sexuality in connection with race or an ethnic group to which she belongs (see, for example, Hall 1991: 230; Oleksy 1998: 80–83). Thus the filmic representations described here are nothing exceptional. Yet, it is worth pointing to specific elements in the Polish system of representation, which have formed a model of sexuality in which woman is Other. As I have mentioned before, what influenced it most was the myth of the Polish Mother, the dominant model of femininity developed in Polish dominant cultural discourse. Among many factors shaping this myth I would like to draw attention to the religious one. The analysis of representations of this myth in Polish art enable one to see how strongly they were based on the tradition of representation of the Virgin Mary. Using this representative model inevitably led to a desexualisation of images of women in Polish mainstream art. Conditioned by a collective historical experience, the individual experience of Polish women, who expected to lose their husbands and fiancés in the numerous uprisings, resulted in what I would call 'a secondary virginity', a punished and suffering representation.

The problem of gender identity does not refer only to women, but to men as well. This originates from particular historical and political circumstances. In partitioned Poland, deprived of the institutions of male power for nearly 150 years, the traditional patriarchal position of men had been seriously undermined. The lack of connection for so long between individual male power and state power has had, as Peggy Watson claims, a frustrating effect on them, leading to a kind of emasculation (Watson 1993: 485).

By and large, one can discern in Polish cultural discourse, because of particular historical circumstances and political factors, the attenuation and blurring of gender role distinctions in terms of individual, as well as collective, self-recognition. Repressing sexual difference within the dominating gender discourse has led to its relocation in areas of feminine marginality, which are defined by racial, ethnic, religious or class Otherness. The Otherness of women's sexuality in these areas was intensified, and at the same time men's fear of it was hidden under the exigencies of other historical pressures. An endangered collective national identity was the reason for the specific fear of the unknown, marked by an excessive rendering of Jewish female Otherness. The plots of these films not only express this fear, but also fully support it.

A common element linking these films is their use of tragic endings, the consequence of the presence of the Other woman and the destructive influence of her sexual power over man. In *The Promised Land*, Lucy Zucker is responsible for the moral fall of Karol Borowiecki, another deviation from the literary original. This is connected with an adoption of the convention of the gangster film by Wajda, noted by Ewelina Nurczyńska-Fidelska (1998: 118–26). He alludes to this generic form using a convention of *film noir* in the construction of the female characters. Wajda assigns the Jewess the role of the *femme fatale* in causing the hero's failure. As Nurczyńska-Fidelska writes: 'Lucy Zucker, a beautiful and sentimental Jewish woman in the novel, makes Karol fall in love with her, but in the film this love-affair becomes a wild passion where sexual desire dominates feelings' (1998: 120). Mildly troubling in the novel, the love affair with Lucy is disastrous for Karol in Wajda's film. During his journey with his mistress to Berlin, her husband takes revenge, setting fire to Borowiecki's factory, thus precipitating his bankruptcy. The only solution for Karol, if he wants to keep his position in the Łódź world of 'cotton celebrities', is to marry Mada Müller, primitive and unattractive, yet with a huge dowry. Karol's moral fall is completed in the last scene of the film, when he orders that protesting workers be shot. The only value that Wajda finally validates in his film is male friendship, which, on the contrary, is questioned by Reymont. In the novel the arson attack is not fully explained. Karol's problems partly result from the intrigues and the disloyalty of his friend Moryc Welt. It is clear that Wajda transforms this plot material into a male narrative, in which the antagonistic element is a 'bad woman'. As this model of treacherous femininity was absent from the prevailing national discourse on the purity of Polish womanhood, it had to be relocated in the marginal Jewess. The destructive power ascribed to a Jewish woman because of her sexuality can be easily extended to the supposedly destructive role of Jews in the history of the Polish nation in general, attributed to them by many Poles.

Another Wajda film, *Holy Week*, negotiates this element in the collective consciousness. Piotrowska, one of the inhabitants of the villa where Irena Lilien finds shelter, represents this attitude. She is deeply convinced that the presence of a Jewish woman in their house will bring bad luck to all (this opinion was not irrational, as during the Second World War people were sentenced to death for giving shelter to Jews). The bias against Irena Lilien becomes personal, because her presence threatens the stability of Piotrowska's marriage. Her husband is obsessed by this young and attractive Jewish woman. However, Wajda presents this fascination as a result of the innocent behaviour of Irena herself, who appears on the balcony wearing only underwear, exposing her body to the spring sun. Irena's sexuality makes her, in Piotrowska's husband's eyes, an object of erotic desire. She protests his advances and he rapes her. Wajda presents a parallel line of action when another neighbour's young daughter falls from a balcony, an action which Piotrowska witnesses. She is convinced that it is Irena's presence that has caused this tragic accident. She rushes into the neighbour's flat and brutally forces Irena to leave. When Irena is beyond the gate, the unconscious child miraculously comes round and opens her eyes. Before leaving, the Jewess curses all the inhabitants of the house, wishing them the fate experienced by the Jews. The last scene of the film, in which the male hero is shot while taking Irena's things from the house she previously lived in, becomes a sign of this curse.

Wajda's *Holy Week* is an example of a text showing the internal contradiction between the area of explicit and symptomatic meanings. Despite the fact that the author's intention was to demonstrate Christian love and the Polish intelligentsia's liberalism, ultimately Piotrowska's anti-Jewish phobia dominates the film (see Madej 1996: 131). Despite her brutal expulsion from the tenement, Irena is not finally doomed, whereas the male hero's death is presented as if a result of her curse. Thus the viewer might be convinced that the direct reason for this death is the Other woman.

This narrative solution one can find in other Polish films. For example, Ryszard Brylski's *Deborah* (1995) ends similarly. The film tells the story of a secret love affair between a Polish painter and a Jewess whom he shelters during the war. He dies, shot in the street by the Germans. In *Farewell to Maria* and *Just Beyond This Forest* the main female characters' death is also linked with help given to Jewish woman and girl. Independently of the realistic motivation of such plots (such events actually took place during the war), all the cases mentioned here deal with the implicit fear of the Other woman and the conviction about her fatal influence on every person who comes into contact with her. This subconscious collective anxiety is released and partially rationalised by means of fictional stories.

The Otherness of Jewish women, represented in the films examined here, is due to the linked factors of gender and race. Although the Jewish woman arouses fear and is rejected, she is a necessary point of reference to a construction of collective and individual identity. The setting of a series of binary oppositions, distinctly separating Us and Them, helps this process of self-recognition and is one of the conditions for constructing a model of identity.

As I have mentioned above, the Polish historical-political experience strengthened the national-racial-religious structuring of the We/They opposition. A more familiar masculine/feminine opposition was weakened and overshadowed by the national cause. This fracturing in the construction process of male subjectivity was the consequence of the partial elimination of sexual difference from the dominating cultural discourse. Therefore, in the structures of male narratives, exemplified by these films, sexual difference is located in Other femininity. As Eva Feder-Kittay states:

> The Other Other is a woman who, like the mother, is female but unlike the mother, comes from some group already marked by salient differences – differences conceptualised as threatening or desirable, as imbuing its bearers with power or rendering them vulnerable prey. Sexual transgressions along the lines of class and race invite dangerous excitement, even disaster, but also

allow men ... who are regarded as One to affirm their mastery or assert their sexuality – especially where upper class male is conceptualised as effete or as lacking a robust sexuality ... . The Other Other, the dark woman, The Jewess, the working-class woman is sexualised – she is conceptualised as unusually voluptuous or yielding, or as perversely exaggeratedly sexual. (1997: 275)

To conclude, placing excessive sexuality onto the Other woman allows the maintenance of the sanctity of the national myths of femininity, while also reinforcing the myth of a historically enfeebled masculinity.

Beyond Stereotypes

Jan Jakub Kolski in opposition to Andrzej Wajda, 'the essential Pole', who, according to Bolesław Michałek and Frank Turaj (1988: 129), is intimately linked in his oeuvre to the idea of the Polish Nation – since his debut *Pogrzeb kartofla (Burial of a Potato*, 1990) is concerned with the various models of Otherness and the dominant group's response to it. Thus in his *Far From the Window* he tried to transcend this one-dimensionality in representing the relationship between Polish and Jewish women. The complexity of the work comes also from its literary prototype: the short story by Hanna Krall, who authored many literary testimonies of the Holocaust.

The action of the film takes place during and after the Second World War. The Polish–Jewish relationship is presented through a complex of gender conflicts without final resolution, and continues in the lives of subsequent generations. The film begins with a close-up of a bridal veil which is followed by a close-up of a woman lying on a bed. Her gaze is directed off-screen. In the next, through her point of view shot we see the object of her look, which is a painting presenting the familiar composition of the Madonna and child. Here, however, the place where the child should be, is left empty. In this opening sequence, Kolski refers to the issue of motherhood in its relation to Catholic tradition, which, as it was demonstrated earlier (see Chapter 1), is an important factor informing the dominant discourse of Polish femininity. However, the stability of this idealised image of femininity is poignantly disturbed through the empty space on the painting that introduces the notion of absence or lack.

The motif of lack is continued in the next scene in which the newly married couple, Barbara (Dorota Landowska) and Jan (Bartosz Opania), are presented in the husband's workshop; he is a local painter who makes signboards to earn a living and who paints canvasses for himself. One can observe the couple's erotic game as he paints her face and body with different colours of oil paint. When he touches her belly with a questioning gesture, she calmly says that she is not pregnant. He does not seem to be worried because of this and jauntily says that they will try again. Barbara seems to be more concerned with this issue, as becomes clear in the next scene where she is shown as praying in front of the 'incomplete' image of holy motherhood. At once she stands up, approaches the wardrobe and takes out a baby's robe, looks at it for a while and throws it back. This situation is photographed from the interior of the wardrobe, which is a cinematographic device to be used extensively later on in the film. When Jan comes to her, she angrily accuses the unfinished painting and almost furiously asks him why he did not finish the painting. 'Looks like she couldn't either', says Barbara to her husband, who leaves the room annoyed. She continues her conversation with the Holy Virgin in the painting, demanding to be heard by her, as she should understand, herself being a mother.

In these sequences, Kolski plays a game with important elements of Polish national ideology. First, he throws into question the notion of family, which is often presented as endangered or destroyed, but this is always due to external factors, such as oppression by enemy forces, whereas here the family is presented as having 'a lack' from the very beginning. Second, the ideal model of femininity based on the myth of the Polish Mother is also questioned due to Barbara's inability to become pregnant. The experience of motherhood, ascribed to the notions of femininity and family idealised in Polish collective consciousness, is erased from the couple's life. This is symbolically reflected through the empty space in Jan's painting.

The following scene initiates a non-realistic mode of narration and introduces into the fictional world the Jewish theme. The sharp and intensive coloured image (slightly flickering like a projection of a silent movie), accompanied by loud and rhythmic music, shows a rolling empty baby carriage with a wedding portrait of Jan and Barbara inside on the front wall. The carriage is passed by a stream of Hassidic Jews carrying their belongings and walking from the opposite direction. This image, which juxtaposes the empty baby carriage and the displaced people, evokes a notion of absence that refers to both Poles and Jews.

The motif of a symbolic Polish-Jewish encounter is subsequently developed in a realistic scene in which a Polish policeman requests that Jan do 'a painting job' for the Germans. When he arrives at the place he is asked to paint over the bloody stains on the exterior wall of a building. These stains are the remnants of the execution of several Jews, a fact signalled by a bloodied armband with a Star of David, which Jan finds and hides in his pocket. Later on, after completing his 'job', he is shown sitting alone in the meadow, his face expressing the horror of what he has seen. In a close-up of his palm we can see the bloodied armband. Then he takes the penknife from his pocket and cuts the palm in which he squeezes the armband. This can be interpreted as a symbolic act of miscegenation, which prefigures the further plot development when a Jewish woman, Regina (Dominika Ostałowska), enters the couple's life.

The first encounter between the two women is presented through a series of their point of view shots. First Barbara sees Regina's legs and her suitcase on the floor, then Regina looks at Barbara. As Barbara approaches Regina, who is hidden behind a door, one can see Regina's blonde hair, red dress and black coat. Interestingly, Kolski's decision as to casting reverses the stereotypical images of Polish and Jewish femininity used in the discussed films. Dark-haired and dark-eyed Barbara does not fit the iconic type of Polish femininity, nor is blonde-haired Regina representative of the Jewish 'dark woman'. As if expecting to face Barbara's hostility, Jan provocatively introduces Regina, emphasising her Jewishness. His wife responds to the situation calmly. However, she refuses to address Regina directly, and, instead, asks Jan to invite her in. He almost forcefully takes the frightened woman into the room, but she runs back to the safer dark zone of the hall-way. In a subsequent conversation, Barbara coolly expresses her anxiety about hiding Regina, whereas her husband insists they help her.

The couple's life, which is already endangered because they are hiding a Jewish woman, becomes even more complicated when Jan and Regina have an affair and she becomes pregnant. Now everybody is entrapped in the situation. None of them can do anything to change it. If Barbara denounces Regina, she would lose her husband as well. Jan cannot leave Barbara as she might denounce Regina in seeking revenge. Clearly, Regina is the most helpless figure and has to accept anything to save her and her child's lives. Thus she accepts a decision to allow Barbara to appropriate the baby from the very beginning of the pregnancy. Using Regina as a constantly accessible model, Barbara begins to act pregnant. First, she produces symptoms of morning sickness by smoking several cigarettes at once and performs this sickness in front of a German gendarme and a Polish policeman, Jodła (Andrzej Pieczyński). She sews and then wears a fake pregnancy. Gradually, she starts to experience Regina's pregnancy in an almost mimetic way. When the latter experiences the baby's movements for the first time, Barbara mimics her gestures and words while having a Sunday walk on the main street with her husband. Her face, lit up with joy and happiness, makes her a perfect figure of an expectant mother.

Therefore, in this surrogate form the initial absence has been filled thanks to the presence of the Other woman, who in order to save her life had to vanish from the surface of the world and hide in the dark interior of the wardrobe, in which earlier Barbara stored her useless baby-robe. Regina is thus not only forbidden from entering the public space, but also within the private space of Jan's and Barbara's house she is located within marginal spaces. This position, however, provides her with a privileged point of view as she often observes what happens through a slit in the wardrobe door. However, here her gaze does not signify her subjectivity, but paradoxically, the opposite – her total objectification, as this is the only space available to her. Moreover, in situations in which she is endangered she can only look, not act. This happens, for example, when the Polish policeman, Jodła, comes to the couple to get a bribe for not denouncing them to the German authorities for hiding a Jew. In this scene, the camera takes on her point of view from inside the wardrobe. Otherwise, she is deprived of the capacity to look, as epitomised in Jan's advice: keep away from the window. This is demonstrated in the composition of numerous shots that show Jan or Barbara looking through the window and Regina hidden in the corner behind the wardrobe.

Closed in the wardrobe, or Jan's workshop, and separated from the outer world, Regina escapes her confinement in her memories or visions which develop the nonrealistic mode of narration, introduced in the scene with the baby carriage mentioned above. We can see a young girl walking across a miniature desolated *shtetl*. In these recurrent sequences Kolski tried to express visually the mechanisms of memory, in which physical space is often distorted due to subjective perception. The *shtetl* is presented as a collection of small houses, like children's toys, or a miniature setting. This device emphasises that the image of the *shtetl* does not belong to the real world any longer, and simultaneously signifies Regina's displacement and homelessness.

Not only is Regina displaced and homeless, she is also dispossessed of everything, as is demonstrated by Barbara's appropriation of the baby. The scene which takes place after Regina gives birth poignantly shows the dramatic twist of these three persons' lives. Regina lies on the bed in the background, Barbara stands with a newborn baby in her arms next to the window in the foreground, whereas Jan occupies the space between them. Regina asks about the baby's sex, but does not get an answer. After a while Jan comes to her and says that it is a girl. Regina wants to see her baby, but Barbara does not seem to pay any attention to this request. She keeps talking to 'her' baby, explaining the external world to her, saying that everything on this earth has its own colour. She remains indifferent to what happens in the room, monotonously continuing her story as if she were in a kind of after-birth shock. When Jan approaches her and asks her to show Regina the baby, she calmly says 'no' and quietly leaves the room.

However, later on Regina is allowed to contact her baby, but only to feed her. Apparently Barbara treats her as wet-nurse. Once, when she retrieves the baby, Helusia, from Regina after the feeding, she says to Regina, 'She is lovely, isn't she', as if she were the baby's mother. She then adds that she will bring her up as a good human being. In response, Regina loses consciousness. Finally, Regina decides to secretly leave her hiding place and her baby, Helusia – most likely for the sake of the baby's safety. In vain Jan follows her in hope of finding her and bringing her back home. When he returns home after some time, he gets desperately drunk, then takes down his unfinished painting of the Virgin and child from the wall, hides it beneath the bed, on which he then has sex violently with Barbara. This scene poignantly demonstrates that the lives of these three have been irrevocably destroyed.

When the narration jumps a few years ahead, we can see that all these wounds of the past cannot be healed. Jan is an alcoholic whom Helusia's presence saves from complete self-destruction; Barbara is a bitter woman who has to accept her husband's love for another woman, and there is an absent Regina who sends parcels for Helusia from Hamburg, where she has finally found her place. In fact, after the end of the war Regina had tried to rejoin Helusia. She sent two men to Barbara and Jan to bribe them and get her child back. They relayed the message that if Regina did not get her child back her heart would be broken, to which Jan replied that if they gave Helusia to her, their hearts would be broken. This dialogue conspicuously demonstrates the intractability of the situation. Symptomatically, when little Helusia saw the two strangers, she hid in the wardrobe as her mother used to do.

Just before his death, Jan reveals the truth to Helusia and says that her real mother is 'that one from Hamburg'. After some time, Helusia, now a young woman, decides to visit Regina. However, she is not welcomed warmly, but, in fact, quite the opposite, as she has to beg her mother to be let in. Finally, Regina decides to open the door; however, she is still full of reservations, if not anger. While Helusia is calmly sitting at the table, she stays behind the chest of drawers, which reminds the viewer of her position behind the wardrobe in Jan's and Barbara's home, nervously smoking a cigarette and recollecting the past. She says to Helusia that she gave birth to her because she had to, as she had to do everything to save her life. She also says that she does not want to remember either her father or those times. Ruthlessly she shouts, 'You remind me of everything. Fear, shame, darkness. I don't want them. I don't! Don't come again!' Helusia responds to it with calmness and only asks Regina: 'Who are you?', to hear: 'A widow.'

A notion of lack, introduced in the beginning of this film, recurs here once again and paradoxically unifies the two female characters, Regina and Barbara, who lead lonely lives overshadowed by memories of the past. Interestingly, Helusia seems to reproduce both of her mothers' lives. After returning from Hamburg she refuses to follow her boyfriend and to emigrate with him to Germany, although she is pregnant. The film ends with an image of two women, Barbara and Helusia, sitting at a table discussing the latter's pregnancy and the future birth of the baby. Perhaps this baby who is to be born will be able to mend a world shattered by the tragic past.

In his film, Kolski, following the literary prototype, makes an effort to go beyond the stereotypical models for depicting Polish and Jewish femininity and instead tries to represent the complex relationship between Barbara and Regina. The film makes the case that the complexity of their interactions stems only partially from racial difference. As Hanna Krall, the author of the story and screenplay, says, 'I don't think in the categories that she is Jewish and they are Poles. This is obliterated in my consciousness. This is a story of three people. Two women, who loved the same man.' Thus she claims that Barbara acted not so much as a Polish woman but rather as a jealous wife (Sobolewski 2000: 15). Nevertheless, she had the possibility of expressing her anger, even if only verbally, whereas Regina had to remain mute in her wardrobe.

Overall, Kolski managed to depart from the stereotypical opposition between the purity of Polish femininity and the dangerous sexuality of Jewish women by invoking the trope of motherhood. What is of the greatest importance is that the tragic experience of motherhood, that is, the loss of a child, traditionally ascribed exclusively to Polish women in national discourse, here is transposed onto a Jewish character. However, she is not idealised as an abstract figure of suffering maternity, as the scene of her encounter with Helusia demonstrates. Clearly, Barbara is also far from the self-sacrificing model of the Polish Mother. However, she is by no means a negative figure. Although she is selfish and cruel to Regina, yet it is she who saves Helusia's life. As Krall says, 'Here nobody is at fault. ... This war's speciality was the creation of situations which could not end happily; and it created questions to which there are no answers' (Sobolewski 2000: 14).

Kolski's film, with its open ending, undoubtedly opens a space for renegotiating the relationship between Polish and Jewish femininity and goes beyond the limitations of national ideology, which stereotypically determine the dominant representations of Other women in Polish cinema. A similar effort was made earlier by Michał Rosa in his debut film, *Farba* (*Paint*, 1997), which concerned a Gypsy woman. The filmmaker departs from the stereotype of a 'dark woman' as a site of sexuality only to problematise it and provide her with a complexity which prevents the possibility of an easy narrative resolution. However, on the other hand, Jerzy Hoffman, in his super-production *Ogniem i mieczem* (*With Fire and Sword*, 1999), offers an image of the Other woman, a Ukrainian Gypsy, as a sexually aggressive 'witch' (see Chapter 6). He contrasted this image with an angelic Polish femininity embodied by the main female protagonist, Helena Kurcewiczówna. To conclude, it can be said that in Polish cinema after 1989 efforts to open a dialogic space between Other and Polish femininities are opposed with images produced within exclusive national ideology.

PART III

Women behind the Camera

CHAPTER 8

Wanda Jakubowska: the Communist Fighter

EWA MAZIERSKA

The first Polish female director to gain national and international recognition was Wanda Jakubowska (1907–98). A measure of her success are the numerous awards she received in Poland and abroad, including the Award of the World Peace Council in 1951 for *Ostatni etap* (*The Last Stage*, 1947). Her career spanned over fifty years, in which she directed fourteen full-length feature films, thus being the longest-working film director in the history of Polish cinema. She performed a series of important administrative and political roles in Polish cinematography. In 1948 Jakubowska became the director of one of three independent production units (Zespoły Autorów Filmowych) and was one of the highest-profile filmmakers to join the Polish Communist Party after the Second World War, representing the party line amongst her fellow filmmakers, and lobbying the Party on behalf of the cinema industry.

Jakubowska is also the most controversial character in the history of Polish cinema and attitudes to her work changed in synchrony with political changes in Poland: while she was generally praised in the 1950s, she was much criticised in the 1980s and 1990s. For a long time her involvement in politics, both on and off the screen, precluded serious examination of her oeuvre and in spite of the fame of her name and persona, she remains a relatively unknown director, both in her homeland and abroad. There are no books devoted to her, and the majority of articles about her work are reviews of individual films and ideological critiques, written in a politically charged atmosphere, in which emotional claims often prevailed over rational argument. She was even omitted from the few Polish publications about female cinema. Apart from *The Last Stage*, which was her feature début, and the children's film, *Król Maciuś I* (*King Maciuś I*, 1958), her films are neither shown on Polish television, nor are available on video, her only prewar feature film and her documentaries are lost. When I viewed Jakubowska's films at a private showing in the National Film Archive in Warsaw, the film researcher who accompanied me drew my attention to the high quality of the prints, jokingly commenting that it is was a good indication that I was the first person to watch them in years. Although Jakubowska belonged to the Polish cinematic mainstream, we can also regard her as a creator of 'minor cinema', as defined by Alison Butler (see Butler 2002: 19–24), because her concerns were typically slightly different from those of her male colleagues operating in the same schools or paradigms. In particular, she showed greater interest than they in the lives and concerns of women and children.

Jakubowska came from an intelligentsia family and began her career as a left-leaning filmmaker before the Second World War. In 1930, at the age of twenty three, together with a group of fellow film enthusiasts, she formed the Society of the Devotees of the Artistic Film (Stowarzyszenie Miłośników Filmu Artystycznego), known simply as START. As well as Jakubowska, the group included the future directors Eugeniusz Cękalski, Jerzy Zarzycki, Jerzy Bossak, cameraman Stanisław Wohl and film historian Jerzy Toeplitz. She was the only woman in the original group. The society lasted for five years and produced only a few films, most of them short, but its influence on the ideology and shape of Polish national cinema, especially after the Second World War, cannot be ignored.

On the one hand, the programme of START was sufficiently wide to encompass filmmakers of different thematic and stylistic interests. Some of its members created experimental films of a world-class standard. On the other hand, its emphasis on depicting reality, demanding state assistance for the film industry to help to eradicate technical deficiencies, and foregrounding the social usefulness of films and their educational value, had a major impact on the ideology of Polish socialist realism in general and on Jakubowska's films in particular (Bren 1986: 22; Zwierzchowski 2000: 51–52). Not surprisingly, after the end of the Second World War the members of START became the most prominent and influential members of the Polish film industry. There were those who genuinely welcomed the change in the political system and believed that the new socialist authority let them create the sort of cinema that they dreamt of before the war. Jakubowska was amongst them.

There is no completely reliable or coherent information about Jakubowska's input into START's programme and activities. Barbara and Leszek Armatysowie maintain that, together with Eugeniusz Cękalski and Jerzy Zarzycki, she was involved in making two *Reportaże* (*Live Coverages*, 1932), flagship productions of the group (Armatysowie 1988: 177). They were short documentaries about various aspects of the everyday lives of Polish people, inspired by the Soviet avant-garde of the 1920s and 1930s. With Cękalski she also made two shorts: *Morze* (*Sea*, 1933) which was a poetical impression about the Baltic sea and *Budujemy* (*We Are Building*, 1934), about replacing the old, dark tenements with new blocks, built by a cooperative. The propagandist function and use of Eisenstein-style *montage* made *We Are Building* look similar to the British documentary *Housing Problems* (1935) by Edgar Anstey and Arthur Elton. In 1937 Jakubowska produced her first independent short, *Ulica Edisona* (*Edison Street*), a poetical étude about street lights without any story-line, reminiscent of 'city films', popular in other European countries in the previous decade. The first feature film included in Jakubowska's filmographies is *Nad Niemnem* (*On the Banks of the Niemen*, 1939). It was not produced by START, which by then had ceased to exist, but by the Co-operative of Film Authors, which is regarded as a continuation of the movement. The film did not survive, not even reaching cinema audiences, as the only copy was destroyed by the Nazis in 1939 during the siege of Warsaw. Consequently, it is not possible to discuss it in greater depth. However, it is worth mentioning the literary source of the film: a novel of the same name, published in 1887 by the famous Polish writer, Eliza Orzeszkowa (see Chapter 1). *On the Banks of the Niemen* is regarded as a masterpiece of Polish Positivism, a literary and political movement whose main idea was to rebuild Poland, nonexistent in the nineteenth century as an independent state, through work, rather than by military action. Orzeszkowa is hardly described as a socialist, but in her books she is always very sympathetic towards the poor and underprivileged. She is also the first feminist in Polish literature: her novel, *Marta* (1873) focused on a woman's right to work and determine her own destiny. In *On the Banks of the Niemen* the women's question is not so foregrounded as in *Marta*, but the novel tends to represent women in a much better light than men, as more altruistic and less preoccupied with material goods than the male characters. The main character, Justyna, who comes from amongst the impoverished gentry, chooses to marry a peasant whom she loves, rather than remain in her social circle which is more affluent, but also snobbish and decadent. One can risk the statement that according to Orzeszkowa a woman is a natural socialist and a fighter for a just society (see Borkowska 1996: 149–99). This idea is also conveyed in many of Jakubowska's later films.

During the Second World War Jakubowska was engaged in the resistance movement, which led to her arrest in 1942. She spent six months in the Pawiak prison in Warsaw and was later transported first to the Ravensbrück concentration camp and then to Oświęcim (Auschwitz), from which she was freed on 18 January 1945. According to her own words, the years in the camps constituted her most important experiences, both in terms of her personal life and her artistic development (Mruklik 1985: 7). Indeed, four of her films are set during the Second World War and three of them deal specifically with the issue of concentration camps. Jakubowska's first feature completed after the war, *The Last Stage* (Figure 8.1), portrays

Figure 8.1 A scene from *Ostatni etap* (*The Last Stage*), 1947, dir. Wanda Jakubowska © Studio Filmowe 'Oko'

life in the women's part of the concentration camp of Auschwitz-Birkenau until it was liberated by the Soviet army. The project was actually conceived during Jakubowska's incarceration; she shared her idea with many fellow prisoners and they passed her their stories to be included in the project. The co-author of the script was fellow prisoner Gerda Schneider, a German, who, like Jakubowska, dreamt of making a film about life in Auschwitz. The completed film has no single main character, but at least three women can be regarded as leading heroines: Marta (Barbara Drapińska), a Polish Jew who works as a translator, Anna (Antonina Górecka), a German nurse and communist, and the Russian doctor, Eugenia (Tatjana Górecka). In spite of their different nationalities, there are many similarities in their views, behaviour and even position in the camp. All have senior posts thanks to their skills and influence and respect amongst their fellow prisoners, which is not the consequence of the task the Nazis ask them to perform, but the way they do it, which is actually contrary to the Germans' intentions. Eugenia goes to any length to procure medicines for her patients, Anna helps her, and Marta organises the smuggling of essential commodities into the camp and tries to uncover the Germans' plans. Their attitude is strongly contrasted with another hierarchy, imposed on the prisoners by the Nazis: the system of 'blockleaders'.

Apart from being individuals, Eugenia, Anna and Marta serve as symbols of the main enemies of fascism: Jewry, communism and the East, in a way which conforms to the socialist realistic ideology. The film conveys the opinion that it was thanks to their cooperation that the Nazis were eventually defeated both on the small scale of the concentration camp and in the war as a whole. Again, this idea of international solidarity is in tune with the communist promotion of internationalism over the welfare of the nation. Characteristically, if Jakubowska shows any group of women in a less favourable light than the others, it is the Poles. The blockleaders are mainly Poles and the greedy, haughty and utterly incompetent wife of a chemist-shop owner, who becomes the new doctor in the female camp, is also Polish. Her character can be regarded as a criticism of the Polish pre-war bourgeoisie, the class that the owners of chemist shops epitomised.

Reaction to the film at the time of its premiere in 1948 was very positive both in Poland and abroad. The reasons for this phenomenal success are complex and it is impossible to establish all of them. However, some factors reappear in the opinions of critics and film historians. Firstly, as Tadeusz Lubelski notes, is simply the subject of the film: the Second World War and the concentration camps. At the time the film was made, Poles were keen to see films about the war. When in 1947 the popular Polish film magazine, *Film*, conducted a survey amongst its readers, asking them what themes they favoured in cinema, the most common answer was the Second World War (Lubelski 1992: 76). One can assume that at the end of the 1940s there was also a desire in many other countries to see the war on screen. Secondly, the strong pacifist message of *The Last Stage* captured the popular mood in both the East and the West, when everyone worldwide needed to console themselves with the assurance 'never again', which ends the film. Over the next decades the mood both in Poland and abroad changed: pacifism was no longer taken for granted and the Soviet Army was associated with an oppressive force, rather than with those who liberated Auschwitz. This affected the reception of Jakubowska's later films, devoted to the issue of the camps. Third – and perhaps the most important reason for the immense popularity and appreciation of *The Last Stage* – is Jakubowska's use of what Tadeusz Lubelski describes as the 'witness's strategy', which means representing a particular reality from the point of view of a person who knows it well, either by having first-hand experience, or by using the insight of other witnesses (Lubelski 1992: 75–83). However, Lubelski persuasively argues that the witness's strategy was intertwined in *The Last Stage* with the strategy of propaganda, typical of socialist realism. The witness's strategy was further compromised by Jakubowska's conformity to certain Hollywood conventions, which prevented her, for example, from showing the emaciated bodies of the prisoners, or their infestation with vermin (Lubelski 1992: 77–83). With the passage of time, and the production of numerous feature and documentary films about camps, *The Last Stage* lost some of its appeal. Still, when Jakubowska died in 1998, she was commemorated mainly as the author of this film, although it is difficult to establish if this was due to a true appreciation of her early work, or rather the critics' unwillingness to recall her more overtly 'evangelical' socialist realistic films, such as Żołnierz zwycięstwa (Soldier of Victory, 1953), or Pożegnanie z diabłem (Farewell to the Devil, 1956).

In 1964 Jakubowska returned to the theme of concentration camps, directing Koniec naszego świata (The End of Our World), based on the novel by Tadeusz Hołuj, who, like Jakubowska herself, had been imprisoned in a camp. The film takes the form of a series of flashbacks. It starts contemporaneous to the period of its production; a car, driven by a Polish man, is stopped by two American tourists, who ask him to give them a lift to Auschwitz. The driver is a Pole called Henryk (Lech Skolimowski), a communist, who was imprisoned in Auschwitz; the woman (Elżbieta Starostecka) is the daughter of a Jew who died in the camp; the other American (Janusz Syketura) is simply a tourist with no personal connections with the Nazis' victims. Henryk not only gives the strangers a lift, but offers them a guided tour of Auschwitz, which allows him to recollect his own past. Most of the screen time is devoted to the representation of the camp when it was 'alive'. The moments when the narrative moves forward to the 1960s, although rare, allow the director to ponder on the attitudes and lifestyle of contemporary Western society, encapsulated in the behaviour of the American. His attitude to Auschwitz is completely that of a tourist. For example, he objects to the way the exhibition is laid out and criticises the work of the camp guides, finding all of them too 'dry' and not entertaining enough. Moreover, he mocks his companion's genuine interest in Henryk's story, constantly asking them to film him, using his expensive camera. The message is that people who think about their own pleasure will not understand the atrocities of the camp, and be unable to prevent a similar tragedy occurring in future. The End of Our World also received good reviews, but did not enjoy the same success as The Last Stage. The reasons for that were largely the same as those that assured the success of The Last Stage: in the 1960s, often described as the time of 'small stabilisation', the Second World War stopped being a 'fashionable' subject. On the contrary, there was a certain fatigue amongst Polish audiences, exposed during the past decade to a large number of films about the war. The viewers demanded movies that were lighter in tone and portrayed present-day Poland.

In the last film, belonging to Jakubowska's 'concentration camp' paradigm, Zaproszenie (Invitation, 1985), contemporary times overshadow the wartime past. The main character of the story is Anna (Maria Probosz and Antonina Gordon-Górecka), a concentration camp survivor, nowadays working as a highly respected paediatric surgeon. The event to trigger Anna's memory is the visit of her old flame, Piotr (Kazimierz Witkiewicz and Leszek Żentara), who now lives in the USA and is a professor of ecology. The reason that they never married was the war. He left their home

town of Cracow in order to fight, and Anna, hearing of his death and per-
suaded by her own mother, married another man, who subsequently died in
the war. Anna takes Piotr to Auschwitz, Sachsenhausen and Ravensbrück,
where she was imprisoned during the war. As they walk through what was
later converted into a museum, she reminisces about her youth.

In the scenes set in the 1980s, Anna is played by Antonina Gordon-
Górecka, who also played the German nurse in *The Last Stage*. In my opinion, her appearance and even her having the same name as the heroine of
the earlier film, is deliberate, signifying Jakubowska's wish to emphasise
that those who survived the camps, including herself, did not change fundamentally: they remained honest, supportive, altruistic. At the same time
the world around them changed a lot, the pursuit of material goods becoming the main purpose of people's lives. In this respect Anna is strongly contrasted with her own daughter, Natalia, who wants to be rich and
successful, rather than to serve others or her country. The ultimate indication of the gulf between their attitudes is Natalia's decision to visit the USA
at the invitation of Piotr and not to return to Poland. *Invitation* also
portrays Jakubowska's disappointment with the official politics, as it was
understood in the 1980s, when people associated it not with ideas, but with
names, and when it was regarded more often as a vehicle of self-advance-
ment than a tool of social improvement.

While in Jakubowska's camp films the evangelical aspect of her work,
concerning communism, might have slipped the audience's attention, being
overshadowed by other messages, particularly the author's pacifism, in her
'contemporary stories' Jakubowska's commitment to the communist cause is
blatant. It is thanks to these films, as well as to *Soldier of Victory*, which will
be discussed later, that she is regarded as a model socialist realist.
Jakubowska devoted more films to the issue of building a socialist Poland
than to any other subject; they include *Farewell to the Devil*, *Historia
współczesna* (*Contemporary Story*, 1960), *Gorąca linia* (*Express Production
Line*, 1965), *150 na godzinę* (*150 Kilometres Per Hour*, 1971) and, to a certain extent, the previously discussed *Invitation* (1985). Her plan to portray
the positive changes, resulting from introducing a socialist mode of production and a one-party political system, was even more comprehensive than
what she managed to achieve. In an interview, given in 1951, she said:

> I would like to make contemporary films, particularly connected with the Six-
> year Plan. I refer to our own, Polish way, of building Socialism. One of my
> projects, based on the script by Marian Brandys, concerns the builders of
> Nowa Huta... I would also like to make a film about Nowe Tychy, which
> changed from a small, sleepy town, into a modern industrial centre, as well as
> films about the birth of industry in Lublin, the Białystok region and many
> other parts of Poland, neglected by pre-war governments. (Nowicki 1951: 6)

The setting of the majority of Jakubowska's contemporary films is,
indeed, provincial Poland which, after years of prewar underdevelopment,

began to catch up with more prosperous regions, largely thanks to the communist authorities which decided to build many factories there. In *Contemporary Story* it is a chemical factory, in *Express Production Line*, a coalmine, in *Farewell to the Devil*, a village, where a cooperative is about to be set up. The conflicts in the films, in a typically socialist realistic manner, revolve around material production, and private lives are strongly influenced – almost determined – by the character's type of work. The first two films belonging to this genre, *Farewell to the Devil* and *Contemporary Story*, are based on real events, which the director learnt about from newspaper reports. However, as with Jakubowska's camp films, the crude facts, probably already coloured by the newspaper journalists, were further 'repackaged' in a way that made them useful tools of communist propaganda. This applies particularly to *Farewell to the Devil*, whose characters fall into the three main categories utilised by the bulk of socialist realistic filmmakers in Poland and in the Soviet Union: a 'master', who never makes any mistakes and knows perfectly how to fulfil the communist ideals, an 'enemy', who tries to upset his plans, and a 'student', who, influenced by his 'master', starts to work for the communist cause (Lubelski 1992: 99). The role of the master is taken by an investigative journalist, the enemy is a rich farmer (*kułak*), who uses subterfuge to discourage his fellow farmers from joining the cooperative, and the student is the *kułak*'s fiancée, who in the end falls in love with the journalist. Similarly, all the conflicts presented in *Farewell to the Devil* can be reduced to an antagonism between the old system, epitomised by private ownership of the land, and the new, symbolised by the large, cooperative farm. Jakubowska is not slow to show certain shortcomings of the social structures, organised according to communist principles. For example, the local party organisation is portrayed as over-bureaucratic and secretive, and we learn that the socialist principles of allocating various goods, such as bricks or fertiliser, amongst the villagers, are flouted. Yet, Jakubowska's criticism is always 'constructive': she never undermines the communist system itself, but attacks the people who twist and abuse it, her purpose being to persuade her audience that it is worth following the party line.

Although Jakubowska's portrayal of provincial Poland in this and other films is strongly coloured by her desire to promote the communist cause, many of her contemporary stories contain a lot of local customs and details concerning the ordinary lives of factory workers. Moreover, often shot on location, with extensive use of long shots and long takes (which seem to be unsuitable means for the arbitrariness of socialist realistic films), the films convey, perhaps against the director's wish, the sleepy atmosphere of small Polish towns, which until the Cinema of Moral Concern of the 1970s were rarely present in Polish movies. With the passage of time some of Jakubowska's films reveal an authenticity that passed unnoticed when the films were made.

As with Jakubowska's camp films, one can detect a certain trajectory in her films about contemporary life in Poland: the first films were the most popular and praised by the critics, while the last ones were scorned by the critics and ignored by ordinary viewers. The reasons for this pattern lie in their subject matter, messages and style. Thus, *Farewell to the Devil* touched upon issues regarded as very important by millions of viewers: why Poles should choose socialism, rather than a capitalist, individualistic system of production. Moreover, in this film Jakubowska portrays an environment where opposition to political change was at its strongest: rural Poland. In addition, the 'witness's strategy', used by the director in *Farewell to the Devil* and *Contemporary Story*, although intermingled with heavy pro-communist rhetoric, and often Hollywood-style acting and cinematography, created an impression that some essential aspects of Polish reality were being depicted accurately. As time passed, the gulf between Jakubowska's films and the dominant paradigms in Polish cinema grew. By the 1970s and 1980s, her films looked dated against the backdrop of the work of such directors as Krzysztof Kieślowski, Feliks Falk, Agnieszka Holland, Marek Piwowski, Krzysztof Zanussi and Andrzej Wajda, many of whom belonged to the Cinema of Moral Concern. The new generation of directors brought with them a new understanding of realism, based on the use of documentary techniques and naturalistic acting. Again, against the backdrop of films such as *Za ścianą* (*Behind the Wall*, 1971) by Krzysztof Zanussi or *Kobieta samotna* (*A Woman Alone*, 1981) by Agnieszka Holland, *150 Kilometres Per Hour* and *Invitation* look unnatural.

Apart from the large number of films devoted to the issue of building and strengthening socialism in Poland, the main reason why Jakubowska is regarded as a socialist realist is her film *Soldier of Victory*. Made in 1953, the year regarded as the zenith of Stalinism in Polish political and cultural life, it is a model revolutionary story, featuring as the main character one of the most famous Polish communists, Władysław Świerczewski, known also as General Walter. Born in 1897 into a working-class family, he took part in almost every important event of the twentieth century in Poland and Europe. He fought in the Russian October Revolution on the side of the Bolsheviks and was sent in 1936 by the Soviet authorities to fight in the Spanish Civil War. During the Second World War he was the chief organiser and leader of the Polish army on Soviet territory. After the war, as defence minister he was responsible for dealing with the Ukrainian underground opposition against Polish authority in the Bieszczady mountains and died in 1948 in unexplained circumstances. A national hero in the 1950s, nowadays Świerczewski is regarded as the person responsible for many military failures and atrocities, including the extermination of hundreds of soldiers of the Home Army.

To present such a rich biography in a way that would educate the viewers in a spirit of communism and satisfy Świerczewski's powerful friends and enemies constituted a major challenge for Jakubowska. The script had to be rewritten many times before it was accepted by party officials and the very process of filming proved very difficult (see Modrzejewska 1991; Madej 1991a, 1991b). The ultimate result is a film made up of two two-hour parts and featuring almost one hundred actors and several hundred extras. Jakubowska covers all important events of Świerczewski's life, from his childhood during the Revolution of 1905 to his tragic death in 1948. When *Soldier of Victory* was released in 1953, it was regarded as one of the greatest achievements of Polish cinema and labelled the first Polish super-production. The reason why the film was acclaimed was not only its subject matter – the life of an archetypal communist hero – but also the director's ability to combine Polish affairs with international history, promoting patriotism and internationalism at the same time. This of course was at a price; the price was psychological subtlety and historical accuracy. All the characters, including the title hero (Józef Wyszomirski), are one-dimensional, either completely good, or extremely bad. In most of the events Świerczewski's political role is hugely exaggerated. This applies particularly to the First World War and the Bolshevik Revolution, where Świerczewski is represented as the second most important figure, after Stalin, in defeating the enemies of both Russia and Poland. All the events in *Soldier of Victory* are shown from a Stalinist perspective. In effect, the world wars and the Spanish Civil War are all regarded as exclusively class wars, with workers and the bourgeoisie fighting on opposing sides of the barricade. According to Jakubowska, during the First World War Polish workers had the same objectives as workers from Russia or Germany, and Polish landlords and factory owners, the same as their counterparts from other countries. The film promotes the idea of constant 'vigilance' against a conspiracy of an international network of spies of the secret society of industrialists from Germany, Britain and the USA, emulating the atmosphere in the Soviet Union and Poland during the political purges of the early 1950s.

After the collapse of communism *Soldier of Victory* was strongly criticised for its political and artistic totalitarianism, which resulted from subordinating all aspects of the film to its propagandist function (see Madej 1991b; Zwierzchowski 2000: 134–42). Although I agree that the sociopolitical values of the film are unacceptable, I resist the opinion that they preclude *Soldier of Victory* having artistic merit. Due to its skilful editing, which ignores chronology and holds in play several different scenes of action and dashing production, especially of battle scenes, *Soldier of Victory* largely succeeded artistically. Moreover, the fierce propaganda not only failed to prevent the aesthetic accomplishment of the film, but was actually conducive to it. The scenes most charged with anti-capitalist sentiment are the best in the whole film. No wonder then, that when several years ago *Soldier of Victory* was re-released by Polish television, one critic compared it to the films of another female filmmaker who successfully combined art with propaganda: Leni Riefenstahl (Atlas 1995: 27).

In the interviews given by Jakubowska in the 1990s, she expressed a certain unease about *Soldier of Victory* and Polish Stalinism. She mentions, for example, a young officer who worked as her consultant in the film production, who was subsequently accused of conspiracy against the communist authorities and executed, and admits that at the time she trusted 'her beloved party too much' (Madej 1991a: 31). Yet, it must equally be stressed that no episode in Polish history, either before or after the collapse of communism, changed her belief that Poland chose correctly to join the community of socialist countries after the Second World War. Several months before her death she said, 'I am an unreformed communist' (Hollender 1997: 25).

It is also primarily in the context of communism and socialist realism that we should view Jakubowska's contribution to Polish cinema for and about children. Education was regarded by the ideologists of socialism as a crucial task for artists, and nobody was more receptive to education than children, whose spirits awaited the 'imprint' of moral values. Not surprisingly, films for and about children formed a substantial part of socialist realist cinema in the Soviet Union, and many of them gained a high reputation. It is difficult to overestimate Jakubowska's contribution to raising the profile of children's cinema, which she did both as a filmmaker and a cinema administrator. She made two films for child and teenage audiences, *Opowieść Atlantycka* (*Atlantic Story*, 1955) and *King Maciuś I*, and as the artistic director of the 'Start' film unit (1955–68) produced many children's films, particularly by the female director, Maria Kaniewska. *Atlantic Story* was regarded as a typical social realistic film and at the time of its premiere was praised in the same vein as *Soldier of Victory* and *Farewell to the Devil*. Indeed, in the plot, which was set on the Atlantic coast of France and involved two boys aged about ten, one from a bourgeois family, one from a working-class background, Jakubowska offered many criticisms of capitalist society. Doctor Oliver (Henryk Szletyński), father of the small and delicate Bernard (Damian Damięcki), who comes to the coast on holiday, is very conservative both in his political views and home arrangements. As a *Le Figaro* reader, he strongly rejects the idea of the French colonies gaining independence and is very strict with his son, whom he rather prefers to spend the whole summer in solitude, rather than to mix with the working-class children. Yet, Bernard strikes up a secret friendship with Gaston (Michel Bustamante), who lives with his uncle (Stanisław Kwaskowski), a woodcutter. The boys, trying to discover who steals their fish, find in a Second World War bunker a hungry German fugitive from the Foreign Legion (Mieczysław Stoor). He tells the boys that he left the Legion because he could not accept its policy of suppressing independence in Indo-China, which resulted in exterminating many civilians. At first Bernard, indoctrinated by his nationalistic father, rejects the story, but is eventually per-suaded by Gaston and his uncle to accept the soldier's version as truthful.

Another subplot of *Atlantic Story* refers to the class struggle in contemporary France. It transpires that Gaston's mother was killed by police during a trade union demonstration, and his father was jailed for participating in the workers' movement. The film ends with Bernard leaving the village where he spent his holiday with his parents. Their car is driven through the crowd of woodworkers taking part in a protest against the employers. Among them is Gaston, his uncle and the soldier, who was given shelter by the workers. Bernard, who notices the demonstration from the window of his car, shouts to his friends that he did not betray them.

The primary aim of the director is to demonstrate that direct contact with the working classes can change a middle-class child into a person who understands the injustices of the capitalist system, even a potential revolutionary. Yet, unlike many socialist realistic films, which were made in the same manner as adult films, disregarding children's attention span and psychology, *Atlantic Story* is not only a film about children, but also for them. The film reveals a good understanding of the expectations of young audiences, especially their need to be entertained. This expectation is fulfilled by the use of a sensational plot, emulating the excitement children feel on holiday when they encounter a mystery. Another way to charm young audiences is the extensive use of locations, particularly the seaside, with sandy beaches, trees, bushes and dramatic waves. The film was shot on the Baltic coast near Łeba, but the critics praised the director and the cinematographer, Stanisław Wohl, for their ability to portray the Atlantic coast as it is in reality.

Contrary to *Atlantic Story*, *King Maciuś I* is treated not as a socialist realist film, but as a 'classic' children's film. The strongest evidence of this is its frequent re-release on Polish television, particularly on 'Children's Day', and the production of a video version. The main reason for its enduring appeal is the literary source of the film: a fantasy novel, written by the famous Polish Jewish pedagogue, Janusz Korczak, who in 1942 died in a concentration camp together with his foster-children. The book and the film presents the fairy-tale adventures of a nine-year-old king (Juliusz Wyrzykowski), including two victorious wars with neighbouring monarchs and trips to the exotic kingdom of a friendly king Bum-Drum. The setting and costumes were all unusually rich and inventive for a Polish production at the time. For example, many props were styled on figures from a pack of playing cards. Battle scenes, on the other hand, were a parody of the Napoleonic wars. There was also a lot of subtle visual and verbal humour, such as adverts for slingshots and films. The film was also praised for its use of modern, atonal music, written by the famous composer, Stanisław Skrowaczewski.

In spite of the plot and setting, *King Maciuś I* is not pure entertainment, as it deals with an issue that was of crucial importance for Korczak, renowned for his progressive attitude to children: children's right to self-rule. Maciuś himself at certain point asks adults and children to change their roles: adults being sent back to school and children deciding the laws in a children's parliament. Both in the book and the film it leads to disaster: the country governed by children falls into chaos. However, on the whole, the authors are not against child democracy; they rather advocate its use in moderation, accepting the principle that the more freedom one has to decide one's fate, the more responsibility one should have. This gentle approach to children and other people under his tutelage informed all Korczak's activities. In order to promote this message, Jakubowska even changed the ending of Korczak's story: in the novel king Maciuś, like Napoleon, is sent to a lonely island as a punishment; in the film he is set free. According to the director herself, *King Maciuś I*, in common with her concentration camp films, was meant to warn about the dangers of war and thus promote peace (Mamrowicz 1984: 15).

Being a communist and socialist realist also had a major influence on the way Jakubowska represented women. However, as with many aspects of Polish reality that she portrayed, other factors also played a significant part in the way in which women were shown in her films. One such factor was the traditionally Polish ideal of femininity: that of the Polish Mother, which was discussed at length in the first part of this book. Another, at which I have already hinted, was Jakubowska's biography, especially her camp experiences, and the postwar reality of ordinary Polish women. The references to the Polish Mother are most pronounced in Jakubowska's war films. Elżbieta Ostrowska argues that in *The Last Stage* Jakubowska at the same time conveyed and manipulated the myth of the Polish Mother, in order to suit communist propaganda. A woman in this film

> symbolises the suffering and heroism experienced by the whole nation. In a climactic scene, a Polish mother is deprived of her newborn baby by a German SS doctor. The despair on her face, shown in close-up, demonstrates the continuing tragedy of Poland. It is worth noting that this traditional representation of Polish women is conjoined at this point with the idea of international solidarity between women of different nationalities, who help each other in the camp. This is included partly because it was useful in relation to the desire of communist propaganda to speak about internationalism at the expense of the interests of the nation. (Ostrowska 1998: 424–25)

The image of a Polish woman giving birth in a camp can be also found in two later films directed by Jakubowska: *Spotkania w mroku* (*Meetings in the Dark*, 1960), which is set in a Nazi labour camp, and *Invitation*. However, its connotations changed over the years. In *The Last Stage* the director foregrounded the suffering of a mother deprived of her child, the mother embodying the suffering of the Polish nation. In *Invitation*, on the other hand, the emphasis is put on birth, which symbolises the birth (or rebirth) of the nation after the atrocities of the war. In *Invitation* the baby (a boy) is not taken away from the mother by the Germans, but saved by fellow prisoners, amongst them Anna, who helped the mother during the birth and after the war becomes a paediatrician. In spite of the extremely difficult conditions of the camp, the boy survives and after the war becomes a successful farmer. He also becomes a kind of spiritual son to both women: his real mother (who became a nurse) and Anna. The transformation of a story of a suffering mother who had lost her child into a narrative of a happy mother who sees her child growing can also be read as veiled praise for a socialist Poland. In Jakubowska's film it is a happy, peaceful country, in which women no longer lose their sons to wars and uprisings.

As Ostrowska notes, 'the myth of the Polish Mother placed woman in a superior position within Polish cultural discourses yet inevitably repressed her own subjectivity' and was 'a fiercely constraining model for Polish femininity' (Ostrowska 1998: 423). The same opinion can be voiced in reference to the representation of women in Jakubowska's 'camp films'. Her interest in the role of women as mothers, and the fact that 'nurturing professions', such as doctors and nurses are the most common female occupations in her films, brings this director close to the ideological position of the Catholic Church in Poland. It also links Jakubowska to another prominent female director of her generation, whose name was mentioned earlier: Leni Riefenstahl. For example, Susan Sontag, discussing *The Last of Nuba*, Riefenstahl's book of photographs, writes: 'Her portrait of the Nuba goes further than her films in evoking one aspect of the fascist ideal: a society in which women are merely breeders and helpers, excluded from all ceremonial functions' (Sontag 1983: 90). Jakubowska assigns to women more prominent roles than those identified by Riefenstahl, but the similarity between the two filmmakers in privileging motherhood remains. Such an emphasis on motherhood by a filmmaker of overtly communist views might appear paradoxical. However, it is worth remembering that the communist governments, in common with the Catholic Church, often placed mothers on a pedestal.

In the remaining films of Jakubowska representations of women are less informed by the myth of the Polish Mother, more by the attitudes to women characteristic of communist propaganda, and by the social reality of women in postwar Poland. The influences were often contradictory, as the communist ideology emphasised the immense opportunities for women in countries that adopted communism – particularly in education, professional work and in areas previously dominated by men – while millions of real women often felt that the new reality brought them more disadvantages than advantages. As in many of the Soviet and Polish films set in the postwar period and belonging to the socialist realistic paradigm, such as *Irena do domu* (*Irena Go Home*, 1955) directed by Jan Fethke and *Autobus odjeżdża 6.20* (*The Bus Leaves at 6.20*, 1953) by Jan Rybkowski, Jakubowska refers to the opportunities of education and professional development which the communist government created for women. There is a significant number of female students in her films and it is suggested that it is largely thanks to educated women that Poland was able to overcome its prewar backwardness and poverty, examples being Ania (Anna Dziadyk) in *150 Kilometres Per Hour* and Franka (Alicja Sędzińska) in *Farewell to the Devil*, both studying agriculture and eager to apply their knowledge to their family farms or collectives. Women in her films often also show a political maturity and insight which their male counterparts lack, as demonstrated in *Express Production Line*, *Farewell to the Devil* and *150 Kilometres Per Hour*. Having said that, I must add that we do not find women of the type most widely associated with socialist realism in Jakubowska's films: women performing typically male tasks, clad in masculine clothes and paying no attention to their physical appearance. Her female characters, with their delicate features and good manners, look almost as if they were transplanted from Hollywood.

In many of her films, perhaps unconsciously, Jakubowska shows us a huge gap between the educational and professional achievements of Polish women and their actual inferior position in society. This glass ceiling is most visible in the situation of Anna in *Invitation*. This brave woman with an obvious talent for leadership did not achieve a status commensurate with her talents and accomplishments, but remained in positions inferior to her less gifted and less hard-working male colleagues. In spite of being regarded as the best paediatrician in the whole hospital, she is only an 'ordinary' doctor. Her male boss, envious of the respect she arouses amongst patients and fellow doctors, undermines her at every step and even tries to force her into retirement. Similarly, the political and industrial establishment that Jakubowska often portrays in her films is all male. Women are reduced to morally supporting men, who make decisions of the utmost importance for their factory, country or party. Consequently, in the films set after the Second World War, men typically hold the main roles and women are cast as secondary characters. Neither Jakubowska's female characters, nor the author herself, condemn, or even question the status quo. The situation where the factory boss or the party leader is male, while his subordinates and helpers are female, is presented as completely natural.

On several occasions Jakubowska treats the men's attitude to women's emancipation as a criterion to distinguish between the progressive (socialist) and conservative members of society. Thus, in *Biały mazur* (*White Mazurka*, 1978), which is set in the nineteenth century, the socialist party demands that women are given equal rights with men, while the reactionary, Polish aristocracy treats the idea as a sinister joke. Similarly, in *Farewell to the Devil* the peasants who are against the setting up of a cooperative in their village want to limit women's role to domestic activities, while the progressive villagers appreciate women's participation in local politics and making decisions that affect a wider community.

As was mentioned on previous occasions, the socialist realistic ideology and aesthetics was a crucial influence on Jakubowska's style. She did not privilege the women's cause and a female point of view, as in her opinion class, not gender, was the principal factor in determining a person's position in society. Nevertheless, she was sympathetic to women and recognised their right to participation in political, cultural and social life. This cannot be said about her German counterpart, Leni Riefenstahl, who perceived women as purely 'natural' creatures, unfit to take part in politics or to create culture. However, it is worth noticing here that even if Jakubowska opposed women's participation in social life, she would find it difficult to reveal it openly in her films without also parting from the ideology of socialist realism.

Conclusion

In conclusion I would reiterate the fact that Jakubowska's cinema was highly ideological. She always tried, and with some success – to use a famous (or infamous) phrase – to be an engineer of human souls, to influence and educate her viewers in the spirit of socialism, pacifism and internationalism. Only a few of her films found a lasting place in the history of Polish cinema, but all demonstrate integrity, which deserves respect, particularly in the light of the unusual length of her career as a director. One could argue that integrity was her main failure: while other directors who started as socialist realists, such as Jerzy Kawalerowicz, Jan Rybkowski and Andrzej Wajda, were able to adapt to new ideas, subjects and poetics – even played a major role in creating new cinematic schools and paradigms – Jakubowska remained faithful to socialist realism. There is also the commonly held opinion that involvement in politics generally compromised her as an artist: she traded her talent as a realist to produce communist propaganda. Obviously, it is difficult to support or contradict this argument, having only one set of films: those made by the real Jakubowska who was a political filmmaker. However, I will risk the statement that politics helped her in her career, rather than obstructed her. First, it enabled her to enter cinema at a time when female filmmakers were not only nonexistent in Poland, but were an absolute rarity in the world. Second, politics allowed her to reach the status of one of the most important and powerful filmmakers in Poland, and a spokesperson for pacifism in the international arena. I suggest that if she was only a female director, however talented, she would have not enjoyed her numerous privileges and simply made many fewer films. She would probably have had a similar career to that of her contemporary, Maria Kaniewska (b. 1911), who had to content herself with making films almost exclusively for children.

Interestingly, in spite of her political beliefs – or perhaps because of her personal integrity in revealing them and sticking to them – as well as self-lessness and friendliness, she remained a popular figure in Polish cinematic circles. Her fellow filmmakers and students liked and respected her and the only malicious personal comments directed at her referred to her unattrac-tive appearance. It could be suggested that she was a maternal figure in Polish cinema and nobody has replaced her in this role.

CHAPTER 9

Barbara Sass: the Author of Women's Films

EWA MAZIERSKA

Barbara Sass (b. 1936) is one of the best-known female directors in Poland. She gained this position in a very short period of time: her début *Bez miłości* (*Without Love*, 1980) made her famous practically overnight. Since then she has been a continuous presence in Polish cinema, although many of her subsequent films were strongly criticised by critics and failed to achieve a larger audience. However, even the most ardent critics of her work admit that Sass has managed to find a niche in Polish cinema, thanks to her consistency in choosing certain topics and problems, as well as to her loyalty to certain actresses, especially Dorota Stalińska and Magdalena Cielecka, who became stars largely thanks to playing in her films.

Sass's road to filmmaking was also one of the most difficult amongst Polish directors. According to her own words, she started shooting films when she was only seventeen and still at secondary school (Śnieg-Czaplewska 1999: 64). In 1960 she began working as an assistant director and since then she has worked with such well-known directors as Andrzej Wajda and Wojciech Jerzy Has. Yet it took her twenty years to become an independent director of feature films; by the time *Without Love* reached an audience, she was already forty-four. Shortly after her début she confessed in interviews that being a 'well-behaved woman' was a major obstacle in persuading appropriate people that she was able to make feature films independently (see Zygmunt, 1989a). It was only when she started to behave as a man that she gained the respect of her colleagues and the funds to make her first film (ibid.) Unlike Jakubowska, Sass was not helped by politics, but one should mention one factor that could have facilitated her road to cinema and aided her through her career: being married to one of the best Polish cinematographers, Wiesław Zdort, who worked with Sass in almost all of her films.

More than any of her women colleagues, Sass is labelled a director of films about and for women, even a feminist. Indeed, she showed more interest in women than any other Polish film director; women are the principal characters in almost all of her films and she often depicts their experiences from their point of view. However, it must be added that Sass's cinema is by no means homogenous, whether in terms of characters, setting, ideology or visual style. We can discern in her work two distinctive strands. In one, which coincides with the early part of her career, she is mainly concerned with the position of women in contemporary Polish society. In the second strand she chooses women from earlier epochs as her main characters, and represents them as melodrama heroines. Melodramas prevail in the second part of her professional life, which is on the whole more versatile. The films dominating these two strands will form the principal material of my discussion, whose overall purpose is to establish whether Sass is indeed a feminist.

Looking for One's Own Place in Contemporary Poland

The first three films of Sass – *Without Love, Debiutantka* (*Debutante*, 1981) and *Krzyk* (*Scream*, 1982) – are often treated as a coherent whole due to such factors as being produced in a short span of time, set in the time concurrent to their production (beginning of the 1980s), having the same actress (Dorota Stalińska) in the main part, and their preoccupation with social issues, especially attitudes and reactions of an individual to the flaws and injustices of the political system in Poland. Due to their social sensitivity, as well as their realistic, almost documentary style – marked, for instance, by extensive location shooting on the streets, in real hospitals, factories and restaurants, a style reminiscent of the 1970s and 1980s films of such directors as Krzysztof Kieślowski and Agnieszka Holland – they are often regarded as late examples of the Cinema of Moral Concern (Bren 1986: 159, 161; Kurz 1999: 37). The director herself contests this classification, regarding them as 'psychological dramas', albeit set in precisely defined social contexts (Maniewski 1996: 6).

Without Love (Figure 9.1) is set in the last period of 'real socialism', when open rebellion against the political authorities had not yet begun, but criticism of the many malaises poisoning social life was widespread. This criticism was directed both against the anonymous, ineffective and corrupt system and against those people who exchanged their moral integrity for more tangible goods: money, high positions, fame. The 'moral concern', to which directors like Kieślowski, Holland or Kijowski devoted their films in the 1970s, resulted from the dilemma, experienced particularly strongly by

Figure 9.1 Małgorzata Zajączkowska as Marianna and Dorota Stalińska as Ewa in *Bez miłości* (*Without Love*), 1980, dir. Barbara Sass © Studio Filmowe 'Kadr'

the Polish intelligentsia: to remain honest by opposing the system and the people who perpetuated it, or to 'sell one's soul' to achieve a better life.

In common with many characters in the Cinema of Moral Concern, Ewa in *Without Love* works in the media, which in the 1970s was regarded as a litmus test of one's political views and personal honesty. Her goal is to become a famous investigative journalist. She also claims that in her journalistic work she is driven by social concern, and intends to denounce corruption and incompetence in social life. Initially Ewa succeeds, securing a permanent post in a magazine, being chosen by her boss to write about topical subjects and offered a scholarship to Italy. However, in pursuing these noble objectives she increasingly uses less than noble methods, which put a question mark over her integrity. Ewa does not mind arranging things in bed, seducing men who are useful to her career, which can be regarded as the kind of corruption she condemns in her journalistic work, and is not shy about sacrificing an innocent individual to write about a 'larger issue'. Testimony to that is her publishing an article about Marianna (Małgorzata Zajączkowska), a young working-class woman who came to Warsaw from the provinces, looking for a better life, but found only a miserable existence in a hostel for factory workers and soon became pregnant. In order to get her piece onto the front page, Ewa included Marianna's picture, which resulted in Marianna's attempt at suicide and the loss of her baby. After this event Ewa's fortunes change for the worse. She is held responsible for this act, disgraced by her colleagues and loses her chance to go to Italy. Lost, lonely and suffering qualms of conscience, she turns to alcohol.

The ending of *Without Love* confirms the opinions of various men who criticised Ewa for her ruthlessness and warned her of the possible perilous consequences of her deeds. By extension, it vindicates the patriarchy that Ewa opposed both in her professional and private life. However, largely through the use of *mise-en-scène* and music Sass reveals various extenuating circumstances for Ewa's behaviour, making the viewer sympathise with the discourse which she embodies in the film. In particular, Sass shows that in Poland of that time one could not act completely honestly, if one wanted to do something good for the country, or for oneself. Ewa's male colleagues, who either because of a higher morality or simple laziness, do not attempt to access the places which she reaches, are unable to write interesting articles. Her difficult situation results also from her gender. All higher positions in Ewa's magazine are occupied by men; female journalists are reduced to making coffee for them. Similarly, men dominate the factories and hospitals; for example, the attendant in the hostel for female factory workers is male and he exercises his power over the women with an air of superiority. Consequently, the viewer is led to believe that moral integrity is a luxury which career women in Poland can not afford. Even Ewa's instrumental and cynical attitude to men, her belief that a woman cannot risk falling in love, if she wants to make something of herself, is partly excused as resulting from her previous bad experiences with men. She once lived in Rome and fell in love with an Italian press magnate. He seemed to reciprocate her affection, but abandoned her when she became pregnant, which drew her to alcoholism.

Ewa's small daughter features in the narrative, but she plays only a minor role in her life. She is looked after by her grandmother and sees her own mother rarely. Yet, Ewa refuses to feel guilty for having other priorities in life than motherhood. She even attempts to instil in her child the same moral 'vices' which she possesses, such as selfishness and strength. The soundtrack, consisting of sentimental music by Seweryn Krajewski and Italian pop, which Ewa listens to continuously and mementoes from Italy,[1] which decorate her flat, together convey the impression that deep in her heart Ewa remains a sensitive woman, able to love, and that it is the man's fault that such perfect material for a romantic heroine is wasted.

Debutante, which is set during the shipyard strikes in 1980, also features a very ambitious woman, who, like her predecessor in *Without Love*, is called Ewa. She is a graduate in architecture from Warsaw, who takes up an offer to work with a famous architect called Jerzy (Andrzej Łapicki) on the project of a sea museum, to be built on the Baltic coast: the arena of most dramatic events in this period. In common with Ewa in *Without Love* her work and private life are intertwined, although in a different way. Ewa the journalist unashamedly used men to achieve professional advantages; Ewa the architect sacrifices her ambition for love. The romance begins when her employer persuades her to move into his house in the country on the pretext that the project needs their close collaboration. She agrees despite being warned by another woman that he uses women for his own goals and discards them when they cease to be useful. The same fate appears to await Ewa: the work regime in Jerzy's house makes her sick from tiredness, and being one of the three women competing for the architect's attention – he lives with his wife Bożena (Bożena Adamkówna) and his secretary Maria (Elżbieta Czyżewska), who is also his lover – puts her in an uncomfortable position. Furthermore, life and work with Jerzy separates her from outside reality, even thwarts her political interests and opinions. In common with many people of her generation, Ewa opposes the communist regime. On her arrival at the coast she addresses the Solidarity conspirators, who put up the posters, 'I am with you.' However, by allowing Jerzy to dominate her life, she inevitably succumbs to his views that politics should be left to politicians and ordinary people should limit themselves to work: a view which was convenient to the communist authorities and which was profoundly challenged by the Solidarity movement. Furthermore, when the people whom Jerzy employs in his design office show an unwillingness to carry on working, because they have not been paid for many weeks, and because, as one of them puts it, 'the country needs houses and crèches, not symbols, such as the sea museum which Jerzy designs' (and which is commissioned by the government), Ewa appeals to them to continue working out of loyalty to their boss, ignoring their arguments. In the end, after he gets drunk at a party and attempts to rape her, she leaves Jerzy and tries to persuade Maria and Bożena to do the same. At this stage it is clear that the museum will never be built, and Ewa's work and devotion would be wasted. Yet, living with Jerzy and his women was not in vain, as she gained knowledge about men. The slight smile on her lips, when she boards the train back to Warsaw, suggests that she will not be fooled again by a man, that she has gained a degree of autonomy. Hence, although *Debutante* is classified as melodrama, the happy ending in this film is not equated with finding love, but with discovering the possibility of life without romance.

The heroines of *Without Love* and *Debutante* are very mobile. They change where they live, as a result of getting a new job or finding a new lover, moving from Warsaw to the coast, or even to Italy, and from hotel or rented apartment to the flat of one's lover. They relish being on the move: Ewa in *Without Love* is so fascinated by distant, exotic journeys, that instead of taking her small daughter to a park, she takes her to an airport, where they observe departing planes. Although the price of constant mobility is the lack of any permanent place to live, Sass's heroines do not mind not having a home and keeping all their belongings in one bag or rucksack. By showing that private space does not mean much to her female characters,

Sass distances herself from the classical women's pictures, in which home is the central setting and an important factor, shaping women's identity (see Cook 1983). More importantly, she also deviates from the traditional ideal of Polish femininity, epitomised by the myth of the Polish Mother, which regarded home as the central value in the lives of women. Mobility, which the heroines in the traditional women's pictures rarely achieve, is typically recognised as a sign of their ability to overcome the constraints resulting from patriarchy and to shape their own fate (Hill 1999: 174–76). However, as Moya Luckett observes, while discussing women in 'Swinging London' films, mobility can also signify less attractive states: displacement, homelessness, confusion, lack of stable identity. It can be constraining, not liberating (Luckett 2000: 239–41). I will suggest that in the first two films Sass ignored the dangers connected with mobility, concentrating on their advantages. For example, women who cannot afford to be mobile, like Ewa's friend in *Without Love* who works as a doctor somewhere in the provinces, or Bożena and Maria in *Debutante*, who feel too powerless and frightened of the outside world to abandon Jerzy, complain about their constraint and are full of admiration for Ewa. Even men, who are usually sedentary, attached to their homes and their desks, envy these women their ability to move – they equate it with freedom and youth, which they have lost for ever. Sass shows that male immobility, not unlike that of women, is also largely the consequence of patriarchy: of having wives who do not work outside the home and of whom they must take care, albeit with reluctance.

Sass's choice of setting, as well as the construction of the female characters and their subsequent iconic status, encourage comparison of *Without Love* and *Debutante* with Wajda's diptych, *Man of Marble* and *Man of Iron* (see Chapter 5). Both Ewa in *Without Love* and Agnieszka in Wajda's films work in the media and fight against the immoralities and absurdities of socialist reality. Yet, their moral trajectories are different. Agnieszka first wants to make an interesting film that will help her to achieve success as a director. Gradually, however, her career and even the film itself become secondary, as she is more committed to fighting for a better society. Ewa thinks more about her own advancement than of the welfare of her country. They also have different attitudes to love and sex. Agnieszka does not have sex with men whom she does not love, while Ewa often arranges things in bed. In common with Sass's female characters, Agnieszka is very mobile, travelling from Warsaw to the furthest parts of Poland. Yet, she eventually settles down, becoming a wife and mother in *Man of Iron*, even the Polish Mother, thus conforming to patriarchal rules of Polish society. By contrast, for Ewa in Sass's films there is never any stability either in a geographical or an emotional sense. One attempt to find success and happiness leads to another, the end of one eventful journey means the beginning of the next one.

There is no doubt that Wajda's character is more virtuous and dignified than Sass's heroines, who come across as selfish, at times even two-faced towards those close to them, and dishonest with themselves – hence the question why Sass constructed her characters the way she did. It is impossible to give a full answer to this, although some factors are worth listing. Firstly, unlike Wajda, who in *Man of Iron* attempted to rediscover national myths, Sass remained faithful to the code of realism favoured by the directors of the Cinema of Moral Concern. In particular, she showed awareness of the corrupting nature of the communist system, the thin line between being on the side of 'Them' – those supporting the system – and 'Us' – the dissidents and conspirators. Secondly, unlike Wajda and other directors of the most distinguished Polish films about women of this period – most notably the director of *Matka Królów* (*Mother of the Kings*, 1982), Janusz Zaorski, who represents female characters as being aware, as Ostrowska put it, that their tragedies are the realisation of 'the collective lot of Polish women' (Ostrowska 1998: 431) – Sass deprives her female protagonists of such knowledge. Thanks to that they are not perceived as participating in the preestablished order and their subjective field of choice feels greater than that of Agnieszka and Łucja Król in Zaorski's film.

Scream, the third film of Sass with Dorota Stalińska in the main role, highlights to an even greater extent the socioeconomic problems facing Polish women in the final years of 'real socialism', and, consequently, their failure to occupy the high moral ground. The main character in this film, nicknamed Perełka, finds herself in an even more difficult situation than her predecessors, which is a consequence of her belonging to the working class or, more precisely, to the criminal margins of Warsaw's poor Praga district. After being released from prison, she gets a job as a low-ranking nurse in a luxurious old people's home. At this stage Perełka is homeless, as she is unwelcome in the shanty house where she previously stayed with her alcoholic mother and her lover, and there is no council accommodation available. Perełka's fortune appears to change when she meets Marek (Krzysztof Pieczyński), a handsome male nurse, who lives in a converted barrack while awaiting a cooperative flat. She moves in with him and initially their romance flourishes, but eventually Marek abandons Perełka without any clear reason. Moreover, her dream of getting a flat disappears, when one of the apparently rich residents in the old people's home refuses to lend her money to bribe the housing cooperative. She kills the old man, which can be read as a metaphorical revenge on all men who let her down, and utters an awful scream: a sign of her anger and desperation.

In common with Ewa in *Without Love* and *Debutante*, Perełka bursts with vitality and almost masculine strength but, unlike her educated predecessors who tried to employ these attributes to advance their careers, she uses them mainly to harm herself. The connotations of mobility also change in this film: here it signifies a lack of direction and above all homelessness, which makes Perełka completely dependent on men. Men, however, as Sass showed on previous occasions, do not fulfil women's expectations, but make them even more unhappy and powerless. This grim diagnosis of Perełka's situation can also be read as an indictment of the political system which abandons the most vulnerable. This system, however, is no longer 'real socialism', as *Scream* is set in 1981, shortly after the brief victory of Solidarity, when, as Krzysztof T. Toeplitz puts it, there were effectively two centres of political power: official (communist) and unofficial (Solidarity) (Toeplitz 1984: 65–66). Yet, in Sass's film the political change makes no real difference to Perełka's life. It can even be argued that in a sense she is a victim of the atmosphere of accusations, characteristic of these times. The man whom Perełka kills is suspected of being a prominent communist figure. If not for this false (as she later finds out) accusation, she might not have chosen him as her victim.

The historical moment in which the narrative of *Scream* is set and its depressing scenario of female life reminds us of *Kobieta samotna* (*A Woman Alone*, 1981) by Agnieszka Holland (see Chapter 10). In both films poor, working-class women are depicted as being completely powerless, disfranchised from wider society and even from their own families. In both they seek refuge in men and initially men promise them happiness and moral salvation, but in the end they are the cause of their total downfall. Moreover, both Sass and Holland associate their heroines' misery with the communist system, which contrary to its pro-working-class rhetoric, let down working-class people, especially women. In both films there is also a sense of pessimism connected with Solidarity; it seems that for 'a lonely woman', such as Irena in Holland's film or Perełka in *Scream*, the new social order will bring few advantages: they remain marginalised as they always were.[2]

The three films previously discussed established Sass and Stalińska as a unique and powerful team in the history of Polish cinema. They owe each other more than anybody else for the launching and strengthening of their careers. However, after completing *Scream* their professional cooperation and friendship disintegrated. Several years later Sass offered Stalińska one more principal role in a film – apparently at the request of the latter, who wanted to play in a film which in some way would document their stormy and multifaceted relationship. The result was *Historia niemoralna* (*Immoral Story*, 1990) (Figure 9.2): a film regarded as full of flaws by the critics, viewers and even the director herself, who claimed that she failed to represent the relationship between Stalińska and herself in a honest way, and instead limited the film's content to gossip (see Grzela 2000: 28–29). The main defect of this picture results from the unreconciled attempt to tell the story of Sass and Stalińska, and at the same time to convey – or at least to play with – the idea (almost taken for granted in the age of postmodernism) that cinema is not the domain of presentation and truth, but representation and falsity. The film takes the form of a film within a film: the director named Magda (Teresa Budzisz-Krzyżanowska) makes a film about

Figure 9.2 Dorota Stalińska in *Historia niemoralna* (*Immoral Story*), 1990, dir. Barbara Sass © Studio Filmowe 'Kadr'

her star, Ewa (Dorota Stalińska), and the main narrative device used by Sass is that of shooting two different versions – or at least two different endings – of the same event: one representing the actress in a better light, one in a worse, and subsequently editing them in a way that further undermines or twists the initial meaning of the events represented. The consequence is a lack of clarity about what Sass wants us to believe with regard to Stalińska's and her own personality, and her relationship with this actress. Despite that, however, we can detect in the film some motifs and issues that pertain to Sass's oeuvre as a whole and are symptomatic of the prevailing discourses on femininity in the period the film was made. Ewa and Magda are typical of Sass's heroines in the sense that, although they forge close relations with other women, they also pursue their affairs at the expense of the happiness of other females. Hence, the friendship between the film director and her actress is marred by their mutual disloyalty and competitiveness. For example, it is suggested that Magda was jealous of the award Ewa received at the festival for a role which she played in her film. At the same time Ewa showed Magda no gratitude for making her one of the most famous actresses of her generation. Also, in common with her predecessors in Sass's films, Ewa is represented as being very mobile. Her love of travelling is epitomised by her expensive Porsche, which she claims was a gift from her father. In reality, after her father's death she almost stole it from her father's second wife, who inherited the whole of his estate. For Ewa the car means more than anything else in her life: only inside her Porsche can she forget about her numerous problems and feel free. The car is also an important part of her identity, confirming her status as a rich and famous woman, which she gradually loses in life. Mobility and vitality, however, not unlike the case of Perełka, are signs of Ewa's restlessness and lack of direction in life, rather than her freedom.

The differences between Ewa in *Immoral Story* and earlier heroines of Sass are as important as the similarities. The most significant is the fact that, unlike the other women in Sass's movies, who despite their numerous vices gained viewers' sympathy, Ewa is ultimately an anti-heroine. Her selfishness, arrogance, grandiose opinion of herself and contempt for those below her, combined with bad manners and bad taste (even her apparent talent is hardly visible in this film) and later her self-pity, do not allow us to like her, even less to identify with her. At times she comes across as totally immoral and repulsive.

Immoral Story was made in 1990, soon after the first democratic government was elected in Poland. The period which followed has been marked by the rise of masculinism and conservative attitudes to women (see Chapter 6). The career or 'liberated' woman, especially if childless, became one of the main victims of the new approach: the object of utter contempt and ridicule of right-wing politicians, Church officials and a large section of the media. The portrayal of Ewa is very much in tune with these negative opinions and images of women. Even the fact that Ewa has an abortion is represented negatively, as a testimony to her egoism and lack of responsibility. It seems to me that Sass not only noticed the new strength of patriarchy and masculinism in postcommunist Poland, but largely internalised it, or at least flirted with it.

Love is Everything

After completing her 'Trilogy' Sass made two films, *Dziewczęta z Nowolipek* (*Girls from Nowolipki*, 1985) and *Rajska jabłoń* (*Tree of Paradise*, 1985), based on the novels by Pola Gojawiczyńska of the same titles, published respectively in 1935 and 1937. Gojawiczyńska's books are renowned for their realistic depiction of the proletarian and petit bourgeois milieus of pre-Second World War Warsaw, which are represented from female perspectives. *Girls from Nowolipki* (Figure 9.3) and *Tree of Paradise* follow the lives of four friends: Franka, Bronka, Amelka and Kwiryna from the time they finished school till the death of two of them. They also contain a strong melodramatic element. These two qualities assured Gojawiczyńska's novels long-lasting popularity, particularly

Figure 9.3 A scene from *Dziewczęta z Nowolipek* (*Girls from Nowolipki*), 1985, dir. Barbara Sass © Studio Filmowe 'Kadr'

amongst female readers, testimony to which is the fact that before Sass turned to them, they had been twice adapted for cinema and television, respectively in 1937 by Józef Lejtes and 1975 by Stanisław Wohl, and their screen versions are regarded as very successful (Dondziłło 1978: 12; Mruklik 1986: 9–11).

The fact that *Girls from Nowolipki* and *Tree of Paradise* are regarded as respectable women's fiction partly explains why Sass, who established herself as a leading author of women's cinema, found in them attractive material for her own work. However, in the light of her previous preoccupation with contemporary reality, her interest in the past came as a surprise. There are several factors that explain this shift in interest. One was a general tendency amongst Polish directors, observed after the introduction of martial law in 1982, of choosing stories set in the past or the future as a way of avoiding contentious issues, or to present them less directly, and in this way evade heavy political censorship. Secondly, there was a rift between Sass and her muse, Dorota Stalińska, which encouraged the director to look for new types of female characters and subjects. Moreover, after Sass completed *Scream*, the critics and the director herself had a sense that she had exhausted a certain type of story, characters and ideas. Turning to literature was meant to alleviate these problems.

Gojawiczyńska depicts the eponymous girls from Nowolipki as strong, ambitious, honest and attractive women, who nevertheless fail to reach their potential. Being an author of left-leaning persuasion and proto-feminist views, she accused the harsh, capitalist and (albeit to a smaller extent) sexist prewar reality for their downfall. Stanisław Wohl preserved and Józef Lejtes even strengthened in their adaptations of Gojawiczyńska's novels the idea that before the war a woman of poor background was sentenced to remain in her constraining and unattractive world. In Lejtes's film it was conveyed, for example, by the recurrent motifs of rapidly closed windows and doors, and the ugly, claustrophobic, inner courtyard to which the girls always return.

Sass conformed to the original narratives but, as Joanna Piątek observes, changed their ideology by putting emphasis on the psychology of the main characters and the role of fate in shaping their lives (Piątek 1986: 11). Fatalism is first revealed by Franka (Maria Ciunelis), the most gifted of the four girls, who dreams about a career as an actress. She tells her best friend, Bronka (Izabela Drobotowicz-Orkisz), 'Neither I nor you are able to close your eyes and "give in", disregarding people's views. Neither are we able to live properly, as others do. The latter life we find too vulgar, too ordinary, too stupid, too suffocating, the former: too clever, too hypocritical, too dishonest. If one enters life with such a "dowry" [of views] as we do, it is enough to end in the gutter.'

Franka becomes a prostitute after being raped by an actor whom she trusted, falls ill with typhus, has an affair with a rich, middle-aged married man and eventually commits suicide. The fate of her friends, Bronka and Amelka (Marta Klubowicz), are hardly any better. Bronka falls in love with her neighbour Ignacy (Krzysztof Kolberger) and her affection appears reciprocated. However, to fulfil his political ambitions he marries a rich and educated woman, while continuing to see Bronka. This solution makes her unhappy and after years of putting up with being only his mistress, she commits suicide. Amelka, persuaded by her mother, first has an abortion after becoming pregnant out of wedlock with her first lover, and soon marries the rich owner of a chemist's shop (Mariusz Dmochowski). She eventually kills him and confesses to her act, not so much out of remorse, but because she feels that there is no meaning in her life; she is haunted by the thought of her lost lover and child. Kwiryna (Ewa Kasprzyk) is the only girl who looks for success outside the private sphere. She inherits a run-down shop from her parents and changes it into a flourishing enterprise. However, she also loses in the end, as her thrift and greed drives a wedge between her and her altruistic husband, Roman (Piotr Bajor). His death from leukaemia, for which she partly blames herself, as initially she did not want to pay for a doctor, demonstrates that a life of professional success is for a woman little more rewarding than a life lived for love.

By emphasising romantic love – or, more precisely, the desire for such love and having a family as the main factors shaping women's lives – Sass distanced herself from Gojawiczyńska and the Polish model of melodrama from the prewar period, which foregrounded sociocultural determinants of romantic love. More importantly, she contravened her own vision of women's place in society, revealed in her 'Trilogy', where the downfall of female characters resulted from a combination of factors that were historical and therefore changeable. Moreover, unlike women in *Without Love*, *Debutante* and *Scream*, who transformed internally under changing circumstances, learnt their lessons and moved on, characters in *Girls from Nowolipki* and *Tree of Paradise* remain the same. As a result, critics argued that they symbolise certain universal types of women, as opposed to historical women (Piątek 1986: 10; Zajdel 1986: 11).

While there is a significant difference in the way women are represented by Sass, men remained the same: selfish, insensitive and conformist. They might be economically and politically powerful, but their emotional impoverishment and almost autistic preoccupation with their own affairs make them unenviable figures. The only exception to this rule is Kwiryna's husband Roman, but his premature death erases him from the narrative, preventing him from making a greater impact on his surroundings.

Comparing the *mise-en-scène* in Sass's 'Trilogy' and her films based on Gojawiczyńska's novels underlines both the continuity and change in the director's representation of female characters. Women in *Girls from Nowolipki* and *Tree of Paradise* live in places that are dark and confining, and, with the exception of Kwiryna, they have little control over their space. Houses and rented rooms that they inhabit do not really belong to them, and their husbands and lovers leave a greater trace of their personalities on them than the women do. In this respect they are reminiscent of the places where heroines in Sass's earlier films lived. Yet, in contrast to them – particularly Ewas in *Without Love* and *Debutante*, who almost invaded public places, filling them with their loud voices and uncontrollable mobility – the girls from Nowolipki are very shy on the streets, in the offices, in the restaurants, even hiding from people's gaze. Such behaviour results partly from their low social status and partly from their unclear conscience: as prostitutes, mistresses or married women lusting after younger men they prefer to stay in the shadows. Their actual confinement is a reflection of their moral confinement. They are happiest in an open space, far from the city, close to nature; their joint excursion to the outskirts of Warsaw constitutes one of their rare moments of pure joy. Yet, such moments are very short and they only highlight the unhappiness of the rest of their existence. Fatalism is also conveyed in the film's symbolism, especially the recurring motif of an apple, standing for woman's appetite for love and sex and her eternal, sinful nature. For example, an apple falls on the pavement at the very moment Bronka throws herself under a car, giving the impression that women sin and are punished simply because they are females. Such symbolism, conveying the idea that women 'belong' to nature, which determines their fortune, hardly appeared in Gojawiczyńska's work; as

Figure 9.4 Magdalena Cielecka as Anna and Olgierd Łukaszewicz as a priest in *Pokuszenie* (*Temptation*), 1995, dir. Barbara Sass © Andrzej Stempowski

previously mentioned, she tended to foreground the sociopolitical components of women's position.

Many motifs present in *Girls from Nowolipki* and *Tree of Paradise* reappear in *Pokuszenie* (*Temptation*, 1995), regarded as Sass's best film of the last decade (Figure 9.4). Set in 1956, the last year of Stalinism in Poland, *Temptation* alludes to a true event, when the political authorities attempted to disempower and disgrace the charismatic leader of the Catholic Church in Poland, Cardinal Stefan Wyszyński, first by imprisoning him, then by sending him a nun, who in reality was a secret service agent with a pseudonym Ptaszyńska, with the task of gaining information from him and seducing him. The authorities failed: the cardinal did not give in to the charms of his female companion, and after the death of the Stalinist leader of the Polish Communist Party, Bolesław Bierut, he left prison enjoying greater respect amongst Polish Catholics than ever before. Sass was not the only director inspired by the story of Cardinal Wyszyński and Ptaszyńska. In 2000 another female director, Teresa Kotlarczyk, made *Prymas. Trzy lata z tysiąca* (*Primate. Three Years Out of a Thousand*). Her film examined the political and moral situation of the leader of the Catholic Church in Poland during his imprisonment against the background of Stalinism.

In her film Sass is less preoccupied with historical accuracy. Unlike Kotlarczyk, she does not use the real names of people and ignores many historical details. The political dimensions of the Wyszyński-Ptaszyńska affair and the views and emotions of the priest are pushed to the background, giving way to a psychological portrait of a young, sensitive woman, who unhappily falls in love. Sass's heroine, named Anna (Magdalena Cielecka), once worked as a maid for a priest (Olgierd Łukaszewicz) who later became very prominent. She was infatuated with him, but her love was not reciprocated. To be closer to her beloved priest, if not physically, then at least spiritually, Anna became a nun and subsequently she was sent to prison for encouraging schoolchildren to oppose communism. The authorities there tried to force her to work for the secret police, to spy on a high-ranking priest accused of an anti-government conspiracy. On her arrival in the military camp, far from civilisation, where the prominent priest is interned, Anna discovers that he is the same man with whom she had been in love. The old love is rekindled in Anna, and the priest himself seems to be tempted by the beautiful young nun, who is completely devoted to him. Yet, in the end he rejects her affection and, in a moment of deepest despair Anna denounces the priest, only to find out that it does not matter any more as the political situation in Poland has changed and the authorities are no longer interested in persecuting the Church.

In common with *Girls from Nowolipki* and *Tree of Paradise* Sass builds her film around the contrast between an imagined life of freedom and happiness and real confinement and misery. Firstly, there is the physical confinement of the camp imposed on its inhabitants by the political authorities. This confinement is suffered by both Anna and the priest, but Sass suggests that being brought up in the country, loving light and fresh air, she suffers more than he, who, as an intellectual, enjoys studying in a solitary cell. Anna's dream of freedom is conveyed by her constant looking through the windows and iron bars and her immense pleasure in observing nature around the camp: trees and animals, particularly birds, whom she also feeds. She herself can be described as a 'caged bird' (a metaphor used extensively in other films of Sass). However, the most painful confinement is psychological and largely self-imposed. Unlike physical imprisonment, this confinement is experienced only by Anna who, by falling in love with a man unable to reciprocate her feelings, and by entering a convent, sentences herself to constant erotic frustration and violation of the values which she promised to respect.

At the same time as exposing love as a destructive force in the life of the heroine, the director exalts it. For example, the priest, quoting the Bible and using allegorical language, glorifies love as the only thing which matters in human life. He means primarily a pure, asexual love of God, but his words can also be applied to the love between humans. Anna herself does not bemoan her being a sexual creature, but only regrets entering the convent, as it prevents her from living in tune with her feminine side. On the whole, Anna is in a nowin situation. She would be doomed, if she gives up her love for the priest, because without love her life would be empty; but by loving him she sentences herself to neverending suffering. This situation reminds us of the circumstances of girls from Nowolipki. Although the priest, like the majority of men included in Sass's previous films, does not reciprocate the woman's affection, this time his inability to love does not make him a moral dwarf. He is 'saved' as a human being by his devotion to God and his service to people who oppose the communist regime; thanks to them he overcomes the temptations of the flesh and finds inner freedom.

The three films discussed in this part of the chapter are set decades before the time they were made, but in common with *Immoral Story* they reflect some changes in attitudes towards women that since the 1980s were revealed by various centres of political and moral authority, such as the state, Solidarity and the Catholic Church. The change consisted of foregrounding a woman's rights and duties resulting from her nature (or, more precisely, what was regarded by these institutions as 'woman's nature'), at the expense of recognising the variety of needs and interests of real, Polish women. Particularly in Solidarity and the Church's discourse on gender, emphasis was put on an 'ahistorical' woman, whose needs are to be fulfilled in the private sphere, as a wife and mother, as opposed to a man whose main role is to act in the public sphere and provide for his family. This return of patriarchy in the official sphere, sometimes regarded as a reaction against corrupting, Western influences on Polish culture, was greeted by women with mixed reactions. Some, particularly those close to feminism, regarded it as constraining and humiliating, because it sentenced them to second-class citizenship. Others, however, regarded it as a chance for gaining freedom from the pseudo-emancipation imposed on them from above, which was the norm in communist times, and which resulted in women's immense difficulty in achieving fulfilment in either the public or the private sphere (Molyneux 1994: 303–30).

It is plausible to suggest that the three films reflect an ambivalent attitude towards the concept of a woman as ahistorical, which was characteristic of Sass and many other Polish women in the 1980s and 1990s. The ambivalence results from the fact that, on the one hand, Sass embraces the notion that a woman is defined primarily by her natural instincts and desires, which culture can temporarily suppress, but cannot change. On the other hand, however, she draws the viewer's attention to the harms inflicted on historical women by accepting such a narrow definition of woman as 'eternal Eve', whose life gains meaning only through men and thanks to them.

Between Identification and Distant Sympathy:
Spectatorship of Sass's Films

In order to answer the main question posed in this chapter, regarding Sass's allegiance to feminism, it is worth considering the spectatorship of her films. I am interested in the ways they assume certain responses from the viewers, their actual reactions, as well as the director's perception of her audience, conveyed in her interviews.

The spectator of Sass's films is addressed through a variety of discourses which often appear to be in conflict with each other. In her 'Trilogy' Sass places a female character in the centre of the narrative: she virtually never disappears from the screen. Moreover, she uses close-ups extensively, subjective shots and other means, suggesting that she intends to present reality from the point of view of the leading woman. The director herself described these films as 'psychological portraits' of strong, determined, young women and admitted that they were addressed mainly to a female audience, expecting the viewer to identify with the position of the central character (Maniewski 1996: 6). This position, as has been previously mentioned, is that of a loser: each film depicts the comprehensive downfall of a woman, comprising a failure in the professional, private and social life of which she herself is largely to blame. I suggest that at the level of narrative the films elicit masochistic identification with the doomed heroine or function as a warning against behaving like Ewa and Perełka (who in the Polish press were typically regarded as independent and liberated women). Asked in interviews why her films contain such gloomy endings, Sass typically replied that they simply reflect the pessimistic side of her personality; the optimistic one is mirrored in her theatre production (Zygmunt 1989b: 12). Without dismissing this explanation I will propose that the pessimism of Sass's narratives can be interpreted as a legacy of Polish Romanticism in her cinema. It is worth remembering here that she learnt filmmaking as an assistant of Andrzej Wajda and Wojciech Jerzy Has, who specialised in creating characters doomed to failure and whose tragedy was depicted as a testimony to their inner nobility.

Yet, in a different discourse, articulated through the appearance and acting of Dorota Stalińska, the films conveyed a different message: that it is acceptable, or even desirable, to act in the way her heroines acted and be selfish, arrogant, even cynical and disloyal. The reaction of young female viewers to *Without Love* at the time the film was first shown in cinema theatres suggested that Sass's heroines were regarded not as villains, but as role models, and their determination to win mattered to viewers much more than their eventual demise. The testimony of such a reception is the immediate stardom of Dorota Stalińska, who in her words off-screen gave the impression of being physically even stronger – as well as more selfish and less sentimental – than her characters, as well as the fact that her physical appearance, marked by large jumpers, bootleg trousers, fast walking and husky voice, began a new fashion amongst young Polish women. Stalińska's strong women, along with Agnieszka from Wajda's films, played by Krystyna Janda, in the early 1980s came to epitomise modern Polish woman – if not completely liberated, at least trying to live her own way. Maria Kornatowska went so far as to suggest that both Janda and Stalińska represented the type of bisexual actresses (Kornatowska 1986: 178–79). I also find it symptomatic that twenty years after the premiere of *Without Love*, female journalists still appreciate the significance of Sass's early films in changing their views on what is proper conduct for a young woman and distancing themselves from the values encapsulated by the Polish Mother. For example, Liliana Śnieg-Czaplewska says that Sass's early films, which she regards as being ahead of their times, encouraged her to fight for herself, to become a feminist (see Śnieg-Czaplewska 1999).

Sass's later films, such as *Girls from Nowolipki, Tree of Paradise* and *Temptation* also, to use Teresa de Lauretis's phrase, address the spectator as a female (see de Lauretis 1987). However, in comparison with Sass's 'Trilogy', their significance in changing viewers' attitudes and behaviour is much less noticeable. In particular, they give no rise to any discussion about the situation of women in contemporary, or, indeed, even past Poland. In the reviews of these films an opinion prevails that they represent a universal, ahistorical situation of a woman. Similarly, although actresses in these films continued to be praised by the critics and rewarded at the film festivals (particularly Magdalena Cielecka, who played Anna in *Temptation*), there is no sign that they became role models or inaugurated new fashions amongst women. Finally, unlike the early films, which attracted audiences counted in hundreds of thousands or even millions, they achieved only moderate success at the box office.[3] My own investigation concerning women's reaction to these films suggests that female viewers sympathise with Sass's characters and pity them, but fail to identify with them. The lack of wider and deeper resonance of Sass's later film amongst women can be explained by their conformity to a conservative notion of femininity. From a feminist perspective, these films are a step backwards in comparison with Sass's early films. The director herself seems to endorse such an assessment of her later work, by increasingly distancing herself from feminism and 'women's cinema', even claiming that choosing women as protagonists of her films is accidental, and that they stand in her films for 'human beings' (see Lenarciński 1994; Grzela 2000).

However, if we place *Girls from Nowolipki, Tree of Paradise* and, most importantly, *Temptation* in the context of Polish cinema of the period concurrent with their production (see Chapter 6), we will notice that they also challenge to a certain extent the prevailing way of representing women, as lacking any subjectivity and dignity. By contrast, Sass in her films demonstrates that women possess subjectivity and analyses it with patience and sympathy.

Note

1. At the time when Sass made *Without Love* Italy became very fashionable in Poland. The songs of Italian pop star Drupi were extremely popular and Italian men were regarded as the sexiest in the world – hence, the dream of many Polish female teenagers and young women to go to Italy and marry an Italian. Sass both plays on these stereotypes and subverts them.
2. From this perspective *Scream* and *A Woman Alone* can be regarded as films anticipating some movies of the next decade, which allude to the disadvantages brought to women by the new political system, such as *Nic* (*Nothing*, 1998), directed by Dorota Kędzierzawska (discussed in Chapter 11) and *Torowisko* (*Track-way*, 1999), directed by Urszula Urbaniak.
3. The director herself largely blames cultural policy in Poland – namely the narrow distribution of her films – for their failure to reach a wider audience (see Pierzchała 1997: 14).

CHAPTER 10

Agnieszka Holland: a Sceptic

ELŻBIETA OSTROWSKA

Krystyna Janda, who played the character of Agnieszka, the young student director, in Andrzej Wajda's famous film, *Człowiek z marmuru* (*Man of Marble*, 1977), recalls working on the part in the following words: 'Nobody knew what this girl was to be like. So Wajda took me to the location at which Agnieszka Holland was shooting her film *Sunday Children* and asked me to watch her' (quoted in Wajda 2000: 168). At that time Holland was indeed herself the ideal prototype of a young, rebellious, female filmmaker, a model figure that was later to be developed as the main heroine of Wajda's film.

Unlike the majority of Polish film directors, who are alumni of the Film School in Łódź, Holland graduated from the Czech film school FAMU.[1] Several reasons determined her choice of Prague. At that time studying at the Łódź Film School was only possible for university graduates, and she did not want to 'waste' her time studying for a degree which was of no interest to her. She wanted to get behind a camera as soon as possible. There were also personal reasons. She was afraid that she would not be accepted at the Łódź School because of negative rumours surrounding the death of her father, Henryk Holland. In the postwar period this journalist of Jewish origin was linked to the new political system. However, after some time he lost his belief in communism as implemented in Poland and was treated as a political enemy. The circumstances of his death are still unexplained. He was either thrown through a window by secret agents who were searching his apartment, or he committed suicide.

While studying in Czechoslovakia, Holland witnessed the events of the Prague Spring of 1968. Overwhelmed by the political atmosphere of those times, she became linked to a group of Polish couriers conveying illegal publications from Paris to Poland via Prague. Though her participation in this action was insignificant, she was arrested and imprisoned for six weeks. She recollects this experience as 'a useful lesson of life' (Zawiśliński 1995: 19). Among her teachers at FAMU were Karel Kachýňa and Milan Kundera. For a while she considered settling permanently in Prague. However, after finishing her studies in 1971, the political situation there completely changed, and she decided, together with her Czech husband, Laco Adamik, to return to Poland.

Her first professional experience was with Krzysztof Zanussi as his assistant on *Iluminacja* (*Illumination*, 1973). 'I was very ungrateful to Zanussi. I worried him to death. I was young then, pretentious, and conceited. I thought I knew everything. As an assistant director I performed all my duties properly, I guess, but as a human being I was unbearable' (Zawiśliński 1995: 24), reminisces Holland. Then followed her collaboration with Andrzej Wajda. She described her first meeting with him this way: 'He seemed to me an incarnation of the spirit of a Polish film director-playboy: cigar, white sheepskin coat, a particular way of speaking. How different he was from all those Czech filmmakers who looked like book-keepers or tailors' (Zawiśliński 1995: 24). She asked Wajda to let her join his famous film unit 'X', and he agreed. However, she did not make a film for quite some time, since the central scenario committee rejected all of her scripts. Nevertheless, Wajda offered her a position as his assistant on the production of *Man of Marble*. Again, the Ministry of Culture withdrew its approval. In response, the whole crew protested, threatening not to work on the production. Although the authorities still refused to change their decision, Holland was allowed to begin work on her previously blocked scenarios. Soon she made her feature début, *Wieczór u Abdona* (*Evening at Abdon's*, 1975), produced for Polish television. Before deciding to emigrate from Poland in 1981 (she was in Sweden when martial law was proclaimed and decided not to return to Poland), she made a number of films on which I will focus in this chapter.

Holland does not perceive herself as a representative of 'women's cinema'. Interviewed in 1995 she said, 'I've never identified myself with women's cinema, not to mention feminist cinema' (Zawiśliński 1995: 43). Her films do not easily fit into such a classification either. Because of the diversity of themes, styles and ideological positions Holland uses the result is a remarkable heterogeneity in her oeuvre. However, one can detect the frequent presence of subject matter and motives that reflect the dilemmas experienced by contemporary women.

Evening at Abdon's, Holland's first television feature, is an adaptation of a short story of the same title, written in 1922 by Jarosław Iwaszkiewicz, a distinguished representative of a modernist trend in Polish literature. In the literary prototype various kinds of oppositions – life-death, philosophy-reality, man-woman – are considered and presented in poetic form, rather than in a logically ordered narrative. Holland decided to clarify this vague structure, while retaining its poetic character. The main character, Abdon

(Marek Bargiełowski), is a philosopher who lives in a small town, Maliny, a place 'where nobody comes to'. He experiences a crisis in his world-view developed through studying philosophy and feels very lonely. His alienation is conspicuously visualised through the *mise-en-scène* of the tight and dark space of his flat and its window, marking a borderline between his inner reality and the external world. Outside reality is presented in a series of static images unfolding before his eyes which attract him, but, at the same time, remain entirely strange and inaccessible. He tries to establish an intellectual relationship with the Rabbi Szymsze, and lends him Nietzsche's *Between Good and Evil*. However, the Rabbi returns the book without reading it and says: 'What is the point of reading this book? It is not a good book.' Abdon's response is full of anger; he accuses the Rabbi of thinking he has a secret and superior knowledge. The Rabbi's denial of the book amounts to a categorical refusal to set up a dialogue and a relationship with the hero. Again, this hiatus is developed by the *mise-en-scène* as the two men talk through the window.

Abdon also suffers from his inability to fulfil his libidinal desire for a local pharmacist's wife, Herminia (Beata Tyszkiewicz). He is unable to express it openly, but can only speak of it as an intellectual construction of love, understood as the meaning of life: the only possible confirmation of the reality of life itself. Herminia, while calmly receptive to Abdon's confessions, prefers a young boy, Michaś (Michał Bajor). This young boy is also for Abdon an object of desire. Michaś and Herminia represent the natural force of sexuality without any feeling of guilt or embarrassment. They do not bother to hide their relationship, treating it as something 'natural' and thus justifiable. The attitude they share seems to be free from the restrictive force of institutional authority, moral law or the super-ego. For Abdon, this 'natural liberty' is both appealing and appalling. He displays a sado-masochistic attitude toward the couple; he invites them to his birthday party, and then provokes them to openly execute their sexual relationship in order to confirm his own disenchantment, which is also his humiliation. This act of open masochism is followed by an act of sadism: the cutting at Michaś's throat with a razor. Abdon escapes from the town, which is shown in a long take filmed from a high perspective. Here he appears on the screen as a helpless figure, like an insect unaware of the fruitlessness of its efforts to escape across an endless terrain. In contrast to Abdon's frenzied actions, those who remain in the town easily return to the previous settled order. Herminia is shown welcoming her husband returning from hunting, while Michaś, still alive, starts flirting with Antonina, Abdon's maid, who takes care of his wounds.

While *Evening at Abdon's* differs significantly from other work by Holland, it introduces issues and motifs found in her later films. Abdon, like many characters in her films, suffers from loneliness and is not able to establish relationships with other people. Among the possible human relationships, love is the most problematic and this will continue to be a key theme of Holland's work.

Niedzielne dzieci (*Sunday Children*, 1976), Holland's next film, was also made for Polish television as part of a series entitled *Rodzinne sytuacje* (*Family Situations*), consisting of a number of medium-length films concerning the problems of the Polish family in the 1970s. *Sunday Children* is Holland's first fully authored work, since she wrote the screenplay as well as directing. The film constitutes an open criticism of Polish reality at the time and is also a penetrating psychological portrayal of the main characters.

The film opens with a sequence of a wedding party taking place in a typical, rather small, apartment block. A newly married couple (Zofia Grąziewicz and Ryszard Kotys), both in their mid-thirties, are surrounded by relatives and friends. The scene is filmed in a documentary style with an apparently accidental composition of frame: a static camera changing its angle in a random way without much concern for providing the viewer with a privileged viewing position. The lack of close-ups denies an individualisation of the characters and an emotional identification with them. The conversations at the table do not help to provide knowledge about the people celebrating the event. We hear isolated conventional phrases, brief remarks on the food being served, and the hosts' thanking of the guests, in particular to an aunt who has come from Great Britain. By and large, camerawork, editing and soundtrack are employed to observe the situation coolly without any attempt to extract individual features. The result is an underscoring of the mediocrity of the couple, as well as the event, an effect reinforced through setting, costume and casting choices: Holland decided to employ lesser-known actors and amateurs. The couple, their relatives and friends are presented as neither rich nor poor, pretty nor ugly, sophisticated nor primitive. They are ordinary people.

After the credits, the couple are shown calculating their monthly budget. Excessively scrupulously they count their money to see how much they will be able to save for the planned purchase of a car. They are shown in medium close-up shot, the man is turned frontally towards the camera, while the woman is seen from the back. They seem to be entirely focused on solving this financial puzzle, without any trace of intimacy between them. This short scene conspicuously demonstrates that this marriage is an economic institution rather than a human relationship based on love, passion or even friendship. Since they are represented as 'an average couple', the viewer can assume that this portrayal of 'family life' typifies Polish society during the 1970s. Anybody living in Poland at that time would be familiar with this image.

Next, another typical scene from the life of the newly married couple is presented: the visit of the husband's parents. Conventional conversations accompany an equally conventional dinner. A nonsensical and banal comparison of the quality of TV sets is inevitably followed by the issue of children, as the man's mother ruthlessly presses for a declaration of when a baby is to be expected. She says that after three years of marriage it is high time to have a child, otherwise people will start talking – expressing the common belief that it is a woman's essential duty to give birth. In her opinion marriage without children does not make sense. Such statements, presented as common sense, confirm the notion of marriage as an economic and reproductive institution, conveyed earlier in the scene of planning the family budget. Symptomatic here is the young couple's readiness to conform to this demand from the older generation. Instead of contesting these ideologies, as one would expect from a younger generation, they seem to be embarrassed, ashamed or even guilty because of their failure to follow these precepts. Certainly, the wife feels guilty, as is demonstrated in a scene where she visits a psychologist to whom she confesses her feeling of being a 'defective woman'. It proves difficult for the doctor to persuade her that this is not true.

In trying to resolve the 'baby problem', the couple decide to adopt a child. They visit an adoption centre only to learn that there is a long list of formal requirements for getting a baby. This could be even more difficult since the couple has special requirements. They want a newly born baby, 'a new brand', as the husband says, in order to pretend it is their own. Worth noting here is that it is the husband who mostly presents the list of wishes and expectations, and who reacts most vehemently to the difficulties in the procedure of child adoption. He shouts that he earns enough money and has impeccable credentials at his workplace, making it possible for them to receive a baby at once. When they are shown all the children waiting to be adopted in the orphanage, the man looks at them in a reproachful way, as if looking at items in a second-hand shop of no special interest or value to him. No wonder that when later that evening he finds his wife in the bathroom, crying with pity for these children, he says: 'You'd be better off pitying yourself.'

While further exploring the possibilities of adopting a child, the husband accidentally meets a young girl who is pregnant and does not want to have the baby. He begins to spy on her and learns that she lives in a hostel for female workers. He arranges a meeting with her friend to learn more about her. Eventually, he goes to her doctor, introducing himself as the father of the girl's child, saying he is not sure whether she is a 'decent' girl. The doctor perfectly understands all these dilemmas and, apparently motivated by male solidarity, checks all her medical tests and finally manages to calm the putative 'father' by demonstrating that she is a 'decent' woman. Now he is ready to begin negotiating his planned 'business deal' with the girl. He offers to adopt her child immediately after the birth, for which he will pay a monthly allowance during pregnancy and an extra sum when the baby is born. The girl accepts all the conditions, and the deal is made.

The wife, while initially uncomfortable with this solution, finally agrees to her husband's plan to feign pregnancy in front of their friends and family. She sews and then wears a fake pregnancy costume and starts buying clothes for the baby. All of these clothes and other accessories have to be 'brand new', as the baby itself will be. The plan goes smoothly up to the final moment. At the moment when the girl is about to give birth, the wife discovers that she is herself pregnant, and hence does not need the 'contracted baby' any longer. The couple does not even bother to tell the girl personally; instead she finds out from the doctor. She ends by leaving her baby in the hospital but without relinquishing her maternal rights. The scene of her leaving the newborn child undermines all the common beliefs on motherhood and maternal instinct. The event occurs after breast-feeding, which, it is commonly believed, guarantees an arousal of maternal feelings. Nothing of the sort, however, happens to this young girl, who, after leaving the hospital, stares at the sun with remarkable relief and joy due to her new-found freedom.

The last scene of the film also calls into question the typical optimistic beliefs about maternal instinct. The girl is officially called to see her child in an orphanage, as she has not appeared for several months. While talking to the doctor she does not reveal any qualms of conscience over abandoning her child. However, neither does she want to agree to somebody else adopting the child. Entering the room with its dozens of children's beds, she is unable to recognise her own baby. The doctor has to show him to her. The girl looks at her son in a rather indifferent way, then she asks why he is crying, and finally lifts him up as the doctor suggests. The baby stops crying and we see in close-up his small fingers playing with the girl's hair. This final image of the film does not bring closure. We do not know whether this contact between the young mother and the baby will change her attitude towards him or not. Holland's film does not encourage optimism, and the viewer faces the bitter truth that the child will enlarge the number of 'Sunday children' who have to spend their childhood in orphanages, being seen only occasionally by their mothers.

The film's documentary style is achieved by means of camerawork and editing, but also by the ways in which the narrative is organised. Although the film has a typical goal-driven narrative, Holland interlaces it with several subsidiary episodes, which are not necessary for the development of the main plot. An example is the scene in which the pregnant girl accompanies her female friends to a dancing party in a restaurant. The camera gazes at the faces of the young people gathered there, trying to hide their lack of confidence with exaggerated gestures of unconstrained boldness. The harsh lighting discloses the defects of their beauty, unskilful and overdone make-up, and the poor quality of their clothes. The lack of dialogue in the scene compels the viewer to focus on these visual characteristics. There is little trace of individuality in their faces or in their behaviour; they are all more or less the same. The young girl with her unwanted pregnancy dissolves into the crowd and faces neither condemnation nor pity. When a man asks her to dance, he does not seem to even notice her bulky pregnant body. Interestingly enough, Holland cuts the episode off here. The viewer does not know whether this dance was just an accidental event, or is followed by a conversation, or perhaps by a couple of dates. Similarly, the married couple's plot-line concludes abruptly with the mere information of the baby's birth.

These cinematographic and narrative solutions distance the viewer both from the characters and the story, requiring him/her to focus on the issues of the film rather than on the plight of the characters. Due to the characters' mediocrity, it is clear that their attitudes to parenthood and consequently, to children, as represented in the film, have nothing to do with any kind of psychological or social pathology. Rather, their demeanour is symptomatic of the general system of values shared by society. Holland ruthlessly reveals the crisis of moral values stemming from the socialist variant of consumerism promoted by Edward Gierek, the leader of the Communist Party at the time. The ease with which the couple decide to 'buy' a baby, and with which the girl 'sells' it, mercilessly uncover the failure of the ideals Polish society was supposed to cherish in relation to the upbringing of children, whether through communist practice, or from the Catholic perspective. This apparent pessimism in relation to the failure of both state and society pervades all of Agnieszka Holland's Polish films.

The theme of motherhood recurs in the film *Coś za coś* (*Something for Something*, 1977), here considered from the perspective of the main female character, a thirty-seven-year-old woman, Hanna (Barbara Wrzesińska), a neurophysiologist working in a research institute. The two short first scenes characterise the heroine and give essential information about her situation. The first is with her lover in bed just after making love. He smokes a cigarette, while she eats an apple. After a while she starts dressing and he enquires whether and when she will phone or return. His begging tone is sharply contrasted with her tough 'no'. The credits follow and we see Hanna in bed, but this time alone as she wakes up, stretches her arms, and grabs an apple from the bedside table. Simultaneously, her husband, Jurek (Tadeusz Janczar), who, as we learn later, is also a researcher, is shown preparing breakfast. She starts talking to him, but at the same time is writing something at her desk: a conference paper.

In these two symmetrical scenes, Hanna appears as an independent, strong and extremely self-centred woman. If she decides to end her love affair, it is not because of a moral dilemma, but rather because she has simply lost interest in it. Neither does she feel guilty towards her husband. The marriage, as it is depicted in the scene, seems to be a typical partnership without the traditional division of the roles of husband and wife. They are mainly friends who like and respect each other and are ready to support each other in their professional careers. Hanna and Jurek seem successful in overcoming the limitations of the traditional conservative model of marriage and family that had been passively accepted by the couple in *Sunday Children*.

A professional career is undoubtedly the priority in Hanna's life. She also expects other people to share this attitude with her, as is demonstrated in the following scenes in the research institute. She is the coordinator of a project that requires all the members of the team to be entirely engaged in their work. She forces one of the female researchers to resign, as she has missed too many working days because of her sick child. In the course of the conversation between the two women, the viewer is confronted with diametrically opposed female positions. For the woman who is to be fired, her maternal duties are more important than her professional career, something Hanna finds almost impossible to understand. She aggressively asks the woman: 'Are you convinced that this world is so perfectly organised that it is worth bringing another human being into it?' Further, she questions all the 'natural' values of motherhood. The woman does not bother trying to convince Hanna of her beliefs, but only says that this is 'a disgusting egotism' and leaves the office. Hanna's face, shown in close-up, reveals a tiny sign of hesitation for the first time in the film. For the first time somebody has drastically questioned her apparently stable point of view. To make the issue even more complex, the woman does not appear to Hanna as a passive victim of maternal fate, or of patriarchal order, but is rather presented as somebody who has deliberately chosen different values in her life and is ready to accept all the consequences of this choice (as the title says: 'Something for something'). On the other hand, Hanna tries to convince herself that her choice does not bring any cost, and there is nothing to regret. Soon her beliefs will be questioned more profoundly.

For research reasons, Hanna meets a would-be suicide. Her 'object of study' is a young woman who has decided to kill herself because of a love affair with a married man. Initially hostile and distrustful, after some time the young woman starts talking about herself and her lover. His marriage, as described by the woman, seems similar to Hanna's marriage. For pragmatic and, in fact, quite trivial reasons, the young woman had decided to fake a pregnancy by him. However, instead of the money expected for a termination of the pregnancy, she received an offer of marriage. Hanna discovers that the woman in fact cannot have children. The 'fake pregnancy' was only of use for monetary gain, and became a terrible burden when she finally realised that her lover loves her and she loves him. The associated fears that had then rushed in had pushed her to the brink of suicide.

In the course of the young woman's story, Hanna becomes more and more convinced that it is her husband who is the lover of the woman. The viewer observes a gradual change in her attitude to the girl, as well as towards the whole issue of love, marriage and motherhood. The woman, initially treated as a mere 'object of research' (Hanna secretly decided to record her confessions), after some time becomes a fellow human being, who, unable to recognise the truths in her life situation, makes a wrong choice.

The encounter with the woman makes Hanna suddenly anxious about her marriage. She is almost completely convinced that it is her husband who is the woman's lover. Her fear accelerates when, in the evening, she does not find him at home as usual, initiating a hysterical search for him. Finally, she learns that she was wrong. When she finds him at home, she bursts out with an unrestrained cry, clearly embarrassing for her husband. Obviously, such an explosion of emotions is not something he is accustomed to. He puts his glasses on and tries to calm Hanna. Rather than sleep in their separate beds, he suggests they sleep together, to which she agrees. The next morning Hanna tells him that she had forgotten to take contraceptives the night before, signifying an apparent change in her attitude towards motherhood. Her husband, however, does not react like the young woman's lover, with joy and happiness. He seems to be entirely indifferent to this possibility and says that he will accept whatever she decides. After he leaves the flat, Hanna starts crying in the bathroom. The last image of the film shows her driving a car, as she smiles and looks calmly relaxed.

Once again Holland offers an open ending. We do not know whether Hanna smiles because she has decided to change something in her life, or because she is pleased that the order of things has not been altered in that her husband has not betrayed her. As in *Sunday Children*, the viewer is left without any solution of the problem dealt with by the film. An open ending allows Holland to withhold herself from formulating explicit judgements concerning these contrasted attitudes. As far as the problem of motherhood is concerned, she seems to be saying that it cannot be treated merely as an obligation for a woman, to be accepted or rejected. Above all, these films question objectifications of motherhood, leading straightforwardly to the commodification of pregnancy and children. Elements of this mind-set seem to be shared by the childless couple and the young mother in *Sunday Children*, as well as by the would-be suicide and Hanna in *Something for Something*.

Something for Something brings to the fore moral dilemmas related to certain occupations. In this film such a dilemma occurs when Hanna decides to secretly record the young woman's confessions. Apparently, she does not see anything reprehensible in this. When asked if this is fair, she answers impatiently that she needs it for her research, as if this explanation overrides moral concerns. This problem had also been addressed in an earlier film, *Zdjęcia próbne* (*Screen Test*, 1976) made by Holland with Paweł Kędzierski and Jerzy Domaradzki. It is also one of the main issues of her next film, her full-length cinema début, *Aktorzy prowincjonalni* (*Provincial Actors*, 1978).

Figure 10.1 Halina Łabonarska as Anka in *Aktorzy prowincjonalni* (*Provincial Actors*), 1978, dir. Agnieszka Holland © Studio Filmowe 'Oko'

Provincial Actors (Figure 10.1) belongs to the trend in Polish cinema called the Cinema of Moral Concern, which developed in the second half of the 1970s. The main representatives of this paradigm, a young generation of filmmakers, including Krzysztof Kieślowski, Feliks Falk, Janusz Kijowski and Agnieszka Holland, wanted to bridge the gap between the official image of Polish reality and the one actually experienced by Polish society. To achieve this aim they chose the realistic convention of cinematic representation, because they believed in the power of the cinematic image to convey the truth of the world, and, above all else, to disclose the reality hidden behind 'real socialism'. Although films of the Cinema of Moral Concern dealt with Polish reality, they were also significantly inspired by various movements of world cinema: British social realism (e.g., Tony Richardson, Ken Loach), cinema direct (Jean Rouch, Chris Marker), and the Czech New Wave (Věra Chytilová, Miloš Forman). The latter's influence has had a strong presence in Agnieszka Holland's works since the beginning of her career. *Provincial Actors*, together with Krzysztof Kieślowski's *Amator* (*Camera Buff*, 1979), are considered the most interesting achievements of this trend. Although these films, like others, depict various pathologies of contemporary political and social life, they go far beyond the mere reproduction of life, by posing important questions regarding the role and situation of an artist in a communist reality. In Holland's film one also observes

the psychological complexity of characters, which in the works of her colleagues was often lacking. Last but not least, she presents the story from
both a male and a female perspective, something that was quite unusual in
the Cinema of Moral Concern (see Kornatowska 1990). Here I will focus
on the female heroine and the psychological relations between the characters, leaving aside matters of political and social criticism, as these aspects
have been extensively analysed elsewhere (see Bobowski 2001: 84–102;
Jankun-Dopartowa 2000: 107–38).

Krzysztof (Tadeusz Huk) and Ania (Halina Łabonarska), a married couple in *Provincial Actors*, are not happy with their life. They live in a provincial town, in a block apartment, as grey as any other place in the
surrounding urban landscape. He works in the local theatre, to which a
director from Warsaw has come in order to stage a Polish national drama,
Wyzwolenie (*Liberation*) by Stanisław Wyspiański. Ania, in turn, works in
a puppet theatre, which, although not a site of 'pure art', has its faithful
children's audience. Both characters are frustrated with their professional
lives but for different reasons. He still dreams about playing leading roles
in the classical repertoire, something that would enable him to play the role
of a spiritual leader of the nation as prescribed by the Romantic tradition.
She has been dismissed from theatre school because of, as her husband
explains it to one of his friends, 'no natural aptitude for acting'. This phrase
was often used as an official excuse to relegate students for political reasons, and so it is possible that Ania was a victim of the student rebellion of
March 1968, suggesting her uncompromising attitude. After completing an
extensive course she becomes qualified as a puppet actor, a profession perceived by many people, including herself, as a surrogate form of a 'real' acting. Yet she is actually more successful than her husband, a fact not
admitted by any character in the film, and relayed to the narrative device.
In the beginning of the film Holland shows two consecutive scenes. The first
one takes place in the 'real' theatre, where almost all seats are empty, and
actors off-stage are complaining that there is nobody to play for. This scene
is followed by a close-up of a small girl whose face expresses an extraordi-
nary curiosity as she gazes at something hidden off-frame. The next shot
reveals the object of her astonishment: she is watching a performance of the
puppet theatre, and Ania is one of the creators of this enhancing reality. The
spontaneous response of the children's audience and their loud applause
contrasts saliently with the silence and haste of the adult viewers leaving
Krzysztof's theatre. If one adds to this the guest performances of Ania's theatre in Warsaw and the award she won at a puppet theatre festival, her professional achievements do not leave any doubts. However, they seem to be
acknowledged only by the narrator, without any confirmation from the
characters. Neither Ania, nor Krzysztof, nor any of their friends, colleagues,
or acquaintances appreciate this success. Ania's work is entirely silenced in
the couple's conversations, whereby the leading role played by Krzysztof in

Liberation occupies the central place in their family life. If Krzysztof says anything about Ania's work, it is always derogatory or ironic, such as 'Hop, skip, on a stick', which he repeats a number of times throughout the film in front of other people. The worst is that Ania seems to accept this disregard for her work. While visiting a friend from school, now a prosperous architect living in a luxury apartment in Warsaw, she does not want to say much about her professional life and answers all questions evasively.

Even if Ania is frustrated with her acting career, she does not try to resolve this problem at the expense of others as her husband does. While she is shown performing various duties, such as ironing or shopping, Krzysztof constantly behaves as if he were acting the role from the play currently being produced. Krzysztof does not exist any longer; there is only Krzysztof playing the character of Konrad, the main protagonist of *Liberation*. His narcissistic identification with the character leads to an emotional detachment from the real world in which he lives, and from Ania in particular. Accordingly, the viewer observes the gradual deterioration of their relationship. Krzysztof's egotism inevitably makes Ania more and more lonely, as she gets nothing in return for the emotional support she provides for her husband. Pharmaceutical tranquillisers are her only accessible solution. She also suffers from a sexual frustration, as is revealed in two scenes. In the first, the viewer sees Ania lying in bed erotically touching her own body; this is followed by a smooth camera movement, and then, in the next shot, Krzysztof is shown, photographed from a radically different camera angle, visually marking the distance between them. Suddenly, he begins to move rapidly and to scream as if he were having a nightmare. Ania wakes him and says 'You're tossing about again. Is it *Liberation*? Take it easy.' Krzysztof gets up, dresses and leaves the flat. Before doing this, he answers his wife's question with a dialogue from *Liberation*.

In the other 'bed' scene, one sees Ania in a silk nightgown. She asks Krzysztof whether he likes her nightgown. He absent-mindedly answers 'yes', then goes to bed, turns his back on her and falls asleep almost immediately. In response, Ania goes to the kitchen, unfolds a camp-bed and goes to sleep. By this gesture, while it may be perceived as immature or even hysterical behaviour, she also signifies her reluctance to make grudges. Her sincerity and straightforwardness sets her apart from the people who surround Krzysztof. Once, after listening to the actors' complaints concerning the Warsaw director's work and his cynical and opportunistic attitude, she asks them why they do not rebel. The answer she receives is, 'What can we do? We are actors, we must act.'

Ania believes she does not have to act, and that her fate is not sealed, so she decides to leave Krzysztof and start her life over. However, when he, having become disillusioned, comes to the puppet theatre in a state of a nervous exhaustion, resulting from his colleagues' acceptance of the Warsaw director's political opportunism, she consoles him and suggests that they move to another city and start over. Yet, this image of reunion does not bring hope, rather the opposite. The viewer knows that there is no way for them to escape this vicious circle of their professional and personal lives. The sick reality of the outer world inevitably destroys personal lives, says Holland in her film.

In 1980, when everybody revelled in the victory of Solidarity depicted by Andrzej Wajda in his *Człowiek z żelaza* (*Man of Iron*, 1981), Agnieszka Holland turned quite unexpectedly to a historical subject and made *Gorączka* (*Fever*, 1980), based on Andrzej Strug's novel, presenting the Polish Revolution of 1905 and the two subsequent years. In this film Holland expresses her own scepticism about revolution, which always raises great hopes but finally brings disappointment. In 1980 such scepticism could not be easily appreciated. In fact, while making *Fever*, Holland was far from playing the role of a warning prophet, as she said several years later:

> I decided to make this film because, after the experience of Czechoslovakia, I was sensitive to the bitter experience of a revolution that was 'sold out.' Otherwise, I would probably not have an interest in this subject. However, *Fever* has been linked to the events of August 1980. And this is irritating. One makes a film about something which is historically distant, and then one sees that this converges with something happening currently. Then one can realise how silly history is. (Holland, quoted in Bobowski 2001: 125)

In *Fever* (Figure 10.2), as in its literary prototype, there is no single main hero or heroine, a circumstance determining the film's narrative structure and its plot construction. We can see the various characters as they are connected through the idea of revolution. The idea is materialised by a bomb, which becomes a fetishised object of desire for all the characters. The bomb is represented in this way in the first scene, serving as the background for the opening credits. We first see it in close-up as somebody's hands gently touch it. Then, the close-up of a man's face is shown; he looks at the object with almost erotic fascination. Suddenly, he cuts his finger, and we see an enlarged image of drops of blood dripping on the bomb and of him sucking his finger in a somehow erotic manner. When the credits end, the scene continues, and a young beautiful woman, Kama (Barbara Grabowska), comes to the man to collect the bomb. His excitement when he sees her through the window, and the way he looks at her and talks to her, disclose his unspoken love for her. However, she seems not to pay him attention, as the bomb is the only thing she is attracted to. If the man's attitude to the bomb can be described as a melancholic enchantment, hers recalls a frenetic ecstasy, triggered by means of the mere presence of the desired object. The bomb, which functions as a revolutionary fetish, is a catalyst in the narrative. As it is passed from person to person, some characters enter the fictional world and others leave it, having been annihilated in some fashion. The first 'victim' of the bomb is its constructor, who is arrested immediately after Kama leaves his flat.

Figure 10.2 Barbara Grabowska as Kama and Olgierd Łukaszewicz as Leon in *Gorączka* (*Fever*), 1980, dir. Agnieszka Holland © Studio Filmowe 'Oko'

The characters in *Fever* represent various attitudes to the idea of revolution. Leon (Olgierd Łukaszewicz), the head of the revolutionary unit, embodies an entirely new type of conspirator in the Polish tradition, and is far from his romantic antecedents who undertook a fight doomed to failure in the name of faithfulness to a 'lost cause'. He is pragmatic, ruthless, and ready to sacrifice anything or anybody to achieve his revolutionary goals. He has no reservations about using terrorism to defeat his enemies.

The character of Kama comes from the previous Romantic tradition and can be perceived as another variant of the Polish traditional figure of the 'mad patriot'. She is in love with Leon. Like Leon, she is ready to sacrifice everything, including her life, for the revolutionary cause. However, she, unlike him, is not able to appraise the situation in a rational and realistic way. These flaws in her character are demonstrated remarkably when she is supposed to assassinate the Russian governor in Warsaw, using the bomb. We can see Kama in a state of unusual excitement as she walks together with Leon around the market the governor plans to visit. She moves chaot-ically from one stall to the next, unexpectedly buys a rocking-chair, then loses the box with the bomb only to find it a few minutes later. Finally, she learns that the governor will not appear there today. Another attraction is offered to the crowd in the market: the open-air projection of a silent movie. Holland presents the fast flow of images: close-ups of Kama's tense face, fragments of the screened movie, and images of a crowd distorted by the stream of light flowing from the movie projector. The fast editing com-bined with a cacophonic soundtrack foreshadows the coming attack of Kama's hysteria, which occurs in a carriage the couple finally manages to get to. Leon reacts to the woman's hysteria with cruelty and reproaches her for 'wanting to die beautifully'. Kama, initially a mad advocate of revolu-tion, who is madly in love with Leon, finally goes mad for real and is sent to an asylum.

The bomb is passed on to other revolutionaries who also treat it as a fetishistic object capable of destroying the old order, a step necessary to build a new one. Among them are: Wojtek Kiełza (Adam Ferency), a naïve peasant who uncritically believes in all the revolutionary ideals and trusts everyone he meets on his way, and Gryziak (Bogusław Linda), an anarchist, who wants to destroy the world for the sake of destruction itself. The for-mer is betrayed and sentenced to death by Russian authorities, while the lat-ter is only able to execute a pathetic parody of a spectacular destruction.

Eventually, the bomb reaches the Russians, its initial target. They are able to cope with it, by diminishing its destructive power to a mere pictur-esque explosion, which does not threaten them, but instead brings a sense of satisfaction. Such a devastating picture of revolution could not be well received in Poland in the euphoria of 1980. As Sławomir Bobowski wrote,

> at a time of great social enthusiasm, of hope for a change for the better, and of the complacency of Polish society proud of the transformations going on in Poland, the remarkable ... artist [Holland] gave a mirror to them in which they did not recognise themselves. ... Holland made a bitter film in a time of faith and euphoria; she showed people-puppets, who only think that they have a say, who believe that they are free and can shape reality according to their own will. She presented the world as a playground of irrational forces of destruction and *libido*. (Bobowski 2001: 125)

Kobieta samotna (*A Woman Alone*, 1981), the next film made by Holland (and the last one made in Poland), retains this sceptical perspective. This time, however, it is used not to analyse the mechanisms of history but the working of contemporary reality. In this film Holland also returns to the issue of motherhood which she had examined in her earlier works. *A Woman Alone* can be regarded as an attempt at rereading the myth of the Polish Mother, which is the dominant structure in the Polish discourse on feminin-ity (see Chapter 1). Holland revisits this myth by abandoning the martyro-logical perspective that prevails in cultural texts which employ this structure.

Holland's film is a portrayal of a single mother, Irena (Maria Chwalibóg), who is raising her only child, eight-year-old Boguś. However, she is not a widow, as the majority of Polish single mothers in the Polish tradition tend to be. Her son is an illegitimate child, whose father is a criminal locked in prison. Irena works very hard as a postal worker, but is paid so badly that she hardly makes ends meet. Her biggest problem is her inability to move to a new flat. The one in which she lives presently – one room without running water or heating – is located in the suburban slums. It was given to her by the local Communist Party committee. Her neighbours, a very poor three-generation family, want to take over her room, and are openly hostile and even aggressive toward her. The heroine thus has to struggle with poverty and is surrounded by enemies or, at best, by people who remain entirely indifferent to her. If one considers the traditionally prescribed significance and sanctity of the family in Polish society, one can see that Irena's situation bespeaks something else. To begin with, her father, an alcoholic, used to abuse his entire family. Instead of respecting and loving him, Irena hated him and was happy after his death. The aunt who raised Irena had been soulless and unrelentingly harsh to her. Even now, as the aunt is dying from cancer and Irena looks after her, she is more demanding than grateful. Irena's care, however, is not entirely unselfish as she hopes to inherit the aunt's flat. She will soon be disillusioned. First, she learns that the aunt agreed to pass the flat on to another relative. Then, after the aunt's death, she is asked to pay for the funeral, as the aunt has donated all her savings to a local parish. Enraged, Irena leaves the aunt's flat without waiting for the end of the ceremony.

The destruction of family bonds thus brings about the destruction of traditional family rituals. Such corrosion is also shown in the episode presenting Boguś's First Holy Communion, in the Polish tradition one of four most important rituals of family life: baptism, first communion, wedding and funeral. Initially, in the scene in church one sees Irena being genuinely moved, and for a while the elevated mood seems to pervade her and her son's lives. However, in the next scene the sublime is rapidly transformed into something trivial. Irena's brother, her son's godfather, and his wife refuse to come to her place for lunch because they lack the time. Boguś, trying to persuade them, says 'Please, come, mum bought vodka and sausages.' Eventually they come, but only for a while, to have vodka and sausages hastily, as if afraid to stay a bit longer and begin to feel sympathy for the lonely woman.

Instead of acting as a spiritual and practical support for the heroine, the family endows her with the status of the 'black sheep'. In her alienated relationships with her colleagues Irena is also doomed to play the social role of the Other. In fact, there is not much opportunity to establish a closer relationship with them as she spends most of her work time delivering the post. However, when she comes to the post office early one morning to collect letters and monies to be delivered, it is clear that she does not have any friends there. She is always seen alone, walking along long corridors, being observed by her colleagues, who are talking to one another gathered in two-or-three-person groups. Later, we learn that they want her to be transferred to a more poorly paid department. Although the action of the film takes place during the Solidarity period, there is no solidarity among the people who surround Irena.

One day she meets her spiritual counterpart, a crippled, ugly and poor man, Jacek (Bogusław Linda), who is a newcomer to the town where she works. He is as lonely as she is, and, similarly, he does not have his 'own place': he rents a room from a family. Both live on the margins of society, and the 'otherness' they share brings them closer together. In the course of their relationship, their alienation from the outer world is fully described. They are detached both from the past and from the contemporary life of the nation. In their experience, tradition exists only as an empty ritual performed by political groupings to legitimise their right to power. The man dreams about emigration to the 'West', where 'people are respected', while she appears to be unpersuaded by this idea. She says to him that she would not leave Poland 'for anything in the world'. However, it is clear that these words are merely a cliché everybody is taught at school, as she has no answer to Jacek's question: 'What's so special about Poland? There is nothing to be found here.' To express such an opinion when the whole society was revelling in Solidarity's victory and in the hope for a better future stemming from it, one has to be thoroughly disillusioned and detached from the rest of society. One line spoken by the heroine perfectly characterises her consciousness of her position in society. 'Who am I?', she asks herself and gives the instant answer: 'Nobody.'

Jacek, however, is convinced that he is a 'nobody' only here, in Poland. Somewhere abroad (in the West, naturally), he thinks, it will be possible to regain his dignity, become 'somebody' and be able to control his own life. Initially, Irena does not seem to share his expectations; she even tries to manifest her patriotism. However, when she loses all hope for changing her life situation, after first being brutally thrown out of the headquarters of the Communist Party committee, where she expected to find help, and later, after failing to receive any inheritance from her aunt, she feels trapped. Jacek's plans seem to her the only possible way to escape her hopeless situation. However, fulfilling these plans is not altogether easy. Since her overwhelming desperation pushes her to do everything to make this 'dream about the West' come true, she decides to steal the money she was supposed to deliver to people, leave her son in an orphanage, and escape abroad with her lover. On their way to the border, they have a car accident, which cannot be reported to the police since they bought the car with the stolen money, and so they find themselves trapped once again. The hopelessness of the woman's situation now reaches its climax. The only escape seems to be death, which comes from her lover.

This single mother from Holland's film does not remind us of the traditional icon of the Polish Mother as it is represented in such films as *Matka Królów* (*Mother of the Kings*, 1982) by Janusz Zaorski, *W zawieszeniu* (*Suspended*, 1986) by Waldemar Krzystek, *Skarga* (*The Complaint*, 1991) by Jerzy Wójcik or *Wigilia* (*Christmas' Eve*, 1985) by Leszek Wosiewicz (see Chapter 2). By and large, the difference results from Holland's replacement of a representational code based on romantic mythology with the code of realism. This replacement powerfully undermines the myth of the Polish Mother. Holland does not accept the traditional representation of motherhood in Polish dominant discourse, and, therefore, does not present the character as a disembodied monument, obliged both by 'nature' and cultural and social norms to bear suffering with dignity. Her 'lonely woman' is of flesh and blood. Holland at last had the courage to demystify the icon and begin to remove it from its pedestal.

Indeed, the single erotic scene in the film is one in which Holland's use of the realist code of representation is the most conspicuous. It takes place immediately after Irena's and Jacek's discussion of their life situation in Poland. At one point he approaches her and clumsily tries to embrace her. In response to this warm gesture, she draws the curtains across the window and begins to undress. The camera shows her in a long shot and the viewer can observe the woman as she calmly takes off all her garments: skirt, pants, bra, etc. Simultaneously, we see the man, who, at the opposite end of the room, clumsily fights with his shirt and trousers. He is also shown in a long shot. Thus, the camerawork reinforces the spatial distance between the characters, and also builds a distance between them and the viewer. The lack of close-ups or point of view shots, which are usually used in erotic scenes in mainstream cinema, prevents the audience from identifying emotionally with the characters. Next, the characters are shown frontally sitting on the bed, next to one another. It is difficult to imagine a more pathetic and sad image of a couple that is about to make love. She is seen frontally in her slip, somehow ashamed of the situation, just as he seems to be, sitting in his socks, dark old-fashioned boxers, and undershirt, with his misshapen crippled leg fully visible. Then we see Jacek's profile in close-up; his spasmodically distorted face drips with perspiration, as also, consecutively, is Irena's face when she comes to orgasm marked with a gesture of physical relief. Intercourse thus serves as a way to relieve tension and pain without any trace of joy or pleasure. The love scene does not last very long; afterwards Jacek clumsily slips off Irena and starts sobbing, as he explains to Irena he has never felt so good. *Mise-en-scène* devices and camerawork employed in this scene produce an effect of sheer naturalism, in strong opposition to the romantic code of representation dominant in Polish culture, as well as in conventions of mainstream melodrama.

The main heroine's sexuality sets her apart from the traditional icon of the Polish Mother who was usually strongly desexualised. Holland's heroine violates the precepts of motherhood even more drastically as she abandons her child and leaves him in an orphanage. However, her deed does not mean a lack of maternal love, as throughout the film she displays a reasonable concern for her son. She believes he is a good boy and sometimes she is even proud of him. She knows her maternal task is to bring him up to be a 'good Pole', although she is not sure what this means these days, as she says to Jacek, since 'our values have been destroyed'. The chaos of the political situation in the country converges with her hopeless circumstances, pushing her to make desperate choices: to steal money, leave Boguś in an orphanage, and to escape Poland.

Irena does not want to accept her miserable life. Instinctively, rather than consciously, she refuses to find satisfaction and masochistic pleasure in a lonely life full of sacrifices. Society reacts with intolerance and a desire to humiliate her because she dares to have individual desires and needs. Her death at her lover's hands could be interpreted as a symbolic punishment, deserved because she has violated the cultural and moral norms considered universal. Thus, Holland discloses the destructive aspects of the myth. Those who do not follow its precepts are met with disdain and repugnance. The bonds of solidarity do not link everybody, says Holland. There are always 'lonely women' who are left aside.

A Woman Alone is the last film made by Holland in Poland. Due to martial law, it had to wait for its premiere until 1987. In 1985, she made her first film abroad, *Bittere Ernte* (*Bitter Harvest*), beginning a new chapter in her directorial career.

Conclusions

It is difficult to recount in a conclusive way Holland's Polish output because of its thematic and stylistic diversity. None of the 'labels' employed by film criticism seems to be able to subsume her work. Although one notices the recurrence of women's issues in her films, the ways in which they are represented and discussed do not allow them to be embraced with the term 'feminist'. *Evening at Abdon's*, *Provincial Actors* and *Fever* are films in which there is neither a dominance of women's themes nor a privileging of the female perspective. In turn, *Sunday Children* and *Something for Something* show Holland's distrust of all ideological assumptions imposed on women, whether conservative or progressive. A general ideological distrust and scepticism characterise all her films, including those made abroad, as is demonstrated both through content and style. All means Holland uses, as stated earlier, are aimed at distancing the viewer from the fictional world of the characters, in order to compel her/him to an individual critical reflection on the issues that are discussed. According to Mariola Jankun-Dopartowa, the main feature of Holland's cinema is ironic distance deriving from various traditions: Polish Romanticism, the writings of Witold Gombrowicz and Witkacy, and the Czech New Wave cinema. No doubt Holland's own historical experience of living in Eastern Europe has also made her largely 'a distant observer' of the past and the contemporary world.

Note

1. All the biographical information comes from: Stanisław Zawiśliński, *Reżyseria: Agnieszka Holland* (1995).

CHAPTER 11

Dorota Kędzierzawska: Ambivalent Feminist

EWA MAZIERSKA

The last female director to be discussed in this book is Dorota Kędzierzawska (b. 1957). In spite of her relatively modest output, comprising several short films and only three full-length feature movies, all made on a relatively small budget, she is regarded as one of the most original Polish filmmakers to emerge after the collapse of communism.

In common with Sass, her road to cinema was protracted. In spite of having a taste of cinema at home, thanks to her mother Jadwiga being a director of children's films, she had difficulty convincing the examining board at the Łódź Film School that she was talented enough to become a filmmaker. After that experience she undertook cultural studies for a year and then transferred to the famous Moscow film school, WGIK, where she studied alongside Vasili Piczul, later renowned for his film *Malenkaya Vera* (*Little Vera*, 1988). From there she returned to Poland, where she was eventually accepted into the Łódź Film School. She graduated in 1981 and in 1991 completed her first full-length film, but not without major problems in securing funding (see Janicka 1995).

Kędzierzawska can be listed amongst those directors unwilling to define their own work in terms of opposition to male cinema. When I interviewed her in the summer of 1999 she was utterly dismissive of the concept of women's cinema, claiming that she neither understood what 'women's cinema' means, nor had any particular interest in or knowledge of films made by fellow women artists. The same sentiment is conveyed in an interview given four years earlier to Bożena Janicka, when she commented: 'Only one thing is specific to the situation of a female director: she must not show her physical weakness. I am a director, the rest does not matter' (Janicka 1995: 21), and to Manana Chyb in 1998, when she said 'I have nothing in common with feminism' (Chyb 1998: 85). However, I will argue that if one can detect in Poland any signs of an emerging women's cinema, which is different from the dominant male models not only in terms of subject matter, but also stylistic approach, then it is in the films of Kędzierzawska. At the same time, in terms of ideology, her films are difficult to pinpoint. By no means is she an uncritical apologist for women.

Kędzierzawska's films focus on those who live at the margins of society: ethnic minorities, children and single mothers, who barely cope with their everyday problems. She often investigates their experience from within, rather than looking at them from the point of view of society. In this sense she opposes the dominant paradigm in official Polish culture, including film – that of Romanticism, which typically neglects the private sphere of human life and concentrates on heroes of both sexes, sacrificing their lives for noble causes, especially the freedom of the country. She also stands in opposition to most Polish young directors of the 1990s, who make films that are misogynist and often without women (see Haltof 1997; Stachówna 2001). Moreover, Kędzierzawska (as Johnston puts it) 'interrogates the depiction of reality' (Johnston 1985b: 215) by the use of formal rupture and visual stylisation, and her type of formalism is also unique at the backdrop of Polish prevailing cinematic traditions.

Kędzierzawska's first full-length feature film, *Diabły, diabły* (*Devils, Devils*, 1991), is set in a village, somewhere in the Polish mountains, on the outskirts of which a group of Gypsy travelers set up their camp, causing a major upheaval amongst the local people. The majority of villagers regard them as hostile and threatening. The ultimate testimony to their hatred is the villagers' attack on the defenceless Romanies, when men, armed with fire-hoses and led by the local priest, drench the Gypsies and their tents. They stop only when a Gypsy man threatens with a knife a teenage girl, nicknamed Mała, who is amongst the Romanies at the time of the attack. Soon after the incident the Romanies leave the village.

Mała (Justyna Ciemny), who is the main character in the film, lives in a modest house with her unmarried mother (Monika Niemczyk). She is enchanted by the Gypsies' way of life and even tries to behave like a Romany. She becomes romantically involved with the man in the camp (Wiesław Szoma), who will later put a knife to her throat. Eventually Mała asks the travellers to take her with them, and when they refuse, she is so sad that she becomes ill. Her old friends, on the other hand, no longer play with her; she becomes as isolated in her own community as the Gypsies were. In contrast to Mała, who before the incident with the knife always played outside with friends, her mother remains indoors, alone or with her daughter, usually working on an old-fashioned sewing machine. She has a sad, tired and dreamy face, and sometimes she stops her work to look through the window, or to stare nowhere in particular. There is little talk and few caresses exchanged between mother and daughter; it even appears that

Figure 11.1 Justyna Ciemny as Mała in *Diabły, diabły* (*Devils, Devils*), dir. Dorota Kędzierzawska © Studio Filmowe 'Indeks', photo: Zdzisław Najda

Mała does not like her mother and rebels against her, but once the girl is rejected by the village community, her mother is the only one to look after her and support her. Even then, however, there is little communication between mother and daughter.

Mała's mother is the first in a stream of silent, lonely and unglamorous working-class women who appear in Kędzierzawska's films. In *Devils, Devils* (Figure 11.1) the director treats her with sympathy, forgiving her lack of time and attention for her offspring. She also subtly suggests that there is a similarity between mothers and daughters; the daughters reproduce their mothers' strengths and weaknesses. Mała, who shows significant independence and lack of prejudices, cannot resist her sexuality and falls in love with a dashing Gypsy, and might imitate her mother's 'youthful mistakes'. The film ends with the image of a girl, aged about three, with blonde hair and archetypal Slavic features, in a meadow, dancing to the Gypsy's song. The girl is Aniela Mikucka, Kędzierzawska's own daughter. The girl's movements are slowed down, increasing their grace. The ending might suggest that there is a chance of reconciliation between Polish and Gypsy culture by the means of learning from each other. Perhaps Kędzierzawska only expresses the hope that the next generation of Poles will be more tolerant, or simply promises that she will bring up her child free of ethnic prejudices.

One of the most striking aspects of *Devils, Devils* is the minimal dialogue. The film is almost silent: images and songs are the main vehicles of

meaning. There is also little action, and what there is, consists of tiny incidents, typically ignored by mainstream filmmakers: a pupil, observing a spi-
der climbing a blackboard, a teacher practising the recitation of a poem in
solitude, a Gypsy woman plucking a chicken, children playing in the
meadow. The whole point of Kędzierzawska's work is to immortalise
moments, which otherwise will passed unnoticed. The tiny incidents, put
together, provide a fascinating insight into the culture of Gypsies. The most
important feature of Romany life, as she portrays it, is communality: they
travel, live, work and play together. Children learn by example from adults,
and then share their experiences and skills with other children. We see, for
example, girls no older than ten looking after babies, and even smaller girls
making pastry. Although Gypsy children perform tasks which in 'civilised'
societies will be regarded as too difficult for them, they enjoy their work very
much, treating it as play, giggling, while doing useful things. The village children find their informal way of education and life in the open fascinating:
they stand for hours near the camp, observing what the Gypsies are doing.
The newcomers encourage the village children to join in; one woman starts
dancing round a teenage boy and after a while he starts dancing himself. The
boy is previously shown to have problems at school, but now his face shows
not only pleasure, but pride. The Gypsy's mode of education by play and
personal experience is contrasted with the formal learning that the village
children receive at school. Both the children and their teacher (Krzysztof
Plewka) seem to be utterly bored and uncommitted to their work. During a
Polish lesson, when the pupils are supposed to learn the work of their
national poet-prophet, Adam Mickiewicz, we see some children yawning,
others playing with the contents of their pencil cases, and the teacher is lost
in his thoughts. Eventually, when the Gypsies come to the meadow opposite
the school, the whole class, including the teacher, abandon their work, press-
ing their faces to the window to observe the newcomers.

In contrast to the Gypsies, who are united and inclusive, the villagers, as
portrayed by Kędzierzawska, are fragmented and exclusive. Different people have different lifestyles and there is little communication between them.
Apart from the children, everybody seems to live in solitude, locked in their
own home and their own ideas. Their isolation and narrow-mindedness is
conveyed by the motif of windows: the villagers constantly look through
the windows and close them to avoid being observed. The village streets are
empty, the only person to be seen there is a weak-minded old woman,
scorned by everybody as a 'witch' (Danuta Szaflarska). The only moment
when we see the villagers as a community is when they attack the Gypsies.
Yet, even then, it is obvious that not all want to participate in the act of ethnic cleansing. Some villagers stay at home, some children, who previously
played with their contemporaries amongst the Romanies, gaze from a distance, surprised, or perhaps even ashamed. Even the men with fire-hoses
look less certain of themselves, as they soak the Gypsies, their homes and

belongings in water. When they eventually leave the meadow, it is not a scene of triumph for the villagers, but one of embarrassment. The villagers' moral defeat is exacerbated by the Gypsies' behaviour: instead of hiding or running from the water, they appear to welcome the unexpected opportunity to bathe. Women wash their children's faces and soak their long hair in the stream of water. Later, however, when it is obvious that the water destroyed their homes, many of them look straight into the eyes at their oppressors, without saying a word. This silent accusation is reminiscent of photographs and documentary films showing prisoners in the Nazi concentration camps.

The priest, who masterminded and led the attack on the Gypsies, appears in the film on several occasions. We see him for the first time when the Romanies pitch their camp in the meadow. His gestures, observed through the school window by the children, leave no doubt that he does not want the strangers to stay in his parish. In another episode he leads a group of girls through the fields, on their way to the church. The girls, hearing the cries of the Gypsy children, amplified by echo, stop and reply one by one. Thus a kind of dialogue without words takes place between the village girls and the Gypsies. The priest disapproves of their behaviour and orders the girls to stop shouting, and to resume their march to the church. The priest also convinces his parishioners that the Gypsies were sent by Satan, which explains the film's title. It can be suggested that the priest, apart from being a bigoted and cruel individual, stands for the whole Polish Roman Catholic Church, whom the director accuses of promoting ethnic prejudice. The accusation has a basis in reality: both before and after the Second World War Poland was the scene of violent attacks on ethnic minorities, and individual priests, as well as the Church hierarchy, played a part in promoting xenophobia. Many attacks on Gypsies, as well as on Jews and Ukrainians, took place in the name of protecting the only 'true faith'. It is worth adding that, according to the director's own words, her main inspiration for making *Devils, Devils* was a conversation she once had on a train with a priest, who boasted that once he drove the Gypsies away from a village using a fire-hose (see Janicka 1995: 21).

Almost all the actors who appear in *Devils, Devils* are relatively unknown (the exception being Danuta Szaflarska, a veteran of Polish cinema, playing the 'witch'); the main part of teenage Mała is given to a complete amateur, Justyna Ciemny, and real Gypsies were cast in Gypsy parts. Some of the actors retain their real names; for example, the teenage boy named Karabin is played by Grzegorz Karabin, which adds to the impression of Kędzierzawska's work being not so much fictional film, as an anthropological document. Particularly convincing and touching are the episodes with children, such as the moment when a small Gypsy child looks at his reflection in an enormous mirror, or the episode of the girls making dough. They add to the impression of the vulnerability and innocence of the Gypsies, increasing the viewer's sympathy towards them.

The period in which the events are set is not spelt out explicitly, but the style of costumes, iconography and the very fact that the Romanies are travellers (by the 1990s practically all Polish Gypsies led settled lives) suggests that *Devils, Devils* is set in the 1960s. The temporal distance increases the impression that the film is a valuable ethnographic document. In its preoccupation with the history of provincial Poland and its unflattering portrayal of rural life *Devils Devils* recollects the work of Jan Jakub Kolski, another distinguished, and in many ways marginal, Polish director to emerge after the collapse of communism, particularly his *Pogrzeb kartofla* (*Burial of a Potato*, 1990) and *Cudowne miejsce* (*Miraculous Place*, 1994).

The main stylistic method applied by Kędzierzawska in *Devils, Devils* can be described as fragmentation. Firstly, the narrative is fragmented: there are no smooth transitions from one scene to another. Succeeding scenes usually represent different characters and places of action. Contrary to Hollywood cinema, where the main function of editing is advancement of the narrative, Kędzierzawska's main concern is to portray what happens in various parts of the village. Accordingly, there is no obvious progression of time in her film; in most cases it is impossible to establish whether sequences take place concurrently. Kędzierzawska also uses graphic and rhythmic editing, at the expense of continuity editing, to give her film an almost musical quality. Images often function as vignettes: much attention is paid to the composition of the frame and frames are frozen to allow for the contemplation of the beauty of an image – for example, the landscape near the village, with hills, river and the forest in perfect harmony, and of the Romany camp, both taken in extreme long shots. The most memorable shots are taken at night, such as an image of the Gypsies around a bonfire, or the movement of their horses. Darkness adds to the poetry and mystery of Gypsy life. In other scenes movements are slowed to reveal the beauty of simple events, such as the first steps of Mała when she learns a Gypsy dance. The narrative is also slowed by the extensive use of Gypsy songs, which is the only music used in the film. Bodies are often shown as fragmented: extreme close-ups are used to portray the movements of legs, hands or mouth. The aim is to register minute changes in human behaviour, especially when they lead to the acquisition of new skills, and to immortalise cultural patterns. The most fascinating are close-ups of the performance of Gypsy dances, giving the impression that Kędzierzawska was attempting to analyse the elements of the dance. Finally, the speech, too, is fragmented. As mentioned previously, there is little dialogue in *Devils, Devils*. Instead, we often see and hear people practising the use of words: one of the pupils reads out loud at school; the teacher, who stutters, practises reciting a poem at home and attempts to write a novel on his old typewriter; eventually Mała parrots the stuttering teacher, pronouncing words in his characteristic staccato manner. In every case we hear or see separate words, or even letters. They function as signifiers separated from the signified. Similarly,

Gypsy talk, both when the Romanies use their own language, and when they speak Polish with their strange accent, function (at least for Polish viewers) as sounds devoid of their meanings. It can be suggested that by restricting herself in the use of dialogue and using words like sounds, rather than meaningful statements, Kędzierzawska puts Polish and Gypsy language (perceived by some Poles as a meaningless babble) on an even footing. Moreover, by showing Poles either stuttering or silent, and Romanies talking a lot, albeit saying things that cannot understand, she elevates Gypsy language over Polish. Another form of fragmentation is the dissociation of sound and image. The images of the villagers and Gypsies are accompanied by Gypsy songs. In the majority of cases it is difficult to establish if the source of the songs is diegetical or nondiegetical and (because of the lack of translation from Gypsy language to Polish) what the connection between the narrative and the songs might be.

Fragmentation is regarded as a modern and postmodern technique. One of the most interesting analyses of its use in modern cinema was provided by Susan Sontag in her essay about *Vivre sa vive* (*My Life to Live*, 1962) by Jean-Luc Godard (see Sontag 1964). Sontag suggests that Godard uses the new language of breaking-up and dissociation to interrogate both reality and cinema, and to extend the borders of the feature film genre. In *Devils, Devils* fragmentation serves two apparently contradictory purposes. One is ethnographic; thanks to it we can better appreciate what constitutes Gypsy culture. Moreover, the perception of Romanies as romantic travellers who defy the rules of civilisation, which nowadays is regarded as stereotyped, even banal, through the use of fragmentation gains unusual depth and persuasiveness. The second of Kędzierzawska's aims, in line with modern and postmodern authors, can be described as formalistic: challenging viewers' habits of watching films, requiring them to question the status of cinematic reality. It is worth mentioning that although *Devils, Devils* is saturated with 'texts', such as the previously mentioned songs, dances or quotations from a famous Polish poem, *Oda do młodości* (*Ode to Youth*) by Adam Mickiewicz, their sources are always noncinematic, typically Gypsy songs and dances. Contrary to *Devils, Devils*, the majority of Polish films of the 1990s that are regarded as postmodern, for example *Psy* (*Dogs*, 1992) by Władysław Pasikowski, *Człowiek z...* (*Man of...*, 1993) by Konrad Szołajski or *Kiler* (1997) by Juliusz Machulski, gained this label through their extensive reference to cinema, often in the form of *mise-en-abime*.

By the use of fragmentation, or, more precisely, various kinds of fragmentation, which were rarely applied in Polish films, Kędzierzawska positioned herself on the margins of national cinema, and even on the margins of Polish postmodernist (postcommunist) cinema. Her marginalisation was twofold: by choice of subject matter (Gypsies and children) and by style. The result was, as acknowledged by some critics (see Demidowicz 1995: 70), one of the most interesting and unusual films made in Poland since the collapse of communism, and in many ways the most radical of Kędzierza-wska's career, but the film remained largely unwatched, attracting in the cinemas less than thirty thousand viewers. Andrzej Wajda (whose opinions are closely followed by the media and hence, serve as a guide for potential viewers), described *Devils, Devils* as 'a film neglecting the audience' (Demidowicz 1995: 70). In an interview with the journalist Bożena Janicka, who was on the whole rather sympathetic to the director's work, Kędzierza-wska was asked if she felt guilty about making films that do not cover their costs, paid for almost exclusively by the Polish taxpayer. She bravely replied 'no', admitting that she only felt responsible for the artistic quality of her film, not for its box office success (Janicka 1995: 21). While appreciating the director's courage to assert her artistic autonomy, it is, however, worth asking the question: Why was *Devils, Devils* such a box office failure? It is impossible to establish all the reasons, but some can be easily detected. One of them was a very poor distribution and promotion of *Devils, Devils*. In many large Polish towns the film was not shown at all. Film promoters and distributors assumed that it was too difficult for ordinary viewers, and too bald in its criticism of Polish society and its most respected institution: the Catholic Church. However, the fact that Kędzierzawska had the courage to portray Poles as prejudiced and xenophobic, and the Church in a deeply unflattering light (something which her critic, Andrzej Wajda, never did), deserves respect.

In *Devils, Devils* Kędzierzawska paid much attention to the child's per-ception of the world. In her next film, *Wrony* (*The Crows*, 1994), children play an even more prominent part. The main character, Crow (Karolina Ostrożna), is a girl about ten years old. Being the child of a single mother, who is poor and constantly overworked, the girl receives neither the atten-tion and tenderness, nor the material circumstances she yearns for. At school Crow does not feel happy either. Humiliated by the teacher and laughed at by other children in her class, she runs away from school and embarks on a journey through her city. She is accompanied by a girl of three or four, nicknamed Maleństwo (The Little One) (Kasia Szczepanik), whom the older girl persuades to leave her home and play as her child. The adven-ture finishes late in the evening. The little girl is returned safely to her wor-ried parents, who embrace her when she appears back at home. The older girl also returns home, but her mother is much less welcoming. The girl asks her to cuddle her, but her request remains unanswered. As she asks over and over again, the camera moves higher and higher. Eventually we see only parts of her arms and her head, surrounded by darkness, which creates the impression of a bird. This crow association is confirmed in the last scene of the film, when the girl jumps about, making crow-like noises.

In terms of action, as with *Devils, Devils*, little happens in *The Crows* (Figure 11.2). The film consists of many tiny episodes, such as the girls vis-iting an old church, where a wedding ceremony takes place, observing

Figure 11.2 A scene from *Wrony* (*Crows*), dir. Dorota Kędzierzawska. © Arthur Reinhart

through the window schoolgirls practising ballet, stealing a loaf of bread from a shop and then eating it on a boat at the water's edge. Yet, together they portray with unusual freshness and subtlety the complex relationship between two children of different ages and social background.

The film was shot on location in Toruń, regarded as one of the most beautiful Polish towns, famous for its Teutonic past and as the birthplace of the astronomer Nicolaus Copernicus. Toruń in Kędzierzawska's film is a mysterious place, with an abundance of dark, narrow lanes, dilapidated but still imposing houses, as well as tolling bells, impressive ruins, and virtually no tenement blocks, which epitomise communist and postcommunist reality. The city in *The Crows* is also an essentially liminal space, as on the one hand it is surrounded by a vast area of greenery, meadows, parks and forests; on the other, it borders the sea (which in real Toruń is the Vistula river). Here the girls find an old boat, where Crow shares with her small companion her dream about a journey to the other side of the world. The beauty and mystery of Toruń is significantly enhanced by the cinematography, praised by many reviewers (see Elley 1994: 24; Jabłońska 1995: 197). The director of cinematography, Arthur Reinhart, uses long shots extensively, low-key lighting, which at times produces the effect of chiaroscuro, and reduces the colour scheme to various shades of browns, or to black and white. Much attention is paid to the composition of the frames, which display the quality of paintings. Some shots resemble black and white portraits of the main characters.

The episodic structure and the emphasis put on the experience of children – which from the feminist perspective can be regarded as virtues – in the eyes of the bulk of Polish film critics were treated as the film's major weaknesses. Even the most sympathetic critics suggested that The Crows is not much more than an extended 'film étude', lacking in any ideology and with little chance of reaching a wider audience (see Janicka 1994: 8). The film had only a limited distribution and did only slightly better in the box office than Devils, Devils.

The characters, narrative and even the symbolism of The Crows are reminiscent of Kes (1969) by Ken Loach. Both Loach's Billy and Kędzierzawska's Crow are neglected by their parents and teachers; they are thin, miserable-looking, rather small in comparison with their peers and rejected by their classmates. This is shown in the P.E. lessons, when both Billy and Crow fail to bring their P.E. kit and consequently are forced to exercise without the proper clothing. Moreover, in both films the children, let down by people, identify (albeit in different ways), with birds. The birds, a kestrel in the case of Kes and crows in Kędzierzawska's film, signify freedom, which the children dream of and cannot achieve in reality. In the case of the heroine of the Polish film (although one can argue that a crow is more benign and less dangerous than a kestrel) the affinity to crows also reflects her sense of rejection and the resulting aggression (Jabłońska 1995: 197). Yet, there are also some significant differences between Kes and The Crows. For example, Kędzierzawska's film is more stylised, fragmented and 'art-house' than Kes. It is also less overtly political: Loach explained Billy's situation by a multitude of social and political factors, such as the poverty of the working classes, the failure of an education system that discourages working-class children from developing their interests and talents, and the macho culture prevailing in English mining communities. Kędzierzawska, by contrast, avoids any discussion of similar issues and puts the blame for Crow's unhappiness almost entirely on her individual circumstances. Most importantly, there are women: Crow's mother and teacher, who force the girl to run away from home. It could be argued that the lack of communication between women of different generations, as represented in Devils, Devils, is changed in The Crows into an open hostility between them. Moreover, by depicting Maleństwo as sweet and trusting and the older girl as moody, cynical and often aggressive and malicious, Kędzierzawska, perhaps unconsciously, represents single-parent families as dysfunctional and advocates a conservative model of the nuclear family, which is also strongly promoted by the Catholic Church.

Of the three films Kędzierzawska has directed so far, Nic (Nothing, 1998) has had the greatest resonance. It was the most awarded film at the 1998 Film Festival of Polish Films in Gdynia, receiving, amongst others, a reward for best director. Nothing was also Kędzierzawska's most popular film amongst ordinary viewers, in spite of its limited distribution. The main reason for its relative popularity is its subject, which is the question at the centre of the most heated political debate experienced in Poland in the post-communist years: a woman's right to have an abortion. As was mentioned in Chapter 6, its prominence followed the introduction in 1993 of a new abortion law, making abortion illegal in most circumstances. Predictably, the new legislation had the most damaging effect on the lives of the most vulnerable members of Polish society: poor women, those with many children, who could not afford contraceptives or had little understanding about their impact, teenage girls and victims of rape. From the early 1990s the number of abortions decreased, but the number of unwanted children and those living in poverty increased, and now account for over one-third of all Polish children. Poland also witnessed a virtually new phenomenon: infanticide. It is estimated that each year in the 1990s fifty to a hundred newborn babies were killed by their own mothers. The abortion debate in Poland is not yet settled as neither side of the political spectrum is satisfied with the current solution. The political right, encouraged and supported by the Church hierarchy, demands even more restrictions on having abortions and stronger punishments for women committing infanticide, while the left wing, represented primarily by women's organisations and the postcommunist party, demand relaxation of the current law. Although *Nothing* (Figure 11.3) cannot be reduced to just another voice in the argument exchanged between supporters and opponents of the anti-abortion law, the debate, concerning a woman's rights versus her foetus's rights, is an important factor in the film's reception. It is also worth mentioning that in spite of the word 'abortion' appearing for several years almost daily in the newspapers, on television and in the discussions of ordinary people, Kędzierzawska was the first director in postcommunist Poland to refer to this issue and she experienced significant problems in securing funding for her film.[1]

The source of the film was a story Kędzierzawska found in the national newspaper, *Gazeta Wyborcza*, about a married woman with three children, who killed her fourth child (see Kubisiowska 1998: 12). Accordingly, at the centre of her narrative is a young family with three children. The husband, Antoni (Janusz Panasewicz), is the breadwinner. His wife, Hela (Anita Borkowska-Kuskowska), looks after the children and does virtually all the housework. The burden of work is particularly heavy as a result of their modest material status: the family lives in a flat with no central heating or washing machine, and every morning Hela carries a heavy bucket of coal from the cellar to the third floor. Antoni not only refuses to help his wife in her everyday tasks, but constantly criticises her for being lazy and absent-minded. Moreover, he is very moody – one minute affectionate, the next, violent and abusive. From time to time he is also violent towards their children, although at the same time he criticises Hela when she loses her temper with one of them. In addition, he likes women and alcohol, and shows no remorse for coming home drunk late at night. He regards it as his right

Figure 11.3 Anita Borkowska-Kuskowska as Hela in *Nic* (*Nothing*), dir. Dorota Kędzierzawska. © Arthur Reinhart

and compensation for his 'loss of freedom'. In spite of her husband's short-comings Hela has no intention of leaving him. There are a number of reasons why she wants them to stay together, such as her fear that she will not manage to support her family without his wages, and her children's emotional attachment to their father. An important factor is also her own love for Antoni, and her refusal to accept that her feelings are not reciprocated. The best indication of her self-delusion is her monologue in the first scene of the film, in which she whispers poetically to her sleeping husband about her love for him. The scene ends abruptly, when Antoni wakes up and tells her to shut up, calling her completely mad.

Life, difficult as it is for Kędzierzawska's heroine, gets much worse once she learns that she is pregnant again. She conceals this fact from her husband, thinking that he will abandon her, or even kill her, if she has another baby. Judging from his behaviour, continuously threatening her with severe punishment if he finds out that she has done 'something stupid', this seems a distinct possibility. Hela tries to arrange an abortion and approaches several doctors, but all refuse to help. Later she tries to get money for an illegal abortion, pawning her wedding ring, but buys it back after Antoni notices its absence on his wife's finger. Subsequently she tries to cause a miscarriage herself by letting her small son jump on her belly and taking hot baths. This, however, only makes her sick and weak. Hela also turns to a priest, requesting a confession, but he has no time for her. Eventually, on New Year's Eve, she gives birth in the bathroom, strangles her baby and then buries him in the local park. The husband watches the birth through the glass bathroom door, but he does not intervene and pretends that he does not know what happened. Afterwards, encouraged by a sympathetic neighbour, Hela leaves home, taking her children with her, but soon is found by the police and brought to court. The judge asks her if there is anything to justify her guilt and she answers 'Nothing'. The answer gives the title of the film, which is, of course, ironic, as there are plenty of reasons why we want to forgive Kędzierzawska's heroine: her difficult family situation, her loneliness and poverty, and, most of all, her inability to arrange a legal abortion.

As in Kędzierzawska's earlier films, the actress playing the main part, Anita Borkowska-Kuskowska, is not a professional: she is a classical ballet dancer. This makes Hela's story even more believable and increases the audience's sympathy towards the heroine. Moreover, as the reviewers observed, she has a pure, gentle face, with long, curly, ginger hair, reminiscent of a character in the pictures of the old masters of the Italian Renaissance (Olszewski 1998: 100), or even of Madonna (Hollender 1998: 16). Borkowska-Kuskowska is often shown in close-up, her fear and anguish perfectly visible to the viewers. It is difficult to accept that she is a murderer of the cruellest kind, as pro-life campaigners try to portray women who have had abortions.

As Jan Olszewski noticed, the film excuses abortion, or even promotes it, as the best solution for women in Poland in a similar situation to Hela (see Olszewski 1998). Yet, the political or ideological significance of *Nothing* is richer than this. By showing Hela approaching representatives of various powerful institutions, such as the medical profession and the Church (social services are not even mentioned in the film), who are unwilling or unable to help her either to get rid of her pregnancy or to keep her child, Kędzierzawska accuses them – and even society as a whole – of letting Polish women down. This accusation is particularly strong in the light of our knowledge that in Poland these institutions are not passive observers of the anguish of thousands of women, but take a more active role as moral preachers and judges, demanding that they sacrifice their personal happiness and ambition to 'fate' and the needs of their families. The film also draws attention, not unlike in *Devils, Devils*, to the lack of solidarity amongst Poles, encapsulated by the doors remaining closed when Hela calls on her neighbours in order to share with them some cakes, baked before Christmas. Interestingly, the doctors are represented in a worse light than the priest. The priest is simply absent when Hela needs him and it is even suggested that he might assist her, if she would wait for him in a church, or see him another day. The female gynaecologist, on the other hand, whom Hela asks for help in arranging an abortion, not only refuses her, but with complete insensitivity insists that Hela should have as many children as she physically can bear: this is the law of God and nature.

Off-screen Kędzierzawska played down any suggestions that her film contains criticism of the current abortion law or of the Catholic Church, and that it promotes women's rights. She even claimed that her heroine's problems result from Hela's own shortcomings (Chyb 1998: 85). However, this attitude, seized on by some Polish critics (Wiktor 1998: 29), can be partly explained by the director's possible desire not to offend the Polish press and 'cinematic establishment', which are predominantly right-wing.

In common with *The Crows* one can notice parallels between Kędzierzawska's film and the work of Ken Loach. Young, poor, pregnant women and mothers, let down by the institutions that are meant to help them, and by their own families, are recurrent motifs in Loach's films, such as *Up the Junction* (1965), *Cathy, Come Home* (1966), *Poor Cow* (1967) and, more recently, *My Name Is Joe* (1998). In common with Loach, Kędzierzawska also refuses to let her heroine enjoy a happy ending; in this respect her films can be regarded as both realistic and masochistic. The motif of female oppression and struggle within a patriarchal family also brings her close to Terence Davies's work, examples being *Distant Voices, Still Lives* (1988) and *The Long Day Closes* (1992). Furthermore, one can see Kędzierzawska's treatment of birth and death in *Nothing* as being closely connected with that in Davies's *Death and Transfiguration* (1983).

There are also important differences between Loach's and Davies's films, and *Nothing*. The loneliness of Kędzierzawska's heroine is more complete and the climate in which she lives even more claustrophobic than in any of the films of the British directors. Moreover, while Loach and Davies are not afraid to show the most appalling details of the lives of their characters, Kędzierzawska withholds graphic description. Even the most shocking event of Hela giving birth and killing the baby is shown with remarkable subtlety, shot from the other side of the glass in the bathroom door. The shapes of the mother and baby are blurred and there are no images of Hela harming her child. Only the end of its crying suggests that the baby is no longer alive. Yet, even that gives more an impression of a loving mother putting her child to sleep, than of her murdering her offspring.

The narrative structure of *Nothing* is almost linear; there are no images or texts inserted for their own sake. Other means, used in Kędzierzawska's earlier films to break up the narrative, such as slow motion, are applied more sparingly and with greater care for the smoothness of the narrative. On the whole, however, as with Kędzierzawska's earlier films, *Nothing* is largely stylised. As many reviewers noted (and some denounced), it is impossible to watch the film without being aware of its form. For example, extremely low-angle and high-angle shots and disquieting compositions are used extensively; at times it feels as if the world is falling on Hela, crushing her. On other occasions it seems as if she wants to commit suicide by jumping from a height. Some critics compared the camerawork and lighting to the masterpieces of German Expressionism (see Malatyńska 1998: 9). Iconography, heavy with symbolism, increases the impression of entrapment and horror. Hela is often shown looking through the window or standing on a balcony. When she looks up, a flight of crows flies over her head making a terrible noise. Their image and connotation also recollect Kędzierzawska's previous film, *The Crows*, where the black birds signified the little heroine's loneliness and her desire to run away from her reality and be free. A carp, swimming in the bath, waiting to be killed for a traditional Polish Christmas dinner, symbolises Hela's new child, who will also be killed around Christmas. The neighbour, who sees the fish alive in the bath, tells Hela with moral superiority that she is unable to kill. On the other hand, the fish, which is itself trapped and half dead, also stands for Hela. The heroine even tells the fish how lucky it is, as her torture will soon be over, while for her there is no end to suffering. As with previous films by Kędzierzawska, images, rather than dialogue, are the main bearers of meaning. As in *Devils, Devils*, sound plays an important function in creating the gloomy mood, particularly the music and the loud noises invading Hela's world, such as the crows flying overhead, or the New Year firecrackers.

The colour range is very limited; practically the whole film is shot in different shades of browns, which, being the colour of autumn, of dying, adds to the sombre mood of the story. This mood is increased even further by low-key lighting. The images are sometimes so dark and different from a normal sense of colour that it is difficult to notice the details of the sparse home furnishings or clothes. They appear inconspicuous, neutral, almost invisible. Kędzierzawska also avoids providing details of the characters' situation. We do not learn what Antoni's job is and in which city the characters live. Even Hela's name is unknown almost until the end of the film. Perhaps it is a sign that Kędzierzawska wants her heroine's story to be less specific to a particular place and time and more universal. Universalism, talking about 'woman', instead of 'women', is often criticised by feminist writers as a way of dispensing with 'real' women, by replacing them with an abstract, distilled from diverse discourses dominant in Western cultures (see de Lauretis 1984: 5). However, I will suggest that if Kędzierzawska attempts universalism, it might be for a different reason, namely to emphasise that her heroine is not the only one to carry her cross: there are many more like her, in Poland, in other countries, in the past and in the future.

Conclusion

The three movies secured a unique place for Kędzierzawska in Polish post-communist cinema, and indeed, in the whole history of Polish film. Her uniqueness results from her attention to the lives of the marginalised and the disadvantaged, who were neglected even by those Polish directors praised for their 'humanistic' or 'compassionate' approach, such as Andrzej Wajda or Krzysztof Kieślowski. The singularity of Kędzierzawska's oeuvre also has much to do with her avant-garde temperament and her concern for cinematic form. This brings her closer to feminist counter-cinema, the masterpieces of cinematic modernism and progressive postmodernism, again – differentiating her from the mainstream of Polish cinema. Yet, Kędzierzawska is not a straightforward champion of women's rights. At the same time as representing the anguish and unhappiness of Polish women, she also stresses the lack of solidarity amongst them, and presents the advantages of a 'complete' family to bring up children.

Kędzierzawska's place in Polish cinema is also marginal in the sense that her films fail in the box office. Instead, they enjoy an extended 'half-life' at specialist cinemas and national and international festivals, where they are often rewarded. Neither has Kędzierzawska any imitators or followers in her native country. However, even as one of a kind, her work is a breakthrough. Her marginality and loneliness as an artist deserve our interest, as they tell us much not only about what kind of artist she is, but also about the shortcomings of Polish cinema.

Note

1. Following *Nothing* Urszula Urbaniak has also made *Torowisko* (*Track-way*, 1999) and Łukasz Barczyk, *Patrzę na ciebie, Marysiu* (*I'm Looking at You, Mary*, 1999) (see Chapter 6), both of which deal with the problem of an unplanned pregnancy out of wedlock. It is also worth mentioning *Farba* (*Paint*, 1997), directed by Michał Rosa, a film about a pregnant teenage girl who blackmails gynaecologists to get money for her travels. *Paint* had its premiere before *Nothing*, but the script of Kędzierzawska's film was written earlier. Yet it was only in the film by Kędzierzawska that the problem of pregnancy found such a tragic solution; in the remaining films female characters come to terms with their inescapable motherhood.

Filmography

1922 *Rok 1863* (*Year 1863*), Edward Puchalski
1928 *Huragan* (*Hurricane*), Józef Lejtes
1930 *Na Sybir* (*To Siberia*), Henryk Szaro
1938 *Florian*, Leonard Buczkowski
1951 *Kobiety naszych dni* (*Women of Our Days*), Jan Zelnik
    Pierwsze dni (*First Days*), Jan Rybkowski
1954 *Autobus odjeżdża 6.20* (*The Bus Leaves at 6.20*), Jan Rybkowski
    Niedaleko Warszawy (*Not Far from Warsaw*), Maria Kaniewska
    Przygoda na Mariensztacie (*An Adventure at Marienstadt*), Leonard
    Buczkowski
1955 *Irena, do domu* (*Irena, Go Home*), Jan Fethke
    Pokolenie (*A Generation*), Andrzej Wajda
1956 *Trzy kobiety* (*Three Women*), Stanisław Różewicz
1957 *Eroica*, Andrzej Munk
    Kanał (*Canal*), Andrzej Wajda
    Zagubione uczucia (*Lost Feelings*), Jerzy Zarzycki
1958 *Popiół i diament* (*Ashes and Diamonds*), Andrzej Wajda
    Krzyż Walecznych (*Cross of Valour*), Kazimierz Kutz
1959 *Lotna*, Andrzej Wajda
1961 *Noc* (*Night*), Tadeusz Makarczyński
1962 *Pasażerka* (*The Passenger*), Andrzej Munk
1963 *Jak być kochaną?* (*How to be Loved?*), Wojciech Jerzy Has
1968 *Pan Wołodyjowski* (*Colonel Wolodyjowski*), Jerzy Hoffman
1971 *Za ścianą* (*Behind the Wall*), Krzysztof Zanussi
1972 *Perła w koronie* (*A Pearl in the Crown*), Kazimierz Kutz
    Poszukiwany, Poszukiwana (*Searching For*), Stanisław Bareja
1973 *Iluminacja* (*Illumination*), Krzysztof Zanussi
1974 *Potop* (*Flood*), Jerzy Hoffman
    Ziemia obiecana (*The Promised Land*), Andrzej Wajda

1975 *Wanda Gościmińska – Włókniarka* (*Wanda Gościmińska, the Textile Worker*), Wojciech Wiszniewski
1976 *Człowiek z marmuru* (*Man of Marble*), Andrzej Wajda
1978 *Bez znieczulenia* (*Rough Treatment*), Andrzej Wajda
1979 *Amator* (*Camera Buff*), Krzysztof Kieślowski
      Dyrygent (*Conductor*), Andrzej Wajda
1981 *Człowiek z żelaza* (*Man of Iron*), Andrzej Wajda
      Dreszcze (*Shivers*), Wojciech Marczewski
      Wahadełko (*Shilly, Shally*), Filip Bajon
      Wielki bieg (*The Big Run*), Jerzy Domaradzki
1982 *Kobieta z węgla* (*Woman from Coal*), Wanda Różycka
      Matka Królów (*Mother of the Kings*), Janusz Zaorski
      Przesłuchanie (*Interrogation*), Ryszard Bugajski
1983 *Stan wewnętrzny* (*Inner State*), Krzysztof Tchórzewski
1985 *Wigilia* (*Christmas' Eve*), Leszek Wosiewicz
1986 *W zawieszeniu* (*Suspended*), Waldemar Krzystek
1990 *Pogrzeb kartofla* (*Burial of a Potato*), Jan Jakub Kolski
1991 *Jeszcze tylko ten las* (*Just Beyond this Forest*), Jan Łomnicki
      Koniec gry (*The End of the Game*), Feliks Falk
      Kroll, Władysław Pasikowski
      Panny i wdowy (*Maidens and Widows*), Janusz Zaorski
      Skarga (*The Complaint*), Jerzy Wójcik
1992 *Psy* (*Dogs*), Władysław Pasikowski
      Wszystko, co najważniejsze (*Everything, That Really Matters*), Robert Gliński
1993 *Człowiek z...* (*Man of...*), Konrad Szołajski
      Pożegnanie z Marią (*Farewell to Maria*), Filip Zylber
      Rozmowa z człowiekiem z szafy (*Conversation with a Cupboard Man*), Mariusz Grzegorzek
1994 *Cudowne miejsce* (*Miraculous Place*), Jan Jakub Kolski
1995 *Gnoje* (*Dung*), Jerzy Zalewski
      Młode wilki (*Young Wolves*), Jarosław Żamojda
      Pestka (*Stone*), Krystyna Janda
      Deborah, Ryszard Brylski
      Tato (*Dad*), Maciej Ślesicki
      Wielki Tydzień (*Holy Week*), Andrzej Wajda
      Za co? (*For What?*), Jerzy Kawalerowicz
1996 *Panna Nikt* (*Miss Nobody*), Andrzej Wajda
      Słodko gorzki (*Bittersweet*), Władysław Pasikowski
      Szamanka (*Shaman*), Andrzej Żuławski
1997 *Autoportret z kochanką* (*Self-portrait with a Lover*), Radosław Piwowarski
      Ciemna strona Wenus (*The Dark Side of Venus*), Radosław Piwowarski

Farba (*Paint*), Michał Rosa
Kiler, Juliusz Machulski
Przystań (*Haven*), Jan Hryniak
Sara, Maciej Ślesicki
1998 *Billboard*, Łukasz Zadrzyński
Demony wojny (*Demons of War*) Władysław Pasikowski
Prostytutki (*Prostitutes*), Eugeniusz Priwiezencew
1999 *Ajlawju*, Marek Koterski
Dług (*Debt*), Krzysztof Krauze
Ogniem i mieczem (*With Fire and Sword*), Jerzy Hoffman
Operacja Samum (*Samum Operation*), Władysław Pasikowski
Pan Tadeusz, Andrzej Wajda
Patrzę na ciebie Marysiu (*I Look at You, Mary*), Łukasz Barczyk
Torowisko (*Track-way*), Urszula Urbaniak
2000 *Chłopaki nie płaczą* (*Boys Don't Cry*), Olaf Lubaszenko
Daleko od okna (*Far From the Window*), Jan Jakub Kolski
Dzień świra (*The Day of a Nutter*), Marek Koterski
Prymas. Trzy lata z tysiąca (*Primate. Three Years Out of a Thousand*), Teresa Kotlarczyk
Reich, Władysław Pasikowski
2001 *Portret podwójny* (*Double Portrait*), Mariusz Front
Przedwiośnie (*Early Spring*), Filip Bajon
Quo Vadis, Jerzy Kawalerowicz
2002 *Zemsta* (*Revenge*), Andrzej Wajda

Wanda Jakubowska (1907–1998)

1932 *Reportaż 1 i Reportaż 2* (*Live Coverage 1 and 2*), together with Eugeniusz Cękalski and Jerzy Zarzycki, short
1933 *Morze* (*Sea*), together with Eugeniusz Cękalski, short
1934 *Budujemy* (*We Are Building*), together with Eugeniusz Cękalski, short
1937 *Ulica Edisona* (*Edison Street*), short
1939 *Nad Niemnem* (*On the Banks of the Niemen*)
1947 *Ostatni etap* (*The Last Stage*)
1953 *Żołnierz zwycięstwa* (*Soldier of Victory*)
1955 *Opowieść Atlantycka* (*Atlantic Story*)
1956 *Pożegnanie z diabłem* (*Farewell to the Devil*)
1958 *Król Macius I* (*King Macius I*)
1960 *Historia współczesna* (*Contemporary Story*)
Spotkania w mroku (*Meetings in the Dark*)
1964 *Koniec naszego świata* (*The End of Our World*)
1965 *Gorąca linia* (*Express Production Line*)

1971   *150 na godzinę (150 Kilometres Per Hour)*
1978   *Biały mazur (White Mazurka)*
1985   *Zaproszenie (Invitation)*
1988   *Kolory kochania (Colours of Love)*

Barbara Sass (b. 1936)

1972   *Ostatni liść (The Last Leaf)*, TV
1973   *Dziewczyna i gołębie (A Girl and Pigeons)*, TV
1975   *Literat (Writer)* in *Obrazki z życia (Pictures from Life)*, TV
1978   *Wejście w nurt (Entrance into a Stream)*, TV
1980   *Bez miłości (Without Love)*
1981   *Debiutantka (Debutante)*
1982   *Krzyk (Scream)*
1985   *Dziewczęta z Nowolipek (Girls from Nowolipki)*
       Rajska jabłoń (Tree of Paradise)
1987   *W klatce (In the Cage)*
1990   *Historia niemoralna (Immoral Story)*
1993   *Pajęczarki (Spiderwomen)*
       Tylko strach (Only Fear)
1995   *Pokuszenie (Temptation)*
1999   *Jak narkotyk (Like a Drug)*

Agnieszka Holland (b. 1948)

1970   *Hrích boha (Jesus Christ's Sin)*, short
1975   *Wieczór u Abdona (Evening at Abdon's)*, TV
       Dziewczyna i 'Akwarius' (Girl and 'Aquarius') in *Obrazki z życia (Pictures From Life)*, TV
1976   *Niedzielne dzieci (Sunday Children)*, TV
       Zdjęcia próbne (Screen Test), together with Jerzy Domaradzki and Paweł Kędzierski
1977   *Coś za coś (Something for Something)*, TV
1978   *Aktorzy prowincjonalni (Provincial Actors)*
1980   *Gorączka (Fever)*
1981   *Kobieta samotna (A Woman Alone)*, TV
1985   *Bittere Ernte (Angry Harvest)*
1988   *To Kill a Priest*
1990   *Europa, Europa*
1991   *Olivier, Olivier*
1993   *The Secret Garden*
1994   *Red Wind*, TV

1995 *Total Eclipse*
1997 *Washington Square*
1999 *The Third Miracle*
2001 *Shot in the Heart*, TV
     Golden Dreams, short
2002 *Julie Walking Home*
2005 *Copying Beethoven*

Dorota Kędzierzawska (b. 1957)

1988 *Koniec świata* (*The End of the World*), short
1991 *Diabły, diabły* (*Devils, Devils*)
1994 *Wrony* (*The Crows*)
1998 *Nic* (*Nothing*)
2005 *Jestem* (*I Am*)*

---

* This film had its premiere when our book was already in production. It is therefore omitted from the discussion of Kędzierzawska's work.

Bibliography

Anderson, Benedict (1991) *Imagined Communities: Reflections on the Origin and Spread of Nationalism* (London: Verso).

Armatys, Barbara and Armatys, Leszek (1988) 'Film krótkometrażowy', in Barbara Armatys, Leszek Armatys and Wiesław Stradomski (eds), *Historia filmu polskiego*, vol. II (Warszawa: Wydawnictwa Artystyczne i Filmowe), pp. 137–203.

Atlas, Janusz (1995) 'Zwycięstwo Wandy Jakubowskiej', *Wiadomości kulturalne*, 5/11: 27.

Attwood, Lynne (1993) 'Women, Cinema, Society', in Lynne Attwood (ed.), *Red Women on the Silver Screen: Soviet Women and Cinema from the Beginning to the End of the Communist Era* (London: Pandora Press), pp. 19–132.

Baczko, Bronisław (1984) *Les imaginaires sociaux: Memoires et espoirs collective* (Paris: Poyot).

_____ (1994) *Wyobrażenia społeczne: Szkice o nadziei i pamięci zbiorowej*, trans. Małgorzata Kowalska (Warszawa: PWN).

Badinter, Elisabeth (1981) *The Myth of Motherhood: A Historical View of the Maternal Instinct* (London: Macmillan).

Bergel, Lidia (1998) 'Życie bez mandatów' (Interview with Władysław Pasikowski), *Film*, 3: 76–79.

Bettelheim, Bruno (1977) *The Uses of Enchantment* (New York: Vintage Books).

Bilewicz, Michał and Pawlisz, Bogna (eds) (2000) *Jidełe*. Special edition *Żydzi i komunizm*.

Bobowski, Sławomir (2001) *W poszukiwaniu siebie: Twórczość filmowa Agnieszki Holland* (Wrocław: Wydawnictwo Uniwersytetu Wrocławskiego).

Borkowska, Grażyna (1996) *Cudzoziemki: Studia o polskiej prozie kobiecej* (Warszawa: Instytut Badań Literackich).

Bren, Frank (1986) *Polish Cinema* (Trowbridge: Flicks Books).

Bronfenbrenner, Urie (1972) 'The Changing Soviet Family', in Michael Gordon (ed.), *The Nuclear Family in Crisis: The Search for an Alternative* (New York: Harper and Row), pp. 119–42.

Brown, Peter (1981) *The Cult of the Saints: Its Rise and Function in Latin Christianity* (Chicago: University of Chicago Press).

Bulgakova, Oksana (1993) 'The Hydra of the Soviet Cinema: The Metamorphoses of the Soviet Film Heroine', in Lynne Attwood (ed.), *Red Women on the Silver*

Screen: Soviet Women and Cinema from the Beginning to the End of the Communist Era (London: Pandora Press), pp. 149–74.

Butler, Alison (2000) 'Feminist Theory and Women's Films at the Turn of the Century', *Screen*, 1: 73–79.

_____ (2002) *Women's Cinema: The Contested Screen* (London: Wallflower Press).

Caban, Wiesław (1994) 'Kobiety i powstanie styczniowe', in Anna Żarnowska and Andrzej Szwarc (eds), *Kobiety i świat polityki: Polska na tle porównawczym w XIX i w początkach XX wieku* (Warszawa: Instytut Historyczny Uniwersytetu Warszawskiego), pp. 43–56.

Caes, Christopher (2003) 'Catastrophic Spectacles: Historical Trauma and the Masculine Subject in *Lotna*', in John Orr and Elżbieta Ostrowska (eds), *Cinema of Andrzej Wajda: The Art of Irony and Defiance* (London: Wallflower Press), pp. 116–31.

Caldwell, Leslie (1991) *Italian Family Matters: Women, Politics and Legal Reform* (London: Macmillan).

Calhoun, Craig (1994) 'Social Theory and the Politics of Identity', in Craig Calhoun (ed.) *Social Theory and the Politics of Identity* (Blackwell: Oxford, Cambridge), pp. 9–29.

Camp, Richard (1990) 'From Passive Subordination to Complementary Partnership: on Papal Conception of a Woman's Place in Church and Society Since 1878', *Historical Review*, 76: 506–25.

Chyb, Manana (1998) 'Sama na huśtawce', *Film*, 10: 84–85.

Coates, Paul (1997) 'Walls and Frontiers: Polish Cinema's Portrayal of Polish-Jewish Relations', *Studies in Polish Jewry*, 10: 221–46.

Cook, Pam (1983) 'Melodrama and the Women's Picture', in Sue Aspinall and Robert Murphy (eds), *Gainsborough Melodrama* (London: British Film Institute), pp. 14–28.

Corrin, Chris. (1992) 'Introduction', in Chris Corrin (ed.) *Superwoman and the Double Burden: Women's Experience of Change in Central and Eastern Europe and the Former Soviet Union* (London: Scarlett Press), pp. 1–26.

Creed, Barbara (1993) *The Monstrous-Feminine* (London: Routledge).

Cywiński, Bogdan (1971) *Rodowody niepokornych* (Warszawa: Biblioteka 'Więzi').

Daly, Mary (1973) *Beyond God the Father* (Boston: Women's Press).

Davies, Norman (2001) *Heart of Europe: The Past in Poland's Present* (Oxford: Oxford University Press).

Davis, Angela (1981) *Women, Race and Class* (New York: Random House).

Demidowicz, Krzysztof (1995) 'Idę pod prąd', *Film*, 3: 70–71.

Dondziłło, Czesław (1978) 'Dziewczęta z Nowolipek', *Film*, 38: 12.

Eberhardt, Konrad (1974) *Film jest snem* (Warszawa: Wydawnictwa Artystyczne i Filmowe).

Ehrenreich, Barbara (1995) 'The Decline of Patriarchy', in Maurice Berger et al. (eds), *Constructing Masculinity* (London: Routledge), pp. 284–90.

Einhorn, Barbara (1993) *Cinderella Goes to Market: Citizenship, Gender, and Women's Movements in East Central Europe* (London: Verso).

Elley, Derek (1994) 'The Crows', *Variety*, 9–16 May: 24.

Falkowska, Janina (1996) *The Political Films of Andrzej Wajda* (Oxford and New York: Berghahn Books).

Farmer, Frank (1999) '"Not Theory ... but a Sense of Theory": The Superaddressee and the Contexts of Eden', in Caryl Emerson (ed.), *Critical Essays on Mikhail Bakhtin* (New York: G. K. Hall & Co.), pp. 378–91.

Feder-Kittay, Eva (1997) 'Woman as Metaphor', in Diana Tietjens Meyers (ed.), *Feminist Social Thought: A Reader* (London: Routledge), pp. 265–85.

Fik, Marta (1989) *Kultura polska po Jałcie: Kronika lat 1944–1981* (London: Polonia).

Fischer, Lucy (1989) *Shot/Countershot: Film Tradition and Women's Cinema* (Princeton: Princeton University Press).

——— (1996) *Cinematernity: Film, Motherhood, Genre* (Princeton, New Jersey: Princeton University Press).

Friedan, Betty. (1963) *The Feminine Mystique* (New York: W.W. Norton).

Fuszara, Małgorzata (1993) 'Abortion and the Formation of the Public Sphere in Poland', in Nanette Funk and Magda Mueller (eds), *Gender Politics and Post-Communism* (London: Routledge), pp. 241–52.

Gaines, Janet (1990) 'White Privilege and Looking Relations: Race and Gender in Feminist Film Theory', in Patricia Erens (ed.), *Issues in Feminist Film Criticism* (Bloomington: Indiana University Press), pp. 197–214.

Gałązka, Ewa (2000) 'Trzeba o mnie specjalnie pomyśleć', *Gazeta Telewizyjna* (supplement to *Gazeta Wyborcza*), 17–23/03: 4.

Geertz, Clifford (1973) *The Interpretation of Cultures: Selected Essays* (New York: Basic Books).

Godzic, Wiesław (1991) *Film i psychoanaliza: Problem widza* (Kraków: Wydawnictwo Uniwersytetu Jagiellońskiego).

Graff, Agnieszka (2001) *Świat bez kobiet* (Warszawa: W.A.B).

Grzela, Remigiusz (2000) 'Słucham moich demonów', *Kino*, 4: 27–29.

Hall, Stuart (1997) 'The Spectacle of the "Other"', in Stuart Hall (ed.) *Representation: Cultural Signifying Practices* (London: Sage), pp. 223–90.

Haltof, Marek (1997) 'Everything for Sale: Polish National Cinema after 1989', *Canadian Slavonic Papers*, 1–2: 137–52.

——— (2002) *Polish National Cinema* (Oxford: Berghahn Books).

Hamington, Maurice (1995) *Hail Mary? The Struggle for Ultimate Womanhood in Catholicism* (London: Routledge).

Hauser, Ewa et al. (1993) 'Feminism in the Interstices of Politics and Culture: Poland in Transition', in Nanette Funk and Magda Mueller (eds), *Gender Politics and Post-Communism* (London: Routledge), pp. 257–73.

Hayward, Susan (2000) *Cinema Studies: The Key Concepts* (London: Routledge).

Helman, Alicja (1999) 'Introduction', in Grażyna Stachówna (ed.), *I film stworzył kobietę* ..., (Kraków: Wydawnictwo Uniwersytetu Jagiellońskiego). pp. 11–15.

Heltai, Peter Andreas and Rau, Zbigniew (1991) 'From Nationalism to Civil Society and Tolerance', in Zbigniew Rau (ed.) *The Reemergence of Civil Society in Eastern Europe and the Soviet Union* (Oxford: Westview Press), pp. 129–44.

Hill, John (1999) *British Cinema in the 1980s* (Oxford: Clarendon Press).

Hollender, Barbara (1997) 'Nie można nikogo nauczyć żyć', *Rzeczpospolita*, 10–11/11: 25.

——— (1998) 'Dramat bezbronnosci', *Rzeczpospolita*, 16/10: 16.

Holquist, Michael (1999) 'Foreword', in Mikhail M. Bakhtin, *Toward a Philosophy of Act* (Austin: University of Texas Press), pp. vii–xv.

hooks, bell (1984) *Feminist Theory: From Margin to Center* (Boston: South End Press).

Iskierko, Alicja (1980) 'Film dokumentalny', in Jerzy Toeplitz (ed.), *Historia filmu polskiego*, vol. IV (Warszawa: Wydawnictwa Artystyczne i Filmowe), pp. 213–49.

Jabłońska, Katarzyna (1995) 'Jestem...przytul...', *Więź*, 2: 197–99.

Jackowski, Jan Maria (1993) *Bitwa o Polskę* (Warszawa: Ad Astra).

Janicka, Bożena (1994) 'Dziecko, elf i ptaki', *Kino*, 12: 8.

——— (1995) 'Sama nie wiem, dlaczego', *Kino*, 2: 20–21.

Janicka, Bożena and Janda, Krystyna (1999) *Gwiazdy mają czerwone pazury* (Warszawa: W.A.B).

Janion, Maria (1975) *Gorączka romantyczna* (Warszawa: Państwowy Instytut Wydawniczy).

_____ (1979) *Reduta: Romantyczna poezja niepodległościowa* (Kraków: Wydawnictwo Literackie).

_____ (1996a) *Czy będziesz wiedział, co przeżyłeś* (Warszawa: Sic!).

_____ (1996b) *Kobiety i duch inności* (Warszawa: Sic!).

Jankowski, Edmund (1980) *Eliza Orzeszkowa*, 4th edn. (Warszawa: Państwowy Instytut Wydawniczy).

Jankun-Dopartowa, Mariola (1998) 'Kobieta jako Mc Guffin', *Kino*, 9: 26–29.

_____ (2000) *Gorzkie kino Agnieszki Holland* (Gdańsk: Słowo, Obraz, Terytoria).

Johnston, Claire (1985a) 'Towards a Feminist Film Practice: Some Theses', in Bill Nichols (ed.), *Movies and Methods* (Berkeley: University of California Press), pp. 315–27.

_____ (1985b) 'Women's Cinema as Counter Cinema', in Bill Nichols (ed.), *Movies and Methods* (Berkeley: University of California Press), pp. 208–17.

Kalinowska, Izabela (2002) 'Oblicza cierpienia: *Nic* Doroty Kędzierzawskiej w kontekście kobiecości w powojennym kinie polskim', in Małgorzata Radkiewicz (ed.) *Gender. Kultura. Społeczeństwo* (Kraków: Rabid), pp. 81–89.

Kaplan, E. Ann (1992) *Motherhood and Representation: The Mother in Popular Culture and Melodrama* (London and New York: Routledge).

Kenez, Peter (1992) *Cinema and Soviet Society* (Cambridge: Cambridge University Press).

Kino, kobieta i... (1991) Special issue of *Film na świecie*, 384.

Klein, Joe (2002) 'What Polish Miracle', *The Guardian* (G 2), 12/06: 2–5.

Knight, Julia (1992) *Women and the New German Cinema* (London: Verso).

Koestler, Nora (1992) 'Kobiety polskie między społeczeństwem tradycyjnym a nowoczesnym', in Anna Żarnowska and Andrzej Szwarc (eds), *Kobieta i edukacja na ziemiach polskich w XIX i XX wieku* (Warszawa: Instytut Historyczny Uniwersytetu Warszawskiego), pp. 31–42.

Kopaliński, Władysław (1985) *Słownik mitów i tradycji kultury* (Warszawa: Państwowy Instytut Wydawniczy).

Kopeć, Jerzy Józef (1983) 'Uwarunkowania historyczno-kulturowe czci Bogarodzicy w polskiej religijności', in Władysław Piwowarski (ed.), *Religijność ludowa, ciągłość i zmiana* (Wrocław: Wydawnictwo Wrocławskiej Księgarni Archidiecezjalnej), pp. 21–63.

Kornatowska, Maria (1986) *Eros i film* (Łódź: Krajowa Agencja Wydawnicza).

_____ (1990) *Wodzireje i amatorzy* (Warszawa: Wydawnictwa Artystyczne i Filmowe).

Korska, Joanna (1998) 'Barbara Sass-Zdort – kobiety pod presją w Polsce lat osiemdziesiątych', in Grażyna Stachówna (ed.), *Kobieta z kamerą* (Kraków: Wydawnictwo Uniwersytetu Jagiellońskiego), pp. 71–85.

Kozioł, Maciej (1992) 'Dominujące wizerunki kobiet w filmie polskim po 1945 roku', *Studia Filmoznawcze*, 12: 225–45.

Kristeva, Julia (1982) *The Powers of Horror: An Essay on Abjection*, trans. Leon S. Roudiez (New York: Columbia University Press).

—— (1986) 'Stabat Mater', trans. Leon S. Roudiez in Toril Moi (ed.), *The Kristeva Reader* (Oxford: Basil Blackwell), pp. 161–86.

Kubisiowska, Katarzyna (1998) 'Lubiłam być dzieckiem', *Przekrój*, 14: 12–15.

Kuchowicz, Zbigniew (1990) 'Postawa wobec kobiety w kulturze szlacheckiej polskiego baroku', in Barbara Jedynak (ed.), *Kobieta w kulturze i społeczeństwie* (Lublin: Wydawnictwo Uniwersytetu Marii Curie-Skłodowskiej), pp. 7–50.

Kurz, Iwona (1999) 'Apetyt na jabłka', *Kino*, 2: 36–39.
de Lauretis, Teresa (1984) *Alice Doesn't: Feminism, Semiotics, Cinema* (London: Macmillan).
_____ (1987) *Technologies of Gender: Essays on Theory, Film and Fiction* (Bloomington and Indianapolis: Indiana University Press).
Lenarciński, Michał (1994) 'Naturę mam dwoistą', *Wiadomości dnia*, 74: 8.
Leyda, Jay (1960) *Kino: A History of the Russian and Soviet Film* (London: Allen and Unwin).
Liehm, J. Antonin and Liehm, Mira (1977) *The Most Important Art: Eastern European Film after 1945* (Berkeley: University of California Press).
Limanowska, Barbara (1996) 'Polemika w kwestii narodowego krokieta', *Pełnym głosem*, 4: 7–14.
Lis, Piotr (1985) 'Człowiek z marmuru', in Jan Trzynadlowski (ed.), *Problemy teorii dzieła filmowego* (Wrocław: Wydawnictwo Uniwersytetu Wrocławskiego), pp. 25–37.
Lubelski, Tadeusz (1998) 'Agnès Varda – eseistka z ulicy Daguerre'a', in Grażyna Stachówna (ed.), *Kobieta z kamerą* (Kraków: Wydawnictwo Uniwersytetu Jagiellońskiego), pp. 11–34.
_____ (1992) *Strategie autorskie w polskim filmie fabularnym lat 1945–1961* (Kraków: Wydawnictwo Uniwersytetu Jagiellońskiego).
Luckett, Moya (2000) 'Travel and Mobility: Femininity and National Identity', in Justine Ashby and Andrew Higson (eds), *British Cinema, Past and Present* (London: Routledge), pp. 233–45.
Łusakowski, Seweryn (1952) *Pamiętniki zdeklasowanego szlachcica* (Warszawa: Państwowy Instytut Wydawniczy).
Madej, Alina (1991a) 'Ja po prostu swojej partii ufałam: Rozmowa z Wandą Jakubowską', *Kino*, 8: 28–31.
_____ (1991b) 'Stalinowskie panopticum', *Kino*, 8: 32–33.
_____ (1994) *Mitologie i konwencje: O polskim filmie fabularnym dwudziestolecia międzywojennego* (Kraków: Universitas).
_____ (1996) 'Wielki Tydzień – wokół opowiadania i filmu', in Ewelina Nurczyńska-Fidelska and Zbigniew Batko (eds), *W stulecie kina: Sztuka filmowa w Polsce* (Łódź: Centralny Gabinet Edukacji Dzieci i Młodzieży), pp. 128–35.
Majka, Jerzy (1980) 'Historyczno-kulturowe uwarunkowania katolicyzmu polskiego', *Chrześcijanin w świecie*, 12: 29–44.
Malatyńska, Maria (1998) 'Nic', *Gazeta Krakowska*, 17/10: 9.
Mamrowicz, Elżbieta (1984) 'W kręgu filmu', *Przyjaciółka*, 10/05: 15.
Maniewski, Maciej (1996) 'Między miłością a dojrzałością', *Kino*, 6: 5–6.
Marszałek, Rafał (1988) 'Kapelusz i chustka', in Zbigniew Benedyktowicz and Danuta Palczewska (eds), *Film i kontekst* (Wrocław: Wydawnictwo Ossolineum), pp. 35–55.
Martin-Márquez, Susan (1999) *Feminist Discourse and Spanish Cinema: Sight Unseen* (Oxford: Oxford University Press).
Mazierska, Ewa (2002) 'Witches, Shamans, Pandoras – Representation of Women in the Polish Postcommunist Cinema', *Scope*, 2 (June). http://www.nottingham.ac.uk/film/journal/articles/witches-shamans-pandoras.htm
Metzel, Zbigniew (1978) 'Sto procent siebie', *Polityka*, 25: 16–17.
Michalski, Cezary (2002) *Siła odpychania* (Warszawa: W.A.B.).
Michałek, Bolesław and Turaj, Frank (1988) *The Modern Cinema of Poland* (Bloomington: Indiana University Press).
Mickiewicz, Adam (1957) *Poems*, trans. Jack Lindsay (London: Sylvan Press).

_____ (1981) *Pan Tadeusz, or The Last Foray in Lithuania*, trans. Watson Kirkconnell (New York: Polish Institute of Arts and Sciences of America).

_____ (1982) *Pan Tadeusz czyli Ostatni Zjazd na Litwie, Historia Szlachecka z r. 1811 i 1812 we dwunastu księgach wierszem* (Wrocław: Ossolinneum).

Miczka, Tadeusz (1996/97) 'Andrzeja Wajdy powinności wobec widza', *Kwartalnik Filmowy*, 15–16: 26–46.

_____ (1998) 'Lina Wertmüller – filmowe bambocjady', in Grażyna Stachówna (ed.) *Kobieta z kamerą* (Kraków: Wydawnictwo Uniwersytetu Jagiellońskiego), pp. 35–51.

Modrzejewska, Ewa (1991) 'Żołnierz zwycięstwa Wandy Jakubowskiej: Protokół z posiedzenia komisji ocen filmów i scenariuszy w dniu 13/05/1953', *Kwartalnik Iluzjon*, 2: 45–48.

Molyneux, Maxine (1994) 'The "Woman Question" in the Age of Communism's Collapse', in Mary Evans (ed.), *The Woman Question* (London: Sage), pp. 303–30.

Morawska, Ewa (1984) 'Civil Religion vs. State Power in Poland', *Society*, 14: 29–34.

Mruklik, Barbara (1985) 'Wierność sobie: Rozmowa z Wandą Jakubowską', *Kino*, 6: 5–9 and 20–21.

_____ (1986) 'Twarzą w ciemność', *Kino*, 6: 9–11.

Mulvey, Laura (1975) 'Visual Pleasure and Narrative Cinema', in Gerald Mast et al. (eds), *Film Theory and Criticism* (Oxford: Oxford University Press), pp. 746–57.

—— (1992) 'Przyjemność wzrokowa a kino narracyjne', trans. J. Mach, in Alicja Helman (ed.), *Panorama współczesnej myśli filmowej* (Kraków: Universitas), pp. 95–107.

Nazarian, Elizabeth (2002) 'The Double Life of Meaning: Ideology and Subversion in Andrzej Munk's *The Passenger* (1963)', unpublished paper delivered at the conference of the Society of Cinema and Media Studies, Minneapolis, March 2002.

Nowakowska, Danuta (1988) 'Women in Solidarity', in *Polish Women's Forum: A Women's Anthology in Polish and English* (London: Forum Publication Group), pp. 51–55.

Nowicki, Z. (1951) 'Rozmowa z Wandą Jakubowską o filmie Żołnierz zwycięstwa', *Głos Wielkopolski*, 28/12: 6.

Nurczyńska-Fidelska, Ewelina (1982) *Andrzej Munk* (Kraków: Wydawnictwo Literackie).

_____ (1998) *Polska klasyka literacka według Andrzeja Wajdy* (Katowice: Wydawnictwo 'Śląsk').

_____ (2003) *Czas i przesłona: O Filipie Bajonie i jego twórczości* (Kraków: Rabid).

Oleksy, Elżbieta H. (1998) *Kobieta w krainie Dixie: Literatura i film* (Łódź: Wydawnictwo Uniwersytetu Łódzkiego).

Olszewski, Jan (1996) 'Ofiara', *Film*, 6: 63.

_____ (1998) 'Anielolica', *Film*, 10: 100.

Ostrowska, Elżbieta (1998) 'Filmic Representations of the "Polish Mother" in Post-Second World War Polish Cinema', *The European Journal of Women's Studies*, 5: 419–35.

Piasecka, Ewa (1998) 'Jestem głupkiem domowym', *Elle*, 1: 20–23.

Piątek, Joanna (1986) 'W cieniu rajskiej jabłoni', *Film*, 20: 10–11.

Pierzchała, Aneta (1997) 'Nie jestem skandalistką', *Życie*, 12: 14.

Piwińska, Marta (1973) *Legenda romantyczna i szydercy* (Warszawa: Państwowy Instytut Wydawniczy).

Piwowarski, Władysław (1975) 'Operacjonalizacja pojęcia religijność', *Studia Socjologiczne*, 4: 151–74.

Place, Janey (1998) 'Women in Film Noir', in E. Ann Kaplan (ed.), *Women in Film Noir* (London: British Film Institute), pp. 47–68.

Prokop, Jan (1991) 'Kobieta Polka', in Józef Bachórz and Alina Kowalczykowa (eds), *Słownik literatury polskiej XIX wieku* (Wrocław: Ossolineum), pp. 414–17.

_____ (1993) *Universum polskie: literatura, wyobraźnia zbiorowa, mity polityczne* (Kraków: Universitas).

Przylipiak, Mirosław (2000) *Poetyka kina dokumentalnego* (Gdańsk: Wydawnictwo Uniwersytetu Gdańskiego).

Rau, Zbigniew (1991) 'Introduction', in Zbigniew Rau (ed.), *The Reemergence of Civil Society in Eastern Europe and the Soviet Union* (Oxford: Westview Press), pp. 1–23.

Reading, Anna (1992) *Polish Women, Solidarity and Feminism* (London: Macmillan).

Roof, Wade Clark (1985) 'The Study of Social Change in Religion', in Philip E. Hammond (ed.), *The Sacred in a Secular Age: Toward Revision in the Scientific Study of Religion* (Berkeley: University of California Press), pp. 75–89.

Roszkowska, Dorota (1992) 'Człowiek z drugiej strony: Kobiety w filmach Wajdy', in Sławomira Walczewska (ed.), *Głos mają kobiety* (Kraków: Convivium), pp. 78–94.

Sadowska, Małgorzata (2002) 'Kino bez kobiet', *Film*, 7: 86–88.

Siemieńska, Renata (1986) 'Women and Social Movements in Poland', *Women and Politics*, 4: 5–35.

Siwicka, Dorota (1993) 'Ojczyzna intymna', *Res Publica Nowa*, 7–8: 70–72.

Sobolewski, Tadeusz (1989) 'Cierpiący posąg', *Kino*, 8: 14–15 and 22–27.

_____ (2000) 'Scalanie świata: Hanna Krall opowiada o filmie *Daleko od okna*', *Gazeta Wyborcza*, 17/11: 14–15.

Sontag, Susan (1964) 'Godard's *Vivre Sa Vie*', in her *Against Interpretation* (London: Vintage), pp. 196–208.

_____ (1983) 'Fascinating Fascism', in her *Under the Sign of Saturn* (London: Writers and Readers), pp. 73–105.

Stables, Kate (1998) 'The Postmodern Always Rings Twice: Constructing the Femme Fatale in 90s Cinema', in E. Ann Kaplan (ed.), *Women in Film Noir*, 2nd edn. (London: British Film Institute), pp. 164–82.

Stachówna, Grażyna (1996) 'Równanie szeregów: Bohaterowie filmów socrealistycznych 1949–1955', in Mariola Jankun-Dopartowa and Mirosław Przylipiak (eds), *Człowiek z ekranu: Z antropologii postaci filmowej* (Kraków: Arkana), pp. 7–25.

_____ (ed.) (1998a) *Kobieta z kamerą* (Kraków: Wydawnictwo Uniwersytetu Jagiellońskiego).

_____ (1998b) '"Pożegnania czas już przekroczyć próg...": Wątki melodramatyczne w filmach "szkoły polskiej"', in Ewelina Nurczyńska-Fidelska and Bronisława Stolarska (eds), *Szkoła polska – powroty* (Łódź: Wydawnictwo Uniwersytetu Łódzkiego), pp. 49–61.

_____ (ed.) (1999) *I film stworzył kobietę...* (Kraków: Wydawnictwo Uniwersytetu Jagiellońskiego).

_____ (2001) 'Suczka, Cycofon, Faustyna i inne kobiety w polskim filmie lat dziewięćdziesiątych', in Małgorzata Radkiewicz (ed.), *Gender w humanistyce* (Krakow: Rabid), pp. 55–63.

Stevenson, Michael (2000) '"I Don't Feel Like Talking to You Anymore": Gender Uncertainties in Polish Film Since 1989. An Analysis of *Psy* (W. Pasikowski

1992)', in Elżbieta Oleksy et al. (eds) *Gender in Film and the Media: East-West Dialogues* (Frankfurt am Main: Peter Lang), pp. 138–49.

Szacki, Jerzy (1994) *Liberalizm po komunizmie* (Kraków: Znak).

Szczuka-Lipszyc, Kazimiera (1994) 'Więzień męskości', *Kino*, 10: 12.

Śliwowska, Wiktoria (1990) 'Kobiety w ruchu pomocy zesłańcom polskim na Syberii w pierwszej połowie XIX wieku', in Anna Żarnowska and Andrzej Szwarc (eds), *Kobieta i społeczeństwo na ziemiach polskich w XIX wieku* (Warszawa: Instytut Historyczny Uniwersytetu Warszawskiego), pp. 207–26.

Śnieg-Czaplewska, Liliana (1999) 'Kaktusy hodują się same', *Twój Styl*, 11: 64–68.

Toeplitz, Krzysztof T. (1984) 'Znaki czasu', *Miesięcznik Literacki*, 1: 65–67.

Turovskaya, Maya (1993) '"Women's Cinema" in the USSR', in Lynne Attwood (ed.), *Red Women on the Silver Screen: Soviet Women and Cinema from the Beginning to the End of the Communist Era* (London: Pandora Press), pp. 141–48.

Umińska, Bożena (1992) 'Kwiat, zero, ścierka', *Kino*, 4: 8–11.

_____ (1996) 'Folk feminizm', *Pełnym głosem*, 4: 15–18.

_____ (2001) *Postać z cieniem: Portrety Żydówek w polskiej literaturze* (Warszawa: Sic!)

Wajda, Andrzej (2000) *Kino i reszta świata* (Kraków: Znak).

Walicki, Andrzej (1982) *Philosophy and Romantic Nationalism: A Case For Poland* (London: Clarendon Press).

Wallace, Michelle (1994) *Invisibility Blues: From Pop to Theory* (London: Verso).

Warner, Marina (1976) *Alone of All Her Sex: The Myth and Cult of the Virgin Mary* (New York: Weidenfeld and Nicolson).

Watson, Peggy (1993) 'Eastern Europe's Silent Revolution: Gender', *Sociology*, 3: 471–87.

_____ (1996) 'The Rise of Masculinism in Eastern Europe', in Monica Threlfall (ed.), *Mapping the Women's Movement: Feminist Politics and Social Transformation in the North* (London: Verso), pp. 216–59.

_____ (1997) '(Anti)feminism after Communism', in Ann Oakley and Juliet Mitchell (eds), *Who's Afraid of Feminism?* (London: Hamish Hamilton), pp. 144–61.

Welter, Barbara (1978) 'The Cult of True Womanhood; 1820–1860', in Michael Gordon (ed.), *The American Family in Social-Historical Perspective*, 2nd edn. (New York: St. Martin's Press), pp. 313–33.

Wiktor, Mariola (1998) 'Nieczułość świata', *Dziennik Łódzki*, 17/10: 29.

Woroszylski, Wiktor (1977) 'Człowiek z kielnią, człowiek z kamerą', *Więź*, 56: 186–88.

Wyka, Marta (1996) 'Projekcje Marii Janion', *Dekada Literacka*, 9: 6–7.

Wyszyński, Stefan Kardynał and Prymas Polski (1978). *Kobieta w Polsce Współczesnej* (Poznań: Pallotinum).

Zajdel, Andrzej (1986) 'Jestem między ludźmi', *Profile*, 6: 11–12.

Zawiśliński, Stanisław (1995) *Reżyseria: Agnieszka Holland* (Warszawa: Skorpion).

Zwierzchowski, Piotr (2000) *Zapomniani bohaterowie: O bohaterach filmowych polskiego socrealizmu* (Warszawa: Trio).

Zygmunt, Sławomir (1989a) 'Pięścią w stół', *Film*, 47: 16–17.

_____ (1989b). 'Optymistka na dzisiaj, pesymistka na jutro', *Gazeta Lubuska*, 292: 12.

Zygmuntowicz, Jan (ed.) (1989) *Józef Piłsudski o sobie: Z pism, rozkazów i przemówień komendanta* (Warszawa: Omnipress).

Żmigrodzka, Maria (1965) *Eliza Orzeszkowa: młodość pozytywizmu* (Warszawa: Państwowy Instytut Wydawniczy).

Index